PUGNARE

George Maher has a rare insight into the comparative workings of the classical and modern worlds. He holds a PhD in the economy of the Roman Empire from King's College London and both a first-class honours BA and MA with distinction in Classics from Birkbeck, University of London. He is a Fellow of the Institute and Faculty of Actuaries and holds a first-class honours degree in Special Honours Mathematics from Trinity College Dublin.

Dr Maher was a Partner at Tillinghast-Towers Perrin, the international firm of management consultants and actuaries, now part of Aon, where he advised governments and corporations worldwide. He continues to practise as a consulting actuary. Dr Maher has served as a director and trustee of the Society for the Promotion of Roman Studies and has taught at King's College London.

This is the first history of the Roman Empire written from a practical business perspective. But it is also about people, because business is about people.

Also by the same author:

The Imperial Roman Economy

PUGNARE

ECONOMIC SUCCESS AND FAILURE

George Maher

KILNAMANAGH

First published in 2021 by Kilnamanagh
Blackwell House, Guildhall Yard, London EC2V 5AE

ISBN 978-1-9996262-1-1

Copyright © George Maher 2021

The right of George Maher to be identified as the
author of this work has been asserted by him in accordance
with the Copyright, Designs and Patents Act 1988.

A CIP catalogue record for this book is available from the British Library.

Typeset by Palimpsest Book Production Ltd, Falkirk, Stirlingshire
Printed and bound by CPI Group (UK) Ltd., Croydon, CR0 4YY

For William, Mitesh, Anne, Monica and Sean

CONTENTS

Chapter 1   Introduction   1

Chapter 2   Expansion   8

Chapter 3   Peace   29

Chapter 4   Money   57

Chapter 5   Cities   85

Chapter 6   Prosperity   113

Chapter 7   Life   141

Chapter 8   Chaos   165

Chapter 9   Survival   199

Appendix   217

Additional Reading   219

Acknowledgements   227

List of Illustraions   229

Bibliography   233

Index   251

Chapter 1

Introduction

Not long after I had started working as an actuary in London, I was on a team sent to Italy to investigate an insurance company in Rome. As I travelled into the city from the airport, I passed sights that I remembered reading about when I was a boy learning Latin at school. I passed what was left of the Circus Maximus, where chariot races had been held in ancient Rome and which is now nothing more than a long field, all its old buildings gone. I passed the ruins of the Colosseum, where at one time tens of thousands of people crowded in to watch wild animals and gladiators fight. I saw towering walls that had been the walls of palaces and administrative buildings, once covered in marble that had long ago been stripped off, leaving just old Roman bricks to stand for almost two thousand years.

Our job was to find out whether the company was profitable or not. That work involved numbers, and I have loved working with numbers since I was a boy. However, as part of my training for this job I had been taught that you cannot decide whether a company is profitable just by looking at numbers. The numbers given to you might be wrong for all you know, or they might seem to mean one thing when in fact they mean another.

I had learned that you must first understand the business: why its customers buy its products and how it competes in its marketplace. You need to know the history of the company, something of its past successes and failures and what it learned from them. You need to know what it is like to work in the business, what pressures are put on staff, how they are rewarded, what type of people become successful there, and what the values are of those who run the business. Only then does it make sense to do any profit calculations, and only then can you understand what the profits mean. For example, the numbers might represent substantial amounts of money produced each year, by people who adapt quickly as the market changes, who direct their energies to winning, look after their customers well and respect each other. Or it might be that the number everyone thinks of as a profit is a one-off, a distortion, or worse still – a delusion.

We met with people from the different departments in the company and learned about the company and how it went about its business and what its values were. We learned also what it was like to work in that city, and we made friends. It was the best form of tourism.

This is a book about the economy of the Roman Empire and so it must include some numbers. But just as we could not understand the business of that insurance company just by looking at numbers, we cannot understand the economy of the Roman Empire just by looking at numbers. In fact, there will be few numbers in this book, but the ones included are those that matter. And just as it was necessary to understand how the people in the insurance company worked together so it will be necessary to understand the people who are the subject of this book: what they believed about themselves, what mattered to them, and what success was for them.

During our work breaks from meeting staff of that insurance company and from doing our calculations, my colleagues and I walked the streets of Rome and saw more of the city. We found a church where, when we went down below street level, we came to the remains of another, older church which had been built over. When we went down further, we came to the remains of an old temple of a religion that had emerged at about the same time as Christianity but had lasted only a few hundred years. There were layers and layers of past life in this city. There were remains of blocks of flats built at about the same time as that temple, blocks of flats once a source of profit to Roman property developers and investors. There were columns still standing that celebrated victories against other nations, tribes seen by Romans as barbarian who for centuries had tried to press in on the borders of this now ruined world.

I learned about this world at school. I had learned about a world of armies, of emperors, and of invading barbarians who had come in and destroyed this world. That history had been a succession of dates of battles I never could keep in my head, which I memorised the night before the exam and forgot the day after. Those dates were difficult numbers for me to remember because I could see no pattern to them. Why should this have happened then and not earlier or not at all? There was, however, a pattern to these numbers which would emerge over time.

The sack of Rome by the barbarians

The illustration shown here tells a version of that story, and a violent version. It shows men who are naked or just covered in fur putting ropes around a statue of a civilised and imposing man to pull it down. Behind those starting to tear down the statue we can see others making their way with fire brands into a temple. This scene depicts destruction. It is true to an extent. Something like this did happen in the city of Rome. In AD 410 barbarians invaded the city. However, the people the barbarians encountered were not rich and powerful; they were not the politicians, noblemen, shopkeepers, and traders who had lived prosperous and peaceful lives here. Long before these barbarian men had entered this city, it had destroyed itself, and most of those prosperous people had left and the markets were quiet. The gold had already been taken from the temples, anything of value had been stripped from buildings and sold or used by the people who lived here. There was poverty in this city for two hundred years before the barbarians came. A city that once had overwhelmed the world with its power and wealth had been reduced, depopulated, and weakened. This it had done to itself.

The story we are told of this city is one of military expansion. That story is also true, but there is more to it than that. What became the city of Rome, a city of great marble temples and civic buildings as shown in the painting, had once been a small town like any other around the Mediterranean. Unlike the thousands of other little towns, it had expanded until more people lived in it than would do in any city on earth until the eighteenth century. Along the way, it gained control of Italy, the first time that territory had been ruled from one place. It then eliminated the Carthaginians, the only other superpower in that world, which was Rome's military and trading rival. It continued to expand until eventually it controlled an area half the size of the United States today. This is not merely a story of military prowess. What mattered was that they knew how to hang on to their gains.

Modern businesses that expand quickly often face problems. The old ways of running things when there is one office and one factory often no longer work when the company becomes a business empire with multiple locations in various countries. The successful companies are those that adapt as they grow and develop new ways of doing things when some of the old ways no longer work. This book will start with what was almost the last part of the expansion of the Roman world and the crises that it then faced. The old ways of running things and making money and getting on in the world worked when there were so many new places to conquer. But when those opportunities started to run out, something had to change.

The typical telling of Rome's story overlooks some of the greatest achievements of those who managed that world. Today, as well, we fail to appreciate some of the things that make our economic life possible. We can be employed in specialised tasks, surgeons, pilots, plumbers, or writers and still get what we really need – food and drink – in the production of which we play no part. We depend on a monetary system without which we could not trade our specialised labour for those essentials. As the Romans transformed themselves, they produced and effectively managed the world's first universal currency as acceptable in North Africa as in Britain, a currency that made possible a new world in which more people than ever before lived in towns and cities, and that made international trade easier. Towns grew across the area they ruled, and new towns were built in places that had never seen towns before. The trading empire that developed meant new opportunities for people to specialise, to better themselves, and become wealthy.

We mark out the developments in our time by saying that they happened because of the policies of a certain prime minister or president. But it was never just the individual. It was the circumstances that made the individual or those who selected and supported the policies of the individual. Just as modern times have had an Eisenhower, an Adenauer, or a de Gaulle, so the Roman world had some outstanding leaders. In following the economic history of this world as it expanded and then declined, I will talk of what they added, or took away.

The Roman world was a competitive one – in war, in politics, and in business. Wealth mattered whether it was inherited, won in battle, or made in business. Social status depended on wealth, but not exclusively. In this world, the individual with drive and access to some capital could succeed, whether a former slave, a migrant to the city, or the descendant of one of the people the Romans had conquered. It was a world in which an individual with creative talent, from whatever background, could find sponsorship, and some of the greatest poetry ever written was produced as that world transformed itself. For those, however, with no money or no means of accessing money, it was a harsh and pitiless world.

There were, however, things that the Romans never experienced which we do. When I was a boy, I was fascinated by physics and chemistry. A small grain of copper sulphate suspended by a thread in a jar of copper sulphate solution grew overnight and in the coming days into a beautiful crystal with flat faces, a particular shape reproduced each time you did the experiment. A key connected to a battery and suspended in that solution became coated with copper, became a copper key. Those experiments were done for the pure joy of watching it all happening and seeing how things worked. What I was doing was copying what individuals had done in the previous few hundred years, individuals who loved the pure delight of discovery, the act of discovery, and the honour of having their names associated with that discovery. These were individuals from different backgrounds – Faraday, from a modest background, who discovered that a moving magnet made electric current run in wires surrounding it; Cavendish, the grandson of the Dukes of Devonshire and Kent, who discovered hydrogen.

This wonderful explosion of knowledge, knowledge generated for its own sake and not for profit, never happened in the Roman world. They experimented, for sure, and developed knowledge in agriculture and produced better grain yields, but what started to happen across Europe from the sixteenth century onwards scarcely happened for them. This is the principal economic difference between their world and ours. The discovery by Faraday, for example, that a moving magnet can induce electric current in wires surrounding it, is the basis for electricity generation from wind turbines and hydroelectric dams, and makes much of our modern economic activity possible. The Roman commercial spirit was as good as anything in our time at making money, but the discoveries never happened, to the extent that they did from the sixteenth century onwards.

We can too easily think that all is progress and indeed that our times are better than the times of those who preceded us, but history is not linear. Aside from the science, the world of Rome was in many ways as good as ours, and the people who lived then were much the same as the people who live now. People have not changed in the last two thousand years or indeed in the last hundred thousand years. There were the same angry and contented people, those with ambition, those content to keep things as they are, those with hope and those without. They all dealt with life as it happened to them and made of it what they could or wanted. Their world of politics, of commerce, of finance, was much like ours. What was argued about in their Senate and what was traded in their markets was different, but the human behaviours in those theatres were much the same, and how to succeed in those conflicts was little different between then and now.

We can look at where things went well for them, and badly, and learn from that. Perhaps some of the things we dread are not so bad after all. And, perhaps, some of the things we think of as harmless are what should bother us most.

We have much to learn from them.

Chapter 2

Expansion

What we believe about ourselves matters. It encourages us to do some things and makes us reluctant to do other things. The Roman people, for much of their history, believed that they were different, deserving of success. They believed that they had a God-given right to dominate. They even believed that how they clothed themselves marked them out as different, and better. These are words that the poet Virgil put into the mouth of Jupiter, speaking about the Romans, in the epic poem, the *Aeneid*:

> his ego nec metas rerum nec tempora pono
> imperium sine fine dedi. Quin aspera Juno
> . . . mecumque fovebit.
> Romanos rerum dominos gentemque togatam.
> sic placitum

> I will set no limit in time or space to what they own.
> I have given them power with no boundary.
> Harsh Juno and I together will favour these Romans,
>   the nation that wears the toga, masters of events.
> That is what has been decided.

Their world expanded until it included all the territory that surrounds the Mediterranean. It extended inland to the banks of the rivers Rhine and Danube and eastwards to what is now Syria and to parts of what is now Iraq. One of the last territories to be added was part of what is now Britain.

Expansion was not just the political annexation of a territory. It brought the benefits of conquest, booty captured in war, slaves to add to their manpower, locals forced to serve as auxiliaries in their armies. It added opportunities for men, and women, to expand their business enterprises, their trading and banking, and opportunities for ambitious young men to start careers in the administration of recently acquired territories or to serve in military garrisons. Senior political figures had remunerative posts as governors. It brought the glory of conquest and added to their belief in themselves. In some cases, the annexation was useful for strategic reasons.

Invasion of Britain

Britain had long been a place to which the enemies of Rome who lived in the northern province of Gaul could retreat. People from tribes in Gaul could, when under attack by the Romans, sail across the English Channel, take refuge there, regroup, and in due course return across the Channel to harry the Romans. The people in Britain with whom they were taking refuge were Belgic, the same nationality as themselves. In that part of Britain, the southeast, life was similar to what it was on the continent. There were towns, roads, and administration, and there were crops in the fields. Traders had established themselves there, exporting metals, animal hides, corn, and slaves and importing European luxuries in exchange.

In other parts, life in Britain was as it had been for centuries: an Iron Age world. People fed themselves on the milk and meat of the cattle they herded, the fruits they foraged for, and the animals they hunted. They clothed themselves with the skins of those animals and, according to Julius Caesar, did not cultivate grain. Separate clans dominated different parts of the island, and the land that each claimed as its own was held in common for that clan. They expected to hunt and forage unhindered across their land, which was held in common and not as private property. Before the Romans came, life in much of Britain, beyond the southeast, was much as it was in North America before the European settlers came.

Dressed to kill

Julius Caesar led the first Roman incursion into this island in 55 BC partly to stop his enemies in Gaul taking refuge in Britain. He sailed with ninety-eight ships carrying troops and cavalry. His first sight of Britain was of native Britons ranged along the cliffs of Dover, united as they seldom were but now joining against a common enemy, the news of whose invasion had been brought to them by the traders. Julius Caesar moved further along the coast and landed. There, his men were attacked but drove off their attackers. Before winter he returned to Gaul, but first secured hostages as guarantees that his enemies in Gaul would not be given refuge in Britain. The following year, the incursion was repeated, now with eight hundred ships. This time Caesar made it as far as the Thames to the point where it could, with difficulty, be crossed by foot. As in the first incursion, he returned to the continent before the winter.

For almost one hundred years after those two incursions, no Roman expeditionary force set out for Britain. Not long after Caesar's second return from Britain, the Roman world started to tear itself apart, and Britain was left alone to continue its largely Iron Age life, with clans warring against one another but no intruder coming from outside their world to disturb that age-old pattern.

When next the Britons saw a Roman expeditionary force, it came from a Rome that had changed from the time of Julius Caesar. It was sent by the emperor Claudius but for the same reasons that had caused Julius Caesar to set out against the island. Those who disturbed the peace in Gaul continued to find safe harbour in Britain and return at will across the Channel. There were also the glory of conquest, and business opportunities.

In AD 43, Roman legions landed, pushed in, and established military camps. Within a few years, colonies were set up around those military camps, small unwalled settlements populated by veteran soldiers arriving from across the empire. After their defeat in battle to the Romans and the loss of their lordship over their territories, the local peoples were taxed in grain and money. They were compelled to clear land to cultivate grain to pay as tax tribute to their oppressors.

Veterans set up businesses supplying the army, importing goods to sell to the army, to one another, and to the Britons – for Roman money. To get Roman money, the Britons needed to trade, and they had little to trade for money beyond the grain they grew or the cattle they raised. They could, however, borrow from the Romans in new towns such as London, borrow to fund whatever they wanted to buy and to pay for the money taxes also levied on them. They offered whatever security the bankers needed.

The amounts of money the Romans lent to the Britons increased with interest and further borrowings, and the debts became enormous. According to a later historian, one Roman senator, Seneca, lent in total HS 40 million, in Roman currency, which is equivalent to between £200 million and £400 million in our terms. (See the Appendix for 1 for this calculation). The sums were lent not by sending over tons of gold and silver coins in ships to the island, although coins were sent, but by transfers through the Roman banking system. As the loans to the native Britons increased, the pressure on them also increased. To repay the loans, the Britons needed Roman money, and to get the money, they needed to farm, trade, or make things that others would want to buy. See the Appendix for this calculation.

Rebellion

In AD 60, some Britons rose up under the leadership of Boadicea, the queen of one of their clans, partly because Seneca had suddenly called in his large loans. Later Roman historians report her speech as it had been told to them or, more likely, as they imagined it. She urged her people and her allies to rise up in defence of their ancient freedoms. She recalled the mistreatments they endured, the injustice of the Romans towards them. They had been robbed of what they owned and forced to pay taxes. Their men were conscripted into the Roman army. The Romans looked to profit from them, to get money from them, and now they must put the land they owned out to pasture or to tillage. Boadicea said that they had no money but were braver than the Romans. They could endure hunger and cold while the Romans must drink wine and eat fine food.

While the Roman army was in the west of Britain on the island of Anglesey, which was a place to which the Britons escaped just as earlier the Belgics had escaped across the Channel, Boadicea led her army against the unwalled towns of Colchester, London, and St Albans and sacked them. About eighty thousand Romans and their allies were slaughtered, and horribly disfigured bodies were put on display, or so the Romans claimed, The Roman general returned from Anglesey. The native Britons gave way in front of the Roman military machine and were routed, and the rebellion was at an end, for a while at least.

Military superiority would give the Romans victory in most engagements, but it would be an endless process. In AD 78, a new governor, Agricola, from Southern Gaul, whose family had been Roman citizens for two generations and perhaps more, arrived in the province, subdued Anglesey, and campaigned across Britain. He now supplemented hard power with soft power, an approach his predecessors had tried but not wholeheartedly. He eliminated some of the abuses permitted by his predecessors, the tricks the author-ities had played on the locals – for example, forcing them to go long distances across country in winter to pay their taxes when suitable tax collection posts were close at hand, a humiliation which meant more than the cost of the tribute they had to pay.

The locals were to be assimilated, like Agricola's family had been a few generations earlier. They would learn to prefer the culture of the invader to their own and that the way to get on in the world

was to follow the Roman way and reject the ways of their fore-
fathers, the ways of leaders such as Boadicea. Just as in Ireland in
the nineteenth century and earlier, so in Britain in the first century
AD: the way for the individual to get on was to abandon the
indigenous language and to adopt the language of the superimposed
ruling class, the language of the professions and of trade, the
language of the law courts, and the language that gave access to
learning. Clothes mark out differences among people, and the
Britons came to see that wearing the clothes that the Romans wore,
abandoning the animal skins in which their people were accustomed
to clothe themselves, was a mark of sophistication. But it also
signalled a change in allegiance. Sons and daughters became
strangers to their parents. It became a quieter world, but the resentment never fully died out.

The Romans replicated towns in an expanding network through
the province. The towns followed the same patterns. There was a
forum to serve as a business and social meeting place, a basilica
where court cases were heard in public, a marketplace, temples,
baths, and an amphitheatre. Between one town and the next a
straight road was built; towns were not more than a day's march
apart. Roads along which the army had priority allowed for the
free movement of people between these urban centres, for business
and for pleasure. The network grew rapidly. Once one town had
been established, another could be started a day's march further
out into the country, sometimes based on old British settlements.
These developments offered a different way of life to those of the
native Britons who wanted it: the learning of new skills and a new
language, a life of trade, manufacturing, administration, politics,
baths, dining, fine food, imported wine, and luxury goods. For the
rest, life could continue as before outside the towns and beyond
the cultivated fields: the old ways of hunting, foraging, and herding
cattle, but now with the oppressive burden of taxation to be paid
in Roman coins and in grain. Across the Irish Sea and to the North,
in what is now Scotland, the old life continued unburdened by the
Roman levies, indifferent to the comings and goings of the Roman
people, and it and the old tribal warfare continued for centuries
after they finally left.

London

London was an example of one of the new Roman towns. The site has natural advantages with a navigable river that gives access to a wide hinterland and easy access to the continent of Europe. Along the river were wharves where ships could berth, ships coming in from across the Channel, from further down the coast of Gaul and Iberia, ships going upriver to trade with the hinterland of London.

The modern City of London is a small area in the centre of the metropolitan sprawl of London and occupies a site of one square mile. It stretches from the Tower of London in the East to the Royal Courts of Justice in the West. It occupies almost exactly the site of

Meeting places, temple

the old Roman settlement of Londinium, the first settlement to have been built on the site. We can still see surviving segments of the walls that the Romans later built around their settlement to protect themselves from attack. They built the first bridge over the river, and the successors to that bridge – London Bridge – have, to within a few metres, been built in the same place. The Roman town expanded rapidly, wooden buildings replaced by stone buildings, and an amphitheatre was built which accommodated more people than any theatre in London even now. The modern city that emerged on the site first settled by the Romans is now one of the premier financial centres of the world.

In 1952, rebuilding began on a site in the City of London that

new way of life

15

had been destroyed in the war. New offices were to go up for an insurance company, built on a bombsite. It was to be taller than its predecessor, and the foundations were therefore to be deeper. As the workmen dug down to make these foundations, they dug deep into the history of the city. They found the remains of the walls of an old building that once stood there and had been destroyed or abandoned long before. At first they thought it was some old Christian church. But on the afternoon of 18 September 1954 they found the head of a god, the god Mithras, identifiable because similar figures have been found all across Europe and further east.

The god of a ruined city

When the discovery was announced, people came and stood in long queues to see the ruins. They looked at what was left of the small temple in which this strange god had been worshipped, one who chased, rode on, and then slaughtered a bull, a god who was probably derived from the ancient god Mithra of oaths and contracts, wore a Persian cap and was hailed by his followers with a Sanskrit greeting. Around this temple were other ruins, too, the effects of the recent war's destruction of the city.

The people who stood in those long queues looked at ruins of their city, their places of work, their houses, and they looked at the ruins of a temple where people had once gathered just as they had gathered in the ruined churches around them. The city of which that temple had once been a part had fallen into ruins. The world of which it had been a part had crumbled. A new world, however, had come up eventually above those forgotten walls, the world in which the people now lived. These old walls, this head of a strange god, were a hopeful sight that life could emerge from destruction.

In due course, a new office block filled the site, and the remains of the temple of Mithras were moved a hundred metres from their original site and left at street level. Some sixty years later, that office building itself was knocked down and replaced by another. The remains of the temple of Mithras were brought in and put back almost exactly where the temple had been originally, two floors below what is now street level. These remains are the centrepiece of a new museum and exhibition centre. The temple is visited by tourists, students, and those who work in the City of London.

The temple of Mithras: restored and respected

The cult once celebrated in that temple had spread during the first century AD and could be found throughout the Roman Empire. After the ceremonies in which the god was praised, with all those in the congregation serving in the roles allotted to them, a meal was served at which businessmen and soldiers, living in this town or visiting on a tour of duty or for trade, chatted, sharing news and gossip. It was as much social as it was religious and as much for business as for anything else. The temple is located near the City of London livery company halls, some of which are centuries old and serve similar business purposes now, for the social gathering of men and women to share information, develop commercial relationships, strike deals, and generally enjoy themselves.

Information

The temple of Mithras is now set in a prize-winning building that also houses the European headquarters of an international organisation, which makes its money, as some other organisations do, largely from selling information – on stock prices and grain prices, for example. The customers who buy that information also hope to profit, to gain advantage. Information is valuable.

Then, as now, information was a source of power. A planned rebellion of Britons, an attack on some town or another, discovered by spies or notified by informants, and the military authorities could move divisions from areas where there was no threat to crush and destroy that attempt. In the urban network they had established, a legion of five thousand men could be spread over all the towns in an area of about a hundred-mile radius with at most a few hundred soldiers in each town. Within a day, any particular town in that area could have the size of its garrison doubled. Within a few days, that town could have a military complement of a few thousand. The road network allowed the army to move around, but it was the information network, and the quick and appropriate response to information coming in, that got the soldiers to the right places, and that allowed a single legion to control such a large area. As much of the legion as was required could be anywhere in the network. Rebellious locals planning a surprise attack on some town with a few hundred soldiers to defend it found a force of a few thousand marching out at them before they arrived. Information made the system highly efficient.

Then, as now, information was a source of profit in the City of London: knowing where you can source supplies more cheaply, what trends are happening in the marketplace, what product is more likely to sell better. Knowing that an investment fund or a bank is in trouble and may have to shut down allows you to get your money out before it is too late. Information on companies about whether the share price is likely to go up or down can make you money. If the information tells you that the share price will go up, then buy now and sell later when the price rises, and then pocket the difference. If it tells you that the share price will go down, then borrow shares in that company and sell them. When the share price goes down, buy back the now cheaper shares and hand them over to whoever lent them to you. Similar profits can be made in speculating on grain, for example, then as much as now. You might, however, be wrong and the price might move in the opposite direction and you lose out. What matters is also the ability to figure out whether what you are being told is true. That ability has not changed since Roman times, or before.

Competition

The City of London is a competitive world. Companies exploit market share, undercut rivals, and innovate to gain advantage over competition. Incumbents lose out to new entrants who offer better products or services. Those companies or divisions of companies that fail in this struggle lose revenues, lose employees, become unprofitable, and disappear into insolvency or the ownership of other companies. This competition is overseen by supervisors who enforce rules and whose responsibility is to guard against behaviours that could tear the system apart. Such supervisors have their own histories of success and failure.

The City of London is competitive not just in businesses working together and competing against each other, failing and succeeding, but also in individuals doing the same. Entry into it is selective, interview after interview, and success after that depends on the skills the individuals develop, the reputations they establish, the connections they make, and the money they accumulate. Family and chance can sometimes help, perhaps in opening a door or two, but their ability to assist a person's upward trajectory is limited. Coming from a background familiar with the workings of this world will help, but mainly what matters is the individual and how he or she learns to survive. It was the same in the Roman worlds of trade, finance, and politics.

Trade

In the excavations in 2012 to 2014 for the foundations of the building that now houses the temple of Mithras, thousands of objects were found from the time this place was governed by the Romans. Objects that had been thrown away as useless because they were broken or no longer needed, objects simply lost: pairs of shoes, single shoes, a broken wooden door, large tiles, keys, legal documents, rings, glassware, weighing scales, nails, gold coins, silver coins, plates, drainpipes, and pottery. Some of these goods had been made in this province because they were simple enough to make and there was enough demand to sustain a local manufacturing business – ordinary shoes, for example, but not exquisitely carved rings. Almost all the luxury goods and the specialist goods came from outside this island, brought here through the Roman trading network, which through the first and second centuries AD became increasingly efficient.

A pendant made out of amber from the Baltic

These valuable objects each have a story. Neither of the objects illustrated here was made in this province. Some such objects came in the personal baggage of those who emigrated to the new province or those moving here on a tour of duty, the governor and his staff, for example. Others came through trade. In some cases, objects may have been pre-ordered by a resident in London, but in most cases these objects were imported by traders who had bought them abroad for sale here, had laid out money in Alexandria or somewhere else in the empire, and paid for them to be transported to London. The objects were made by people looking to earn money for themselves, and they were moved around the world by other people also looking to make a profit.

The god Serapis from Egypt

Trading is a profitable business but a risky one. The profit comes from buying goods at one place and selling them later, sometimes at another place, for a higher price. The risk comes from not being able to sell the goods for more than they cost you, and if you bought them on borrowed money, then that risk includes bankruptcy. The skills are in knowing what will sell where and at what price, and in people skills – sales and negotiating. Expertise in the product being traded matters, but price is often the main factor. What makes a trading business profitable has not changed since Roman times.

A merchant, then and now, buying fine wine from Italy, for

example, and shipping that to London for sale makes a profit if he can sell it there for more than the wine and the shipping cost him. But there is competition, other suppliers, and if there aren't competitors now, then the prospect of large profits on each shipment will bring them in. If others manage to find a better source before you, or just do a better deal, and get the same quality wine cheaper and look to offload the merchandise for less than you charge, then your profit is reduced. If they can sell it for less than your costs, then you are probably out of business.

If your suppliers' harvests fail and your competitors import from a different region, then they get the business this year and you do not, and perhaps the customers they get from you this year stay with them next year. If tastes change or there is a better wine available from some vineyards you have just discovered, and you get in before your competition, then there is an extra margin for you.

Knowing what is happening in the world of your suppliers and in your markets makes the difference, as does your ability to figure out what to do with the information and to act quickly. Goods came into the Roman town of London and goods left it too, traded from there as they were in every town and city in the empire, a multitude of little businesses, and some large businesses, making money, keen to know what was going on in their part of the world and beyond.

Finance and the law

In the excavations on the site of the temple of Mithras in London, documents were discovered, some of which are financial contracts.

Legal contracts such as these were written in wax, which was contained on wooden boards, such as the one above, about the size of a wallet. Two boards like this, which folded over, were tied together and sealed, and that was the legal document. The writing was done with a stylus. Where the writer pressed too hard with the stylus, the marks intended only for the wax carried through to the wooden casing below the wax and have survived. The words of whatever contract was written can be recovered from these marks, sometimes with a lot of work, filling in the gaps, almost like a detective story or solving a crossword.

One such document is this financial contract, which was entered into on 8 January AD 57, about fourteen years after the conquest of Britain, when trade was now well established in this new territory. Translated from the Latin, which was the business and legal language of the island, it reads:

> I, Tibullus, the freedman of Venustus, have written and say that I owe Gratus, the freedman of Spurius, 105 denarii for the price of merchandise which has been sold and delivered. This amount I am due to repay him or the person whom the matter will concern . . .

It is a legal document executed between two former slaves. The first, Tibullus, has bought merchandise valued at about £3,000 in our terms, from Gratus. Tibullus has received the goods but has not yet paid. Whatever the goods were is not recorded and does not matter; what matters is the money. The document acknowledges that this amount is owed and is payable to Gratus or to whomever Gratus transfers his rights to this money. Tibullus does not have the money now to pay for these goods but will have when he sells them, and it suits Gratus to make this sale and get his money later rather than make no sale. The document could be made over to someone else, some financier, who might accept it for, say, £2,500 and then later recover the £3,000 from Tibullus.

The site of the temple of Mithras is close to where nineteenth-century discount houses stood. They were specialist banks, some of which survived into the late twentieth century, and served the same purpose as the banking houses that existed when the temple of Mithras was built.

In the nineteenth century, fine china, silver, cotton clothes, and other goods were exported from Britain, to places around the world such as India. A shipment of goods might be valued at, let us say, £100,000 in our terms, the amount to be paid when the consignment reaches the buyer. For the merchant this is money tied up that he cannot use to buy more china, and there is the risk that the buyer overseas might not pay or, if he does, he might delay. Such merchants went to the discount houses located in the city and presented these bills. A bill for £100,000 might be accepted by the discount house for, say, £90,000. The merchant has money that he can now use for further trades. The discount house makes £10,000 when it collects the funds due. What made the money for the discount house was its information on the creditworthiness of buyers overseas as well as its having the capital to lay out and the willingness to take the risk that the money laid out might not be recovered. All of this facilitated commerce.

This mechanism was just the same in Roman times. It was not that the later European financiers and traders copied them but that the same business problem gave rise to the same business solution.

This wooden object found near the temple of Mithras was once valuable and changed hands for our equivalent of thousands of pounds. It enabled different parties – a manufacturer perhaps, a trader who was willing to take risks but had limited capital, and a financier who was happy to lend money on good security – all to do business and make money. Separately these three parties would have found it difficult to do what each did best. Without the financier, the manufacturer might not have made the goods and the trader could not have done his business, and without the manufacturer and trader there might have been little opportunity for the financier to make his profits.

The document was valuable not because the different parties trusted one another. It was valuable because of the law. By executing a contract in their legal form, Tibullus made himself liable, and if he did not pay up when due, then there was a way to get him to pay. Law was administered in the basilica, and one of these was built in the forum at London. The official responsible for the administration of the town appointed a judge, and the case was heard in public. If Tibullus did not pay the thousands of pounds he owed, then whoever had accepted the debt could take a case against Tibullus, to be heard in public. Just as today, the forces of the state could take over and compel the sale of whatever property the debtor had to make good on his obligations.

There was local law, which could be used and was used but there was also Roman law, which was universally applied. A trader coming to London from some other town in the Roman world knew what the law was, how it worked, and how it was administered.

Political advancement

Expansion brought other opportunities beyond those afforded by conquest, by trade and finance. The military control and the local administration of the overseas territories offered opportunities for career advancement and in some cases for financial reward. An ambitious young man – political positions were limited to men – looking to build a career might through family or other connections find his way to an overseas province to serve on the staff of the governor there, perhaps be paid for his work and in any case gain experience, serving an apprenticeship. He could also notice the work and position of the handsomely remunerated governor and might set his mind on one day getting to a similar place of authority, respect, and remuneration. Family and other connections would not, however, be enough for that. The world of politics and administration was just as competitive as were the worlds of trade and finance.

In the time of Julius Caesar, the first step on the road to becoming governor was to stand for election to be one of the *quaestors*. These were in effect elected auditors who administered the state finances centrally in Rome and were allocated as necessary to the provinces. Julius Caesar, for example, started his political career as a quaestor allocated to review the finances of Spain. A young politician who successfully stood for election as the most junior of magistrates, that of auditor, automatically became a member of the Senate. Entry to that body was also subject to a minimum wealth test, which during the first century BC was HS 0.4 million, in their currency, or between £2 million and £4 million in ours and, provided he continued to pass that test, the politician remained a member of the Senate for life.

That requirement meant that, by the age of about thirty, the ambitious man had to have funds of several million pounds in our terms. It did not, however, limit the post to those who came from rich families, or whose wealth might come from the spoils of war, from business or inheritance. Roman women could operate businesses, some were wealthy through inheritance or because they belonged to wealthy families. Thus, marriage to a wealthy woman could help one pass the wealth test. Cicero, for example, was one such man. Wealthy Roman men also adopted young men, and that was another route. Augustus, for example, was the adopted son of Julius Caesar.

The electorate was the Roman citizenry, divided into geographic constituencies, in elections that took place in the fields outside the city of Rome. It was an electoral college, much like the US Presidential electoral college; the candidate won the election by the number of constituencies that voted for him rather than the total number of citizens who voted for him.

Canvassing was as it is today: meeting and greeting, speeches, getting supporters to bring their own supporters along with them, calling in favours, getting news of their achievements out, getting news of their rivals' failures out, exaggerating all of it if that was how they wanted to play the game.

The men who were ultimately successful had built up reputations over time, proving themselves in front of the great men of the city – as a young man, for example, taking on and winning a case against some governor, many years their senior, who had abused and tried to profit from his position. The candidate was expected to have some military experience by his mid-twenties, allocated to a minor position in a legion, serving an apprenticeship under some general or another, and building a reputation.

After his one year in office, and a one-year break, our ambitious young man could stand to be elected to be one of the *aediles*, an administrative officer, and to be allocated tasks such as supervising the city's water supply, the sewers, or the repair of the temples. If the individual was incompetent or his electoral competition were better at their work, then he did not get the job and they did. If the water supply failed while he was in charge of it, then he was unlikely to be able to move on to the next step of this career path. Some man much younger than him who also wanted to establish a reputation could take a court case against him on behalf of the public and win.

Later, again after another one-year break, he could stand to be elected to be a praetor and, if successful, be given administrative responsibility for Rome, presiding at the law courts of the city, supervising the officials junior to him, and exercising power of veto over their actions. The people who voted in the election for this position were the same as those who voted for the more junior magistracies, but in the election for the senior magistrates, the votes of the wealthy counted for more than the votes of the poor. After this year of service, the praetor was usually appointed by the Senate to be a governor of some province.

Only after all of that could he, if nominated by the Senate, stand for election to be consul, the highest executive office of the state. Two consuls were elected each year as equal heads of state, each with a veto on the actions of the other and a veto on the actions of all magistrates junior to them. While in office they were the commanders-in-chief and led any military campaigns, with the financial rewards that success brought, in booty and slaves. Having finished their one-year term of office, they could again be allocated by the Senate to serve as governors of a province.

The Roman poor had a limited say in the election of the senior magistrates, but then well into the nineteenth century – and in some countries into the twentieth century – the poor did not have any vote at all. In any case, in the Roman world the poor voted equally with the rich for the junior magistracies, and they voted on legislation, setting the laws used by traders, for example, wherever they did business across the Roman world. Women had no vote in the Roman elections just as they did not in nineteenth-century Europe or elsewhere. The system was meritocratic as well as accountable. Those who reached the top had served in different areas of public administration, finance, managing infrastructure, law and in the military, and their competence or incompetence was judged by the people they governed.

It was a world that encouraged competition but feared the dominant man and dreaded the emergence of a tyrant. People understood the deep-set longing that some have for power and the dangers of that passion. With few exceptions political offices were limited to one year, and no magistrate was given absolute power: every magistrate was subject to someone else's veto. This constitutional settlement was broadly in place around the time of Julius Caesar when the Roman world was tearing itself apart in civil war, as competition for wealth and power became excessive.

In 49 BC, five years after the second of his incursions into Britain, Julius Caesar returned to Rome. He had become pre-eminent because of his success in the Gallic wars, but there was rivalry between him and Pompey, another successful general, both of whom were becoming used to military power, which in the past had always been temporary. The Senate tried to limit the rivalry and voted that Pompey could keep his men but that Caesar should dismiss his. In response, Caesar seized a town in Northern Italy and marched on Rome, with an army whose loyalty he had bought. Caesar had permanently doubled their pay, in defiance of the right of the Senate to control the state's finances. Once doubled it could not be undoubled, an enormous imposition on the resources of the state. In Rome he seized the state treasury, the aerarium, defying the magistrate who tried to prevent him by ordering a blacksmith to break the locks. He seized the treasury with its state records, accounts, and funds for his use and to pay his soldiers. There was great unrest in Rome as the people now ignored the orders of the magistrates and as the consuls and most of the senators fled.

Now Caesar defeated Pompey in battle, and he celebrated that victory in the traditional triumphal display with which Roman generals had celebrated victory over foreign enemies, a display that, applied to one of their own, was offensive to many. It was becoming a tyranny, and Caesar was hated for the royal power he now took on. The old constitution and its carefully regulated affairs were no longer working, and he was assassinated, stabbed to death by his political rivals and those who resented the changes he had brought to their ancient constitution.

Chapter 3

Peace

Any political system can collapse or come close to collapse. In the seventeenth century, England was in civil war between two religious factions, with one supporting Parliament and the other supporting the king, a civil war which ended with the execution of the king. In the nineteenth century, the United States turned on itself in a civil war in which about six hundred thousand people died. In Ireland in the early part of the twentieth century, two sections of the population and two political parties, one of which supported a treaty with Great Britain and the other which opposed it, went to war with themselves.

These were times of fear, times when nobody knew what the future would be like, which side would win, whom to support, and who would die next. A new order, however, emerged over time; then all became different and peaceful again.

The civil war that continued after the assassination of Julius Caesar brought its own terrors but ultimately a peace. The competition for wealth and power changed, and a new creativity came into the world. Poetry and histories were written that celebrated what had been great about their world before the disorder, how they had endured worse and survived. These works looked back towards their ancestors and their achievements, also forward to the future and how their own world would be remembered. The atmosphere changed and with it the opportunities for growth. Peace brought confidence and investment in the hope of future returns.

Creativity took over the landscape as new buildings transformed towns and cities.

Disorder

The seizure of power by Julius Caesar was not the first time the established Roman order had been unsettled. In 63 BC a dominant individual had attempted to take control of the state. Catiline, scion of a noble family with a long history but which for generations had not numbered a consul among its members, tried to reach the top of this world legitimately and, when he failed, provoked revolution. Money was at the heart of it. His family was ancient but not wealthy, and his accumulated debts were enormous. Others were in the same position.

Catiline surrounded himself with those who also wanted revolution, those, for example, who had also contracted enormous debts, such as veterans who had wasted the booty won in war and were eager for civil conflict, or senators who belonged to a faction other than that dominating the Senate and who preferred to see government overthrown than to be out of power themselves, or with young men who preferred uncertainty to certainty, war to peace.

Privately he rallied his most loyal followers, saying that the state was in the hands of a few powerful men who offered poverty to those they did not favour. Those tyrants built luxurious villas, he said, whereas he and those like him had only the necessities of life. They have palaces but we have miserable homes, he said. They have fine paintings and statues; we have poverty and debt. He proposed that debts be abolished and that the rich be declared enemies of the people, with their wealth confiscated.

Twice he tried for the consulship, and twice he lost, and then he plotted to assassinate Cicero, his successful rival for the consulship. The Senate offered citizens a reward of HS200,000 which is between £1 million and £2 million in our terms, for information on the plot and got no takers. Catiline came to the Senate, protested his innocence, and was shouted down.

Now he turned to armed conflict and marched against Roman legions with an army of two legions, but was defeated. Many of

Catiline isolated in the Senate

those who had defended Rome went onto the battlefield and, turning over the bodies of their adversaries, found a friend, a guest, family. Others found their personal enemies.

The Roman state had been in turmoil before that. In fact, its very constitution reflected past turmoil and the settlements that had followed such disruptions. Several centuries earlier, the constitution favoured the aristocracy, families such as Catiline's. All power rested then with a section of the population whose ancestry was noble and ancient. It was the members of this elite section, the patricians, who framed and enacted laws, and the high officials of the state were drawn exclusively from their membership. The other section of the population, the plebeians, had no role in the government of the state but formed the greater part of the population.

In 494 BC, in response to discontent about the burden of debt, the plebeians withdrew from the city of Rome. In effect, the entire working population went on strike. Deprived of the services of the plebeians, the patricians found that life had become impossible. Thus, the constitution of the state was amended, and a plebeian assembly was instituted. The post of tribune was created; these men would be elected by the plebeian assembly and would have rights of veto over any act of the other officials. This assembly had the

31

power to pass legislation that bound the plebeians. In 287 BC, the plebeians again went on strike, and from then on the laws passed by their assembly were as valid as any other.

At the heart of the society were conflict-resolution mechanisms: the Senate, the vigorous meetings for elections, the campaigning in elections, and a willingness to change. Conflict had also been resolved through changes to the Roman constitution, which, like the British constitution, was only partly written and largely unwritten, comprising accepted conventions and precedents as well as uncodified case law and statute. The constitution had been adapted when the plebeians rebelled in the fifth century BC, for example, but in the first century BC, the Roman state was increasingly threatened by internal armed conflict and the constitution was not being adapted to deal with those threats.

Fear

Since the seventeenth century, bits of an inscription set up towards the end of the first century BC have been found scattered all over Rome. Some bits were found in the riverbank; others had been re-used in catacombs. Some pieces remain missing. They were once part of a memorial measuring just over two and a half metres high and one and a half metres wide, an inscription set up by a man in memory of his wife.

This praise will be a consolation to me

The words are from the funeral eulogy of a rich senator for his wife. The names of neither the husband nor the wife have survived, but it is known as the Laudatio Turiae, in praise of the man's wife, Turia. Their love and his grief are alive now for any person who reads this recreated inscription. During the reign of Augustus (27 BC–AD 14) people passed it on the road and recognised it as the statue a husband had put up to honour his wife.

At a loss without her wisdom and protection, he describes the past fear and upheaval of the civil wars, the confiscation of property, the forced exile, and her resourcefulness. Her parents had been murdered before their wedding, and she brought the murders to justice. While he was in exile during the civil war, some people tried to overturn her father's will and take control of her assets, but she understood the law and defeated them. Other men tried to profit by the civil war and break into their house while the husband was in exile, but she defended their home. When he was pardoned by Augustus, Marcus Lepidus, another senator, tried to prevent his return. Loudly and forcefully she defended her husband and made sure everyone knew he was pardoned. His life was preserved, and Lepidus suffered. He remembers all this with gratitude:

> Let me display before the eyes of men my public acknowledgement that you saved my life.

Both Turia and her husband survived into the peace of Augustus, but he outlived her.

He erected the memorial so that all who walked past it would know his love for her. He would mark her as special by the monumental size of this work and represent her by a statue in front of it. But this would not undo his loss. He was helpless without her and says so.

> . . . along with you I have lost the tranquillity of my existence. When I recall how you used to foresee and ward off the dangers that threatened me, I break down under my calamity and cannot hold steadfastly by my promise. Natural sorrow wrests away my power of self-control and I am overwhelmed by

sorrow. I am tormented by two emotions: grief and fear, and I do not stand firm against either. When I go back in thought to my previous misfortunes and when I envisage what the future may have in store for me, fixing my eyes on your glory does not give me strength to bear my sorrow with patience. Rather I seem to be destined to long mourning . . .

I pray that your gods will grant you rest and protection.

This long civil war was a time of fear and uncertainty. In 43 BC, Cicero, who had defended the state against Catiline's rebellion, was accused of being an enemy of the state. Augustus argued in his defence, but Cicero had opposed Mark Antony in this civil war and lost because of that. His decapitated head was put on display, the tongue pierced through with pins on the orders of the wife of his political opponent. Order had broken down, and law was replaced by the whim of the powerful.

It was a time of economic collapse. There was nothing noticeably new being built, and the existing infrastructure was not being maintained; the aqueducts, for example, which supplied the city of Rome, fell into disrepair. People had other things to think about, such as survival and the protection of their own property.

Competition

This was a society fundamentally based on competition, and it was largely meritocratic. Each year, elections were held for different positions, and people successful in these slowly made their way up the well-established career path, being given responsibility for the military, infrastructure, and judicial power, eventually becoming joint heads of the state. The reputational rewards of these competitions were great. A man who reached the highest executive position and was elected consul had his name applied to the year in which he served. The year we number as 4 BC the Romans dated by calling it the year in which Gaius Calvisius and Lucius Pasienus were consuls, and every year was named in this fashion. The successful man had his name carved into the inscriptions that listed the names of all consuls going back centuries, lists that survive to this day.

The financial rewards, however, lay elsewhere: in conquest. Steadily and progressively over the previous centuries, the territory that fell under Roman power was extended, and generals successful in these conquests were, if the Senate approved, awarded a triumph in Rome. During this celebration, the general paraded the spoils of conquest: the captured treasures, the captive enemies – some soon to be slaughtered in front of the people on the steps of the temple of Jupiter Capitoline. Conquest brought status, but more than that.

When Julius Caesar enslaved a million Gauls, as he claimed, he created great human misery. Sons and daughters saw their mothers for the last time. The embrace that a young man or woman might remember from childhood, comfort in pain, would never be experienced again. Worse than death were the horrible imaginings of where she was and how she lived and the never-to-be-forgotten sight of her tears, her backward glance, the sound of her misery. Men who might have been glorified in their triumph over their enemies or console themselves in battle that their honour would be remembered and that death was not to be feared were dragged under the yoke and put to the work of beasts.

Making money from misery

These enslaved Gauls were not educated like the Greeks. There was no place for them as civilised slave tutors in a rich man's house, who might, though slaves, preside over the domestics and progress to the management of their master's affairs. Many of the Gauls were treated as cattle: they worked on farms, shackled and manacled at night and fed the carefully calculated rations that would sustain them in their labour but not excessively burden the profit-and-loss account. They were useful labour for the silver mines, deprived of light as much as of hope and, if the calculations of income against capital loss merited it, could be worked to death. This great sum of misery, which the enslavement of these people created, was, however, monetisable. These prizes of conquest were disposed of, for cash, in private treaty sales and at auction. This increase in the supply of slave labour depressed the price of this commodity, but the monetary value was enormous. If we value the labour of one of these slaves at an equivalent, say, of £20,000 per annum and if they were bought for a price of five years' income, then the total capital value that accrued from the slaves captured in Caesar's conquest amounted to £100 billion in today's terms, which was distributed amongst himself, his fellow generals, the common soldiers, and the state as he wished and as approved by the Senate's auditor, the quaestor, responsible for oversight of his financial dealings. The conquest of Gaul brought unimaginable wealth to Caesar but, once conquered, Gaul would never again produce such sums. The annual tax tribute of Gaul of HS40 million, in their terms, or between £200 million and £400 million in our terms, would continue to accrue to the state and be managed by the Senate, but never again would Gaul produce these spoils of conquest.

These opportunities were now, in the middle of the first century BC, drying up, and the number of provinces, which had been increasing for generations, was now reaching its limit. Other provinces would be added later, Britain in the west and Dacia in the east, for example, but the rate of increase was slowing. A military society that organised some of its elections according to constituencies reflecting ancient military divisions of Rome had reached the point at which the old systems no longer worked. It was difficult for new men looking for wealth and prestige to get it in the old way. The constitution was now adapted, and the Roman world began to be transformed into one in which trade and finance, rather than conquest and political competition, would become the principal opportunities for prosperity, as we shall see.

The beginning of a transformation

Esteem within the social group, ceremonial dignity, and distinguishing dress can matter more than naked power and mere wealth. For example, the leading citizens of the City of London carry ceremonial privileges. When attending ceremonial events, the Lord Mayor wears eighteenth-century court dress. He is one of the aldermen of the City, who, like the senators of Rome, are politically successful and established individuals of their city. The other aldermen enter such events in procession dressed in clothes that, in appearance, have changed little since the Middle Ages, and are each accompanied by their own mace bearer. The heads of the livery companies, successors to medieval guilds, which once were powerful organisations in the City, also attend such events dressed in clothes that are archaic. Most of these individuals have little political power nowadays, and few have the power that their medieval predecessors had. But they still compete eagerly for their positions because of the status and ceremonial dignity that those positions bring.

From the time of Augustus, the old forms continued, as did the elections that had taken place in the fields outside the city of Rome. The substance, however, had changed. Tribunes, consuls, and other magistrates continued to be elected and retain their ancient dignities. Consuls walking through the great open spaces of the Roman forum continued to be preceded by twelve lictors. The real power, however, slowly moved elsewhere, and there was no threat in the transition.

This was not the last time that change happened gradually rather than by revolution. For instance, every year the City of London celebrates just such a transformation of a democratic institution into a system of appointment – a celebration of, essentially, the loss of substantive power. The election of the Lord Mayor of London takes place annually in the Guildhall in the City of London, as it has done for centuries. The electorate that gathers in the Guildhall is composed of the members of the ancient city companies of merchants and craftsmen, together with members of more modern companies such as the banks and insurers. In practice almost all nowadays are business men and women who work or have worked in the City of London.

The forms are still the same, but the substance has changed. The once rowdy contests that took place some centuries ago have now morphed into a gentler show. Three candidates present themselves, and as the first name is called out, the assembled company shouts out, "Later!" A second name is called out, and the shout is "Next year!" When the third name is called out, the shout is "All!" meaning that all assent. During the following year's election, the two candidates from the previous year move up a step, and a new candidate will hear "Not yet!" in response to their name. When we enter the Guildhall every year, we know beforehand the results of the election in which we will freely participate. Indeed, knowing the names of the three candidates, we also know the results of the election that will take place in the following year and in the year after that. And we are all content.

Those who stand for election have been selected by a committee of aldermen, the City's equivalent of the Roman senators, and the power of deciding the Lord Mayor is with them and not us, the electorate. Nevertheless, a residual power remains. We might object and would do if the aldermen acted in breach of precedent or against the interests of the City. A similar and gradual change in the structure of power happened in Rome as the powerful worked to reshape the constitution, to avoid the chaos that had threatened their common welfare during the civil war – and as they sought to rebuild what their experience had demonstrated to them was possible.

Augustus was the ultimate victor of the civil war that followed the assassination of Julius Caesar, defeating Mark Antony in a naval battle in 31 BC. He had the opportunity to put himself in the position that his adoptive father had held for such a short time. But perhaps he had learned the lesson of his adoptive father's career; the danger of being seen to be in a position of supreme power in the Roman world, the rivalry and resentment that such a position incites, and the insecurity. Or perhaps he preferred a subtler power and a different legacy. In any case, he did not seize power for himself but made gradual changes and allowed power to shift. From the date of his victory he served yearly as consul elected by the people of Rome in the traditional manner until 23 BC, when the Senate and people of Rome offered him the position of consul for life. He refused the offer. They offered him the position of dictator for life, and he refused that offer too.

Then in 23 BC Augustus accepted from the Senate and people of Rome the power associated with an ancient position – but he declined the title. He removed himself from the competition for position and display and allowed that to continue without disruption to the public order. Some centuries earlier, the position of plebeian tribune had been created, a position with no executive power. Now the Senate and people of Rome enacted a law which gave the powers of a tribune to Augustus for life: the right of veto, the right to present legislation, without the title.

He held those powers for thirty-seven years. Others continued to compete for and be elected to the ancient positions, enjoy the ancient dignities and privileges that came with those positions, but he could overrule any of them. In the alteration of the balance of power, the Senate willingly participated in a new creation, a head of state in place for life. It was to be clear, however, that the Senate, the council of respected elders, and the people had consented to this change in the balance of power, or at least everyone maintained the appearance that this consent was necessary.

Augustus set an example – or at least proclaimed that he followed this approach – of not asking for the powers that were transferred to him. They were always to be offered, and he might refuse these powers. In the new constitutional settlement, there was to be no appearance of taking power to oneself. Towards the end of his life, this man who lived modestly in Rome boasted that while others were as powerful as he was, none matched his authority. What he said and did mattered, because of the example he had set.

In time, even the appearance that elections continued and that the people determined who was in charge was abandoned. Not long after the death of Augustus, the Senate issued a decree and started the transfer. Now the elections for the highest positions, those of praetor and consul, would no longer take place in the fields outside Rome. The Senate itself would decide who was to hold those positions. The assemblies of the people would still meet to elect the junior magistrates and to pass laws, but power was shifting, much as over time it moved from the assembled citizens of London to the elders of that city. The constitution would continue to adapt, but for the next two hundred years it was the Senate that gave legitimacy to whoever occupied the position of leading citizen, to Augustus in his lifetime and his successors thereafter.

The wealth and power of the Senate

The wealth controlled by the Senate was considerable. For centuries it had tax revenues from the provinces and revenues from customs and other taxes and duties. With these streams of funds, it had monetary power as well as the power that came from its natural authority in society. The payment of the army came from these revenues, which further cemented their power.

Then, as now, there was a need to control the finances of the state, and this control had for centuries been firmly and securely with the senators. No state expenditure had been possible without their approval, just as in modern democracies the executive needs the legislature to approve budgets. The most senior executives, the consuls, had discretion in the use of the funds voted to them but received the funds only if the Senate approved. The state financial officials – the quaestors, the lowest-ranking officials – could ask for funds from the Senate for specific purposes and needed its approval. Every five years the Senate voted funds to the very highest official of the state, the censor; these funds were used for the repair of public buildings and for new works.

The funds that came into the state had been continuously increasing because of war. When a new territory was conquered, there was booty which was distributed as the spoils of conquest to those who had participated in the venture and to the state. But there was a second gain, which was the tribute or taxes that came annually from the new province. That gain was the property of the state. The state assessed the tax that should come from the new territory, and that was collected on its behalf. There was an advantage to war beyond the mere glory of the conquering general: the future enrichment of the state through the flow of tax. Substantial tax revenues, for example, had been acquired by Pompey through his eastern conquests, substantially more than had been produced by Caesar's conquests of the poorer western provinces of Gaul. Indeed, when Julius Caesar raised the pay of the army, he awarded them a pay level that would not have been possible without the recent conquests of Pompey.

These were enormous flows of money, which, during the first century BC, roughly doubled the revenue managed by the senators and managed by them clearly for the benefit of the state. Money brings temptations, and the man in charge of fund allocations is always tempted to divert some of that flow in his direction. From time to time, and with varying effectiveness, the Senate introduced rules that restricted their members' involvement in business, much as in modern times the business affairs of members of parliament are considered a matter of public interest.

These allocations of funds took place in a debating chamber much the same as that of modern parliaments and congresses, and debate was as fierce and passionate as it can be in those chambers. When Cicero had in 70 BC argued for the impeachment of Verres, who had been governor of Sicily, a Roman province, he was clear, as reported in his oration, *In Verrem*:

> This man whom I have brought for trial is your opportunity to restore your reputation as judges, your opportunity to regain the respect of the people of this city and your opportunity to do what our allies expect. Impeach this embezzler of public funds, this harasser of our Middle Eastern provinces, this exploiter of our laws and this ruin of our province of Sicily.

At stake here is not just the reputation of the Roman people or the security of their rule over the provinces, which depended on populations that peaceably accepted the yoke and must not be goaded. More at stake were the revenues of the state; the more Verres took while governor of Sicily, the less there was to be transmitted to Rome.

The destruction and disorder that had followed the civil war made it evident that the old ways of doing things needed to change.

A settlement was reached within the Senate that established a new procedure. The arrangement come to by the Senate, of which Augustus had been a member since the age of nineteen, was a new division of responsibilities. Until that time Italy had been governed directly by the Senate, and all the provinces had been governed by men of senatorial rank and appointed by the Senate and sent abroad as governors, men who had already proved themselves at home by achieving the high rank of praetor or consul.

A change to this ancient practice was now adopted by the Senate. The negotiations and deals between individuals that led to this agreement are lost to us; what happened behind their closed doors is as much unknown to us as the private meetings, individual conversations, and political agreements that precede the formation of modern state and corporate settlements. Some would have been motivated by fear that recent terrors would be repeated, some by fear of losing their wealth. Some might have believed that any agreement was better than none, and they simply desired peace. Others might have been alarmed by the prospect of thwarted ambition and yet others might have welcomed the prospect of change and the novelty of doing something different. However, the outcome of their deliberations was clear, and the settlement they reached reduced the power and revenues of the Senate and increased those of Augustus. In reality, it achieved a new balance of power which was to serve all well for over two hundred years.

The responsibility for the government and revenues of the provinces would now be split. The Senate would retain the government of Italy and the core provinces that surrounded it, but the government of the provinces that contained the borders of the world under Roman rule would fall to one man, and that was Augustus. The provinces of, for example, Gaul, won by Julius Caesar, and Syria, won by Pompey, and other provinces were to be governed by men directly appointed by him and not by the Senate. With the exception of Egypt, they were to be members of the Senate who had served as praetors or as consuls, but their first loyalty was to be to him.

The opportunities for material advancement from conquest had lain in the invasion of the territories that lay beyond the borders of the world ruled by Rome. Entry into those territories was now

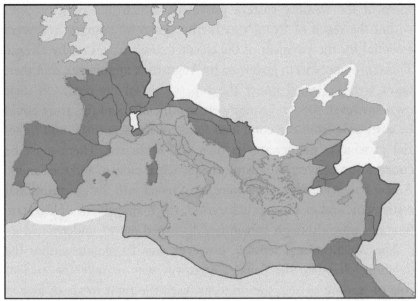

The separation between the imperial (in red) and senatorial (in pink) provinces

through provinces that were governed by the appointees of Augustus, and he was to set the limits of Empire. There was to be no further expansion without his approval and, after 19 BC, no general, other than the emperor, was to be awarded a triumph – that is, no general other than the emperor could parade through Rome displaying the booty and captives he had won in his successful conquests. With that, competition among the elite changed. The Senate retained its centuries-old dignities and respect but was no longer a route to material advancement – nor was it now the *only* route to political advancement. The governorship of some great and wealthy provinces lay outside its power of patronage. There was something in all of this for those who wanted peace, for those who were ambitious for the dignities of the Senate, and for those whose ambitions lay elsewhere.

The old treasury, the aerarium, which had been managed by the Senate since time immemorial, would continue to exist, collect its customary revenues, and disburse sums under the usual senatorial oversight. It would receive the revenues of the provinces governed by senators and the revenues of the remaining provinces, those governed by Augustus. The revenues included taxes that came from some of the wealthy eastern provinces, which had been brought within the reach of Rome's extractive grasp by Pompey and were essential for the payment of the elevated army wages set by Caesar. Those provinces were governed by Augustus's appointees, and their taxes were collected under the supervision of his men. On their own, however, these revenues were insufficient, and the army could be paid only from the combined funds of the senatorial and imperial provinces; neither on its own was sufficient. There must be cooperation between Augustus, the principal citizen, and the Senate. A new balance and tension were introduced into the constitutional settlement, and as long as it survived, the management of the state finances was, although sometimes disturbed, never undermined.

The constitutional tension, however, was to remain within the debating chamber, the Senate. Augustus was to take the ancient role of leading citizen, the princeps, with the right to speak first in the meeting of the Senate, and he held that position for forty years. One of the wealthiest of its honoured citizens, with power over all the border provinces, would participate in an assembly that ultimately made or broke reputations. The Senate, and its leading citizen, might also from time to time remember that the Senate had the power to condemn to death those it considered enemies of the people, a power it would later exercise against Nero.

A new confidence

With the new system of settlement came new peace and confidence, also renewed creativity. Literature flourished with writers such as Livy, Virgil, Ovid, and Horace. Until then, almost all the great literature read by the Roman elite were works that had been produced in Athens or other parts of Greece, written by people who were not Romans, and written in Greek. Now the Romans produced their own works in their own language. How they saw themselves changed: they were not just masters in war but also capable of excellence in other arts. These works celebrated their history, how they had grown by assimilating other peoples rather than being exclusive, how they came from people who took risks, survived and thrived. They celebrated change and looked to the future, which would remember them. These were the values of an enterprising people.

A great new history of the city and its achievements was commissioned, and Livy laid out what had happened through the long centuries from the foundation of the city to his day. The stories were so old that they survived only as legends, those from one hundred or two hundred years before, which were documented in histories. Their facts and figures documented in the voluminous and ever-growing state archives were combined with what was retained in living memory to create a series of many volumes. Much of what survives today was transmitted through the copying and recopying of medieval monks. The history tells the story of how Rome around the time of its foundation in the eighth century BC brought in women from another tribe, inviting them with their families to watch games and marvel at the wonders of their great city and its magnificent walls. They needed these women because the Roman population, swelled by an influx of men seeking refuge, could not sustain itself. As the story goes, the Romans first forced their guests to stay but then the women consented against the will of their parents and made their lives in the city, persuaded by the greatness of what their children would inherit.

Virgil told a history too, but a different one. In his long poem, the *Aeneid*, he tells a story that borrows enormously from the structure of Homer's *Odyssey* but tells the other side of that story. The journey of Aeneas is the journey of a man leaving Troy, a man who fought on the losing side, who journeyed away from home to somewhere new. It is not the troubled and adventurous journey of Odysseus returning home from Troy, a victor, but rather the journey of Aeneas with its dangers: battered at sea, many of his ships lost, rousing his men to struggle in the storm when they might live or die, rousing them with the words from the *Aeneid*

> We have known troubles before and have endured
> worse . . .
> Someday, perhaps, it will be a joy to remember even
> these things . . .
> Press on and save yourselves for a better future

and coming, after their own adventures, to a country where a new Troy was to be founded. After war with those who lived in this country, Aeneas and those who survived with him intermarried with the people of this country; their stock was grafted onto the native plant, and a new people, the Roman people, was formed.

Ovid wrote poems of transformation. These *Metamorphoses* took ancient legends and stories and reassembled them for the education and delight of people living in a changing world. How Narcissus, looking into a pool of water and seeing the face of a beautiful boy, fell in love with himself. The nymph who loved Narcissus and whose love was never to be returned wasted away until nothing was left of her but her voice, and the voice of Echo returns words shouted in valleys; it is a voice with no words of its own.

The literary revolution included Horace, the son of a freedman, a slave transformed from servitude at the will of his master, whose son would have all the rights of a man whose ancestors had been free for centuries. The poetry of Horace lives on many hundreds of years since it was written.

> I have raised up a monument
> more lasting than bronze,
> nobler than the pyramids in their royal place.

Words that survive in their original Latin, in translation and in the adaptations of Shakespeare, in Sonnet 55:

> Not marble not the gilded monuments
> Of princes shall outlive this powerful rhyme.

Because almost all the bronze artefacts of the time of Horace have long since been lost or recast and nothing remains of those works, and because the words of Horace survive in translation and adaptations, then it is fair to say that Horace had a point.

It was not just literature that marked a change. Monuments told a new story. When Augustus's will was read out on his death, it described the memorial that was to be established in his memory and to proclaim his values. Copies were to be set up throughout the area over which he had established himself as ruler. These memorials spread the news of what could be done, described the magnificence of the capital and the nature of the peace he had established. The effect was inspiring, overpowering, even encouraging.

The most complete version of this inscription survived until recently on the Temple of Roma and Augustus, which was set up in what is now Ankara, Turkey. This inscription covered the inside and outside walls of the temple and was written in the original Latin as well as in Greek, which was the more common language in the region. Its setting is religious, but the religious outlook was different from our notion of what a religion is. Most modern societies have a separation of church and state, which are seen as two different institutional structures with separate governance. Here there was quite simply no difference. There was one power structure, and the man who held the highest magistracy could hold the highest religious office. Augustus held the title of pontifex maximus, a term at the root of one of the titles of the Pope. Nor was the Roman religion one of belief. It was a religion of form. There were things the state expected you to do, and while doing them you could believe whatever you chose to believe. The temple on which the inscription was carved is dedicated to two gods: Roma, who is the personification of the capital city, and Augustus, who on his death was declared by the senior citizens of Rome, gathered in the Senate House, to be a god, the ultimate reputational reward. Augustus was to be honoured as a god, whether you believed he was or not.

The monument told stories. Eighty silver statues had been set up in Rome, showing Augustus standing or on horseback or in a chariot. He had all those statues melted down and the silver sold. With the money produced by the sale of that silver he bought gold offerings, which he presented to the temple of Apollo, taking care that those offerings honoured the donors of the statues as well as himself. It celebrated self-effacement, and if the reader cared to know what this god looked like, they could find his handsome image on any of the gold and silver coins that had been minted while he lived. It told other stories, of how another Roman leader had looted the treasures of temples in Asia but Augustus had restored to the temples what had been taken from them. The visitor to the temple could read of how in thanksgiving for his successful military operations in Spain and in Gaul the Senate had voted for an altar to be set up in Rome dedicated to the Pax Augusta, the Augustan Peace.

The wealth of Augustus

The memorial also describes his wealth – which was comparable to that of the richest people now alive – and how he had applied that to philanthropic ends. It lists the sums of money he distributed to the people, the army, and in donations to temples, and it describes the building works he financed. The distributions were philanthropic and restrained. The monies given to the people were not lavish handouts to satisfy a mob. They were donated on only six occasions over a period of decades and amounted to a few thousands of pounds in our terms per recipient on each of those occasions. The largest donation he made for the benefit of the soldiers was the initial outlay for a new pension fund. These amounts came from his own wealth and were in aggregate enormous. The total amount distributed to the people and soldiers in his lifetime, according to this inscription, was HS2.4 billion which is between £12 billion and £24 billion in our terms. In addition to these sums were the amounts he expended on the construction or repair of temples, and other endeavours.

The billionaire Augustus

Part of Augustus's wealth came from inheritance. He was the adopted son of Julius Caesar, who left him a large part of the fortune he had won as the spoils of conquest, including his share of the roughly £100 billion from the sale of slaves from Gaul. Part of Augustus's wealth came from his own and other conquests, including his share of the rich treasures of Egypt. Much of the personal wealth of the Pharaohs, gold and silver accumulated over centuries, was taken to Rome. Augustus also received donations. The rich left him legacies in their wills, and in total he received HS1.4 billion from that source or between £7 billion and £14 billion in our terms.

In time this wealth, his patrimony, became an estate that passed from emperor to emperor, not as a personal inheritance but as property to be used by the holder of the office. A new treasury was established to manage these assets, which gave the emperor a great power of patronage.

The building programme

The wealth of Augustus was comparable to that of the state, and he set about using it in a way that was exemplary. The vast wealth of Augustus was applied to the rebuilding of temples and to the building of basic infrastructure such as roads and the systems supplying water to the cities. During the period of his reign, he poured vast sums into the city of Rome. This tremendous flow of funds into one city was transformative. Everyone felt the change in atmosphere from the terror that had come before. The city was alive with activity. There was a feeling of renewal as old buildings were restored and of fresh life as new creations emerged. The opportunities for work drew people to the city, and stories of what was happening flowed out. New techniques were being acquired by those who flooded into a city that had new demand for labour.

The aqueducts, which had fallen into disrepair during the civil war, were mended, and new ones were built. The aqueducts had existed for centuries, but now more and more were built, and from the time of Augustus until a few decades after his death, their construction continued. This enabled the water supply to more than double, bringing with it more opportunity for life within the city. Soldiers involved in the aqueducts' construction learned how to make them and carried that expertise far and wide.

Large parts of many of these aqueducts remain standing today. Through these aqueducts, water flowed great distances from the far hills surrounding Rome. They are civil engineering marvels. For an aqueduct to function properly, it must have a uniform gradient. That is to say, if over one kilometre it drops in height by one metre, then over the next kilometre it must drop by exactly the same amount. Any divergence from this, and the water overflows. In a gentle endless stream, the water flowed and sustained the city.

Building infrastructure and improving city life

These marvels towered over the citizenry. They were a representation of the state and what their benefactors brought to them. The orderly repetition of their arches and, hidden from sight, the endless, gentle flow of clean water supporting life in the great city, provided cleanliness, encouraged the building of baths – later to be mocked by Seneca – and, just as important, made it possible to flush the great sewers, some still in use today. No city had seen such a steady, regular flow of unpolluted water in such volumes, and none would see it for many centuries to come. This water was not taken from rivers, which could be polluted upstream, but from clean, lovely springs off the mountains, to cool the city during the dreadful Roman summer.

We must, however, remember that these structures needed maintenance. A break somewhere could stop the flow all the way along. An attack upon part of the aqueduct, and the whole thing was useless because it must function the whole length or not at all. Theft of the water by individuals for their own use disrupted communal flow. There was therefore an elected official in charge of the aqueducts. The beautiful structures that towered over the city were symbols of a democratic structure – or at least the peaceful and symbiotic relationship between the authorities and the citizenry. If there was a problem with the aqueducts, people knew who was responsible. This was reassuring.

The water that flowed into the city was a public good, but it also created opportunities for private individuals. The houses that are shown in the illustration are modern constructions but are roughly the same height as those that existed in the city at the time the aqueduct was constructed. Blocks of flats, with shops on the ground floor, were built by private individuals, and the accommodations were rented out by landlords such as the senator Cicero. The more than doubling of the water supply generated opportunities for profit. It is easier to rent out flats, for example, if the prospective tenants know that there is a ready supply of clean water in the district.

Life for those who lived in those flats was more exciting than before. The city was a building site. New buildings were going up, and old ruined buildings were being repaired. Augustus restored the theatre of Pompey and built a theatre, which he dedicated to his nephew, Marcus Claudius Marcellus. He completed the forum of Julius Caesar and the basilica between the temples of Castor and Saturn. He built the forum of Augustus from war booty.

These projects were carried out in a system of public/private partnership that had existed for centuries.

The state authorities put out to tender contracts for the building of these structures and contracts for their maintenance, policed the structures, and where necessary agreed to variations with contractors. Men in Rome grew wealthy from the construction sector and found prestige in being able to associate themselves and their families with the great buildings of the city. In a world where wealth was a prerequisite for admission into the highest order of society, construction and other commercial and financial enterprises were entry points into the elite.

The structures that Augustus claimed in his Res Gestae to have erected were not built by him personally; in most cases they were not built on his direct personal initiative or subject to his personal oversight. What he brought was money and vision. The rest was provided by the system that had worked for generations, one that had enabled the Senate, the ruling body, and the individual citizens together to provide oversight, labour, and material. The approach used in the construction of state buildings was now applied more generally, and this was different from that used in other societies. These great buildings were not erected by conscripted labour diverted from farms when the agricultural season was over, as was the case for the Egyptian pyramids. Rather, private individuals freely participated in the work, each using his abilities and resources as best he could to his own profit. Contracts for public buildings were put out to tender and funded through the Senate. These contracts covered not just the construction of public buildings but also their maintenance – and not just public buildings but all areas of public life: collecting taxes and running mines, for example.

These contracts were valuable. With the funds to build a temple or maintain a harbour, a man of business and skill could make a fortune. More competitive than his rivals, he might secure contracts that, managed efficiently, would produce revenues exceeding costs

– and the difference went to him. As always, the successful winning of a contract brought kudos and the completion of the building pride. These contracts had always been numerous, and many people were involved in this construction business because, then as now, enterprises subcontracted, needing support from other enterprises, and some excelled at one thing and others specialised in different matters. Some contracted directly with the censors who allocated contracts; others acted in partnership with the lead contractor. Still others stood as guarantors, while another group provided financing.

The system that Augustus used was already in place: the knowledge of how to draw up, negotiate, and enforce contracts, and the construction skills. All these projects required materials that needed to be sourced, and the sourcing was yet another means of profit for traders, shippers, and manufacturers.

The works that Augustus initiated were funded in part from the treasures of Egypt. He had the choice of using the precious metals that came his way by right of conquest to commission gold and silver statues and magnificent works of art or to give as donations to sanctuaries. Instead, he chose to coin it. The works in his great building programme were paid for, in part, by coins manufactured from the treasures of Egypt. During his reign, the contribution that he made to the money supply of Rome flowed through the hands of the men he contracted with and into the hands of those who worked for them and then further on and around. Opportunities for trade and commerce increased.

And, as the treasures of Egypt were melted down, coins were minted and the money supply increased. As a matter of policy, the newly created money was directed largely to infrastructure projects, investments that improved future productivity and the construction of which involved manpower and expertise from all sectors of the economy. This was an enormous economic stimulus.

Professionalising the army

Before AD 14, veterans of wars had been awarded lands. Because the land in Italy was already settled, these awards could be given only after farmers and shepherds had been evicted – that, or change their status from owners to tenants, or settle the veterans in new overseas colonies. In Virgil's exquisite *Eclogues* he describes the lament of the shepherd for the lands he had previously occupied.

> O Lycidas, we have lived to see the day when
> an interloper owns our little field.
> Something of which we had never been afraid has
> happened.
> An interloper says:
> 'These are mine! Get out of here, old farmer!'
> We are conquered and distraught.
> Luck changes everything.
>
> We send these little goats to that man.
> May they do him no good.

The shepherd mourns the loss of his land he loved. The young goats he reared are now no use to him. He is landless and cannot lead them out to pasture.

> You, Tityrus, lying under the spreading branches of a
> beech tree,
> are practising your woodland songs on the slender
> panpipes.
> We leave the gentle fields and our ancestral lands,
> We flee our native country.
> You Tityrus, lazing in the shadows of the tree,
> are teaching the woods to re-echo your call to the
> beautiful country girl.

Augustus had established his peace not just by force but by authority. He commanded the loyalty of the army, but the regular salary of the soldier was maintained at the level set by Julius Caesar and was not increased. A pension fund was constructed to reward long service.

The pension fund provided a lump sum of HS12,000, equivalent to between £60,000 and £120,000 in our terms, after twenty years' service, later increased to twenty-five years' service, to the ordinary soldier and higher amounts to the Praetorian Guard. Its value to the legionary can be assessed using the factors that the Roman lawyers used in inheritance-tax valuations. According to these valuation factors, the lump sum would have bought an annual lifetime income of about two thirds of the pre-retirement income.

The cost of this change in the remuneration structure was considerable, but the state finances were largely insulated from the change. A third treasury, the aerarium militare, was established in AD 6, with its own records, assets, and revenue streams and to be overseen by a board of three former praetors. This treasury was funded through an initial capital injection from Augustus's own funds of HS170 million, which is equivalent to between £850 million and £1.7 billion in our terms, and thereafter by a one-percent tax on sales by auction plus a five-percent tax on inheritances. An increase in the number and value of auction sales or in the value of personal estates increased the income of the treasury; a thriving economy helped keep this treasury solvent. The initial funding was sufficient to pay the benefits due in the first one or two years.

The introduction of the benefit represented a fundamental change in how the army worked. No longer did the soldier need to look to booty as a way of funding his post-service life, nor did the state have to confiscate land at home to reward returning veterans. A disciplined army could exist now without needing to wage aggressive wars to provide the career success its soldiers needed. Yet more important, the successful payment of the end-of-career bounty depended on the smooth operation of the state in collecting taxes and not on the ability of individual generals to conduct wars and share the prizes. Order, not chaos, was what the soldier now needed. The new benefit was also payable only at the end of normal service; early discharge was financially ruinous. Rebellion was now a costly option, especially for the older soldiers nearer to discharge, who risked losing the main financial benefit of their service. The structure was an added instrument of disciplinary control. With the exception of an increase in pay of soldiers in AD 84, which had no great impact on the state's finances, there was to be no further increase for close on two hundred years.

The soldier overseas now could dream different dreams. When in later times the soldier mixed with businessmen in the London Mithraeum, conversations about how business worked and how trading opportunities could be exploited had a new interest to him. In time he would have his HS12,000 and might be able to use this to buy goods needed in London from traders he had met in Cologne, for example. And the time to retirement from service gave him – if his mental constitution was suitable – the opportunity to learn how others made their mistakes with money and what he might best do to avoid falling victim to the temptations that forever have ruined the newly enriched.

Not everyone had this mindset and wanted to profit in this way, but those who did, could. Others had the opportunity to return home with their 120 gold coins, buy land in their home locality, and live on purchased land rather than on confiscated property. Others could place these coins into the safe keeping of bankers and thereby provide investment capital to those who needed it. In time, generations of former soldiers were set up to be small holders or traders, all with an interest in a stable law-abiding society.

Chapter 4

Money

The Trillion-Dollar Coin

In our modern monetary system, central banks make money out of thin air. For example, in the United States, the Treasury has the power to fully determine the face value of a platinum coin. It can have a platinum coin minted with metal content worth a few dollars and call that coin a billion-dollar or trillion-dollar coin. By the very act of saying that such a coin is a trillion-dollar coin it becomes worth a trillion dollars. There is no person and or corporation in the United States with wealth sufficient to take that coin, but the President could deposit the coin with the Federal Reserve, which would have to accept it as worth a trillion dollars and transfer that amount to the account of the Treasury. The balance sheet of the Federal Reserve after the transaction would be completely in order. On one side of the sheet would be a liability of a trillion dollars; on the other side would be an asset, that little coin pronounced worth a trillion dollars. By the mere declaration that this object was a trillion dollars the President would have created sufficient money to fund the United States military for more than a year, without having to raise taxes.

No such coin has ever been issued, which is fortunate. The easy creation of money by central banks has destroyed the economies of whole countries, such as Germany between the wars and Venezuela at the present time. Such an action has destroyed jobs, prospects, and livelihoods, and it has created the worst civil unrest. This marvellous magical modern-day process of governments valuing an asset at what they wish and then depositing it with a central bank is one way of creating wealth nowadays.

The currency we use is partly paper, partly metal, and partly electronic. We use banknotes and coins, but mostly our currency is fictional: numbers recorded in electronic files, patterns of electric impulses, or simply the belief that the numbers we see on bank statements will someday allow us to buy things. Much of our money is made by the same magic that causes a platinum token to be worth a trillion dollars. Regularly, central banks accept assets from governments and corporations, value them as they see fit, and then credit the accounts of those who have handed them over. A central bank, such as the Federal Reserve in the United States, can, for example, accept a bond issued by a corporation, value the bond at US$1 billion and transfer US$1 billion to the account of that corporation, money which can be used to buy goods and services. It is irrelevant to this process whether there is anyone who would willingly pay US$1 billion for that bond or indeed whether there is anyone who wants it at any price. The functioning of our system depends on these fictions continuing.

While there were no banknotes in the Roman world, documents could acquire monetary value by the mere fact of the words written on them – and be transferable: see Chapter 2. The Roman banking system, as will be described later in this chapter, also could create money out of thin air, as our banking system does. In both our and their cases, commerce depended on this creation of money and its proper management, and on trust.

Trust in a currency

When we enter a shop and hand over paper money and receive change, there are a lot of things that do not happen. We do not question the relative value of the 'copper' and the 'silver' coins we get in return, and we do not even mind that they are debased versions of what once would have been handed over in change. We accept them because we believe, without thinking, that others will too. The belief comes from trust in a system that has operated since before we were born.

A five-year-old child today in whichever country she lives is capable of recognising that country's legal tender, will eagerly accept gifts of coin used in that country for routine purchases, and will reject as trinkets coins that her contemporaries in other countries will value. She will know how to convert her coins into desirable goods.

In the nineteenth century in Ireland, millions of people hardly ever saw money. They worked land that was not theirs, and the rewards they took from that land were the potato crops they grew. They acquired a few copper coins from the odd sale of this or that and used those coins to buy the few things they needed beyond the food they grew. During the time of the Famine, one such person who happened to come into some money and who was paid in a banknote took that note to a pawn shop and pawned it, receiving less than the value of the note. And if he never redeemed his pledge, he probably was not the less happy for that. What those in the town saw as money he saw as useless paper.

A coin on its own is not money. It is just an object. Roman coins were money once but are not money now. They are still valuable for their metal content or to collectors but are no longer money. They are useless for buying things in today's world; for example, no shopkeeper will take them in exchange for a newspaper. Once these coins were used for buying and selling because of the embedded belief that they were valuable and that others would accept them also. When that recognition and those beliefs were gone, the coins ceased to be money. Coins for which men were once murdered are now mere curiosities.

Creating a currency

The Roman monetary system, and that used in England and other countries until well into the twentieth century, was based on three coin types: gold, silver, and copper or bronze. Illustrated overleaf are the coins used in the time of the emperor Vespasian during the first century and the coins used in the eighteenth century in the time of King George the Second.

In both cases, the image of the ruler is shown with a legend naming him. The gold coins and the silver coins are about the same size. There was a relationship between the silver coins and the gold coins. One gold guinea in the time of George the Second was worth twenty-one silver shillings. One gold aureus in the time of Vespasian was worth twenty-five silver denarii. Shopkeepers in the times of both these rulers knew what change should be given for a gold coin, and their customers did too. This trust in the rate at which bits of valuable metal will be exchanged did not emerge easily or by chance.

Gold, silver and copper coins of the first century and the eighteenth century

In fact, the creation of the Roman monetary system, the first to use gold and silver coins, which were exchanged in fixed and universally accepted amounts, came from the need to solve the problem of how to calculate a soldier's pay, and was made possible by the great increase in the supply of gold available to the Romans after the conquest of Egypt.

Prior to the fourth century BC, the Roman army was largely

remunerated on the basis of booty captured. It had been a volunteer army drawn from the Roman citizenry. Soldiers did receive payments, but these were rather nominal. The soldiers' motivation lay in the glory that attached to victory and in the booty that fell to them when foreign lands were conquered and the captured riches were distributed amongst the soldiers.

By the first century BC, the army had become professional. After the Roman state gained control of the Spanish silver mines, soldiers were paid regular amounts, and soldiers became accustomed to this system. This changed control over the soldiers; they now depended not only on opportunities for conquest, but also on a regular and orderly flow of money. The change also meant that money was regularly being distributed into the economy. The soldiers were not being rewarded with captured objects that might be valuable but not what they needed. Their reward was money, which everyone wanted.

When Julius Caesar doubled the pay of the soldiers in the middle of the first century BC, he doubled the number of silver coins that needed to be transported to the camps, some of which were in unstable border provinces, far from the mints where coins were produced. There was also the difficulty in finding that amount of silver. The soldiers did not need to be paid in new silver coins; some of the pay came from coins handed over by local taxpayers, and sometimes the actual payment of the coins was delayed. Nevertheless, the doubling of the pay of the soldiers created an enormous demand for new silver. Every four months, more than eighty tonnes of silver had to be found, from taxes or newly minted silver. That amount of silver was not regularly available.

The solution was to start payment not just in silver but also in higher denominations of gold. Instead of the eighty tons of silver, only seven tonnes of gold would have to be distributed every four months, less than one tenth the weight. Even that amount of money was not easy to come by. Rules were introduced which limited the amount of cash that soldiers could hold in the camps where they were based, forcing money into circulation and creating opportunities for the authorities to recover money through taxation. Accounts were also set up in the camps for individual soldiers, with pay credited to them as book entries rather than coin, which limited the amount of coin that needed to be transported. The supply of gold coins, which had been relatively rare, increased, as did the state demand for more of them to be made.

There remained, however, a further opportunity to regulate the monetary system. When Julius Caesar started to make payments to soldiers in gold coins, there was no fixed and universal rule for how many silver coins you must get for one gold coin. That was a matter for negotiation and made buying and selling more difficult. As well as negotiating the price of the vegetables you were buying, you needed to negotiate on what change you should be given. You never knew how much your gold coin was worth until you did that negotiation, and, because you used silver coins every day to purchase basic supplies, you never could be sure whether you had enough money or not.

Augustus fixed the rate between these two coins by decreeing that one gold coin was worth twenty-five silver coins. He could just as well have decided that one gold coin was worth twenty silver coins or thirty silver coins, and it would have made little difference to commerce, just as we could have one hundred and twenty pennies in the pound or cents in the dollar and it would make little difference to commerce. What matters is that there is one rule and it is accepted by everyone. That rate would be used when the state collected taxes, and soldiers would demand that rate when they went into the marketplace.

Then as now there was a need for bankers and money changers. At the end of most business days, today's shopkeepers deposit their day's cash takings at the banks or have security firms do this for them. Banks accept the coins and notes and, when the amounts are large, charge a fee for doing so. The same happened in the towns and villages of the Roman Empire, and traders who had too many gold coins and needed silver coins visited money changers who, for a fee, exchanged gold coins for silver coins and silver coins for gold coins. These money changers were required to follow the fixed rate that Augustus had set between the gold aureus and the silver denarius.

Thus, for the first time, a monetary system had been created in which high-value coins and low-value coins of different metals were used together in a fixed relationship that was universally accepted. The lump sum paid to the soldier on discharge amounted to one hundred and twenty gold coins, which could easily be carried on his person, and any one of those could be converted into silver coins at a rate he knew and did not have to guess at. Those silver coins could pay for his daily needs.

The silver denarius was used in daily transactions. When, for example, in the Bible story of the miracle of the loaves and fishes in the Gospel of Mark, Jesus challenged his disciples to feed the crowd of five thousand, his disciples asked him if they were to go into the marketplace and buy two hundred denarii worth of bread. One silver denarius would have bought enough bread to feed twenty-five people. Copper coins were used to give change for silver coins. The illustration above shows the reverse of a Roman sestertius commemorating the capture of Judea and the reverse of an English half-penny showing Britannia. There were smaller copper coins. A few of those smaller copper coins would be enough to buy a family the bread it needed for a day. In the Bible, in the Gospel of Mark, the daily wage of a worker is one silver denarius, which would feed and house a small family. Between them the silver and copper coins shown in the above illustration are all that was needed for daily life.

The gold aureus was useful as a store of value because it could be used for large transactions and also be converted into silver coins for daily purchases. A good number of gold coins that the soldier received on discharge could be used to buy a small plot of land.

The bankers

It was not just soldiers who had accounts. A widely used banking system had emerged before the time of Augustus.

Until well into the twentieth century, world banking practices were no different from what they had been in the time of the Roman Empire. When I was a boy, I opened an account at College Green branch of the Bank of Ireland in Dublin. I signed my name on a card on which an account number had been written by hand, and I filled in the "occupation" blank with "schoolboy". I was given a small blue book, which noted the amount I had handed over. Whenever I had some money that I wanted to save, I brought that money into the bank and handed over the coins. The teller then noted the new balance in the blue passbook and also went to the very large files kept behind the counter and recorded the new deposit there. This system of manually recording the handing over of monies and providing written evidence of the deposit is the same system used in the time of the Roman Empire – and used throughout the world until very recently. And, as happened in Rome, I was paid interest.

Bank of Ireland, Dublin: doing business in Ireland the Roman way

There were additional similarities. Money was transferred between the branch in College Green where I banked to other branches around the country and to branches of other banks around the world. These transfers were made, when I was a schoolboy, by using telexes in which my branch sent instructions to the other branch. Nowadays those instructions are sent electronically. Before the telex was invented, they were sent by letter, as they had been in Roman times. My account was small, and I knew nothing of these transfers, but they were important to trade and commerce.

These transfers happened as follows. My bank, for example, had an account with a bank based in London, and had I wanted to send, say, £100 to a friend in London, my bank in Dublin would have reduced the number in my blue passbook by £100, made a manual adjustment in its files behind the counter in College Green in Dublin, and telexed London to ask them to reduce their account there by £100 and increase my friend's by £100, which the people in London would have done with pen and ink. I would have had £100 less in my account in Dublin, and my friend would have had £100 more in his account in London. The bank would have charged me a small fee for making the transfer, and my friend's bank would have charged him a small fee for accepting the transfer.

Banks in the time of the Roman Empire had similar relationships with different areas around their world. For example, a trader travelling from Rome to Alexandria to buy goods there to sell back in Rome did not need to carry money with him. All he needed was to carry a document from a banker in Rome instructing a banker in Alexandria to make a fixed sum of money available to the trader. The trader travelled with the equivalent of one of our cheques or bankers' drafts.

Having purchased goods in Alexandria and having transferred funds to the individual with whom he had done business in that city, he returned home. No coins needed to accompany him on his journey there and back to Alexandria, and indeed very few coins have been found on Roman shipwrecks that happened before AD 250.

The money transfer system operated across the Mediterranean basin and into the provinces governed by Rome. It enormously facilitated commerce because it removed the need for the physical transportation of coins over long distances, which is risky and expensive even now. The system also made it easier to carry out large transactions. Nobody buying a house today goes along to the seller with a van full of banknotes and coins, and nobody in the Roman world looking to spend large sums on land needed to bring along tons of metal. The Roman bank network enabled large financial transactions to be carried out and large sums of money to be advanced to a trading business.

All this was possible because of a common legal system that operated across this area. The proof of deposit issued at Rome looked the same as one issued in London or Alexandria and was enforceable in the same way. The trader travelling from Rome to Alexandria was not travelling to a country whose laws he did not know and whose system of redress he did not trust. The Roman authorities, moreover, were aware of the risk that trusting individuals might be gulled and lose their money; modern financial services regulators are aware of those same risks today. Roman banks were therefore required to keep records of the amounts of money that individuals paid in and those they withdrew. These records were similar in nature to those manual records kept in College Green when I was a boy, and the Roman banks could be required to produce their records as evidence in legal cases.

The banks that existed in Roman times were partnerships, much as many of those that operated in nineteenth-century Europe and elsewhere. Rich men put up their capital, took in deposits, and lent out money. Some modern banks continue to operate like this, for example, C. Hoare & Co in the United Kingdom, which has no shareholders and is backed by the capital of the descendants of those who founded it in the seventeenth century.

This banking structure, which operated through business meetings in public places and which was embedded in legal structures, was sufficient for the creation of money beyond that in circulation as coin. This is similar to what happens nowadays in our banking system. Central banks create money out of thin air and issue it to the retail banks that lend us money and where we deposit our savings. When those retail banks lend us money, which is then deposited back into the banking system, new money is created.

When we count up the supply of money in a country, we count the notes and coins in circulation. We also count the deposits at banks that can be withdrawn on demand. These deposits are as much part of the money supply as notes and coins in people's pockets.

Banks create money in the following fashion. Let us suppose you deposit £1,000 with a bank. Suppose the bank uses the £1,000 you have deposited to make a loan of £1,000 to someone who buys an antique table from a dealer. Suppose the antique dealer then deposits that £1,000 back with the bank. There are now two deposits: yours of £1,000 and the dealer's deposit of £1,000. The amount of money has increased by £1,000. Most of the money in our economies is created by this second, apparently magical process. When banks lose confidence or for other reasons reduce lending, then the amount of money shrinks. It was the same in the Roman banking system.

As the banks grow by lending more and more of their deposits, then more and more of their assets are loans that they have made to their customers, and less and less is ready cash. If too many depositors want their money back, then the banks may run out of cash. If the loans go bad, then the banks may not be able to repay their depositors, with potentially devastating results.

Failure of trust

The Roman banking system faced the same risks as our own.

In 2008, queues of customers formed outside the branches of a medium-sized United Kingdom savings institution. Customers were queuing to withdraw the money they had deposited with Northern Rock, not because they needed it for their immediate use but because their trust in the institution had failed. They believed that if they did not withdraw their money now, they might not be able to in the future. This was the rational thing to do because the bank had lent almost all its assets as property loans and had kept little by way of cash in reserve. Trust had failed, and those who came first in the rush would get the cash. But the most important depositors did not stand in the queues outside the bank. Northern Rock had borrowed large sums of money from investors on terms that allowed the investors to ask for their money back with little notice. Those large sums of money had been lent out on long-term mortgages, and the cash to repay those large investors could come only from other investors placing money on deposit. With none to be found and almost no cash left, the bank shut its doors.

Initially the misery that faced individuals was limited to those who had banked with Northern Rock. The problem, however, was becoming widespread; the general trust on which the banks depended was deteriorating through suspicion and wariness. If queues were to form at other banks and if they too had to shut their doors, then that misery would spread further into the population and be compounded and bring civic disorder to a country which had long been peacefully settled.

If the transfer systems run by the banks no longer functioned, then the payment of salaries by companies and the payment to companies from sales would stop, and with it much economic activity. Government intervened, providing guarantees and taking some banks into public ownership. Banking institutions once again used the money-creating magic that could make a trillion dollars out of a platinum coin, and cash flowed from the Bank of England into the threatened banks to assure that trust would prevail over suspicion.

The queues that had formed outside Northern Rock formed elsewhere in the world, and for good reason. Across the world, property prices had been increasing steadily and dramatically, in the United States and in the United Kingdom, for example. The wariness of losses that would occur if those increases reversed was superseded by the blind optimism that they would continue forever. When property prices started to fall, loans started to fail, and banks now had two problems: little cash in their offices and losses from loans that would not be repaid. To exacerbate all this, large insurance companies had given out guarantees that loans would be repaid, guarantees that could not be met in full. In the United States as elsewhere, government intervened, and cash was manufactured, and guarantees were given.

The world has since recovered, but the problems it then faced were not new. In AD 33, the economic system of the Roman Empire faced a crisis.

The large expenditure of Augustus had led to an enormous increase in the supply of money. At great cost, he had executed great infrastructure projects, such as aqueducts, and laid out funds on the reconstruction of temples and on the construction of his forum. He paid for all this by the regular minting of large quantities of gold and silver coins, creating new money. The people he paid with money used it to buy goods and services in their turn. It all added to economic activity. As his reign had progressed, construction had slowed down and was almost at a standstill during the reign of this successor, Tiberius. There was no great building programme under Tiberius, and the flow of money out of the treasury and into the hands of contractors, builders, and merchants slowed. The collection of taxes continued, along with seizures of land from supporters of Sejanus his former deputy, and that money started to accumulate in the treasury. As more and more accumulated, there was less and less out in the towns and villages for traders to source goods and for citizens to buy them.

With less money around, prices, including land prices, started to fall. With less money around, interest rates rose and loans for trading ventures – voyages to Alexandria to fetch goods back to Rome, for example – became more expensive and less affordable. It was the fall in land values that hurt most. Land was an asset of the elite; it brought status, and as the price of land fell, the elite felt it. To solve the problem of their declining asset values, those members of the elite acted, and they acted against the bankers who were, they believed, the source of their problem – for, after all, it was the bankers who were charging the now exorbitant rates of interest, which had increased from 4 percent to 14 percent.

The Senate therefore required the bankers to renegotiate loans, reducing the rate of interest charged. They also required the bankers to invest two thirds of their asset base in Italian land, in the hope that the increased demand for land would drive prices back up.

Compelled to charge lower interest rates, the bankers called in loans, but their borrowers did not have cash readily to hand, having invested the money they had borrowed in trade ventures and the like. Bankruptcies of borrowers followed. Forced sales, including sales of land, were needed to make good the funds owed, and prices fell still further. Bankers seeing the price of land collapse further held off their purchases of land, hoping for even cheaper prices. The problem was now out of control.

As in 2008, so in AD 33 the state intervened with cash to restore order to a system at the edge of collapse. Of the vast sums of money held by the treasury, Tiberius advanced HS100 million in their terms or between £500 million and £1,000 million in our terms, interest-free for three years to the bankers, and the system stabilised itself, as ours did.

This was the soundest fiscal policy of Tiberius, whose aim had been to increase the wealth of the treasury. At the time of his death (in self-imposed exile), the treasury held HS2.7 billion or our equivalent of between £13.5 billion and £27 billion, sums accumulated from taxes collected and not spent and from the proceeds of confiscating the mines.

Infrastructure spending

The Roman powers-that-be had learned the importance of fiscal policies to the well-being of the citizens. Taxing without spending did not work. Spending was essential to the well-being of the system.

The following graph shows the infrastructure spending of the first five emperors, the Julio-Claudians. The dramatic reduction under Tiberius is clear.

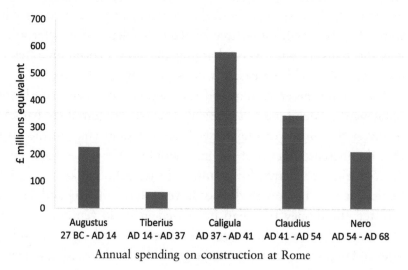

Annual spending on construction at Rome

During the reign of Caligula, which lasted from AD 37 to AD 41, spending started again with the construction of an aqueduct, which would be the greatest addition to the city's water supply for almost two hundred years. Other expenditures, less beneficial to

70

the population at large, were incurred, and palaces were constructed. The aqueduct, started under Caligula, was completed under Claudius, after whom it was named.

Capital expenditure continued under Claudius, who reigned from AD 41 to AD 54, with the completion of the aqueduct started under Caligula as well as additional new aqueducts. A new phase of construction began, and new kinds of works were attempted for the first time. Some distance outside Rome lay Fucine Lake, a large body of water with no adequate outlet; it had become a stagnant breeding place for malaria, and it frequently flooded neighbouring land. A tunnel 5.6 kilometres long was built to drain this lake, creating 15,000 hectares of fertile land that, planted in grain, could feed about 100,000 people. The project provided employment for roughly 3,000 labourers over eleven years.

Building tunnels: improving productivity

The second major project started under Claudius gave Rome new access to the world it had conquered. Rome had no port; ships waited out at sea near Ostia and then either made their way upriver to Rome and discharged goods there or unloaded goods at sea onto smaller craft, which finished the journey upriver. Construction began for a port, a sheltered area where ships could dock protected in case of storms, wharfs where they could unload, and warehouses where goods could be stored. The project took almost twenty years to complete and extended into the reign of Nero. The volumes of goods that could enter and leave the city increased, as did the harbour fees generated by all the activity.

When Nero succeeded Claudius in AD 54, he changed the focus of public spending. Capital expenditure continued but at a much-reduced level and those public works were much more likely directed towards entertainment rather than improving the economic well-being of the city. Amphitheatres and public baths took precedence over aqueducts. The great outdoor space used for chariot racing and other competitions was rebuilt.

New Money

The massive injection of money into the economy that had happened since the beginning of Augustus's reign some eighty years earlier had changed the social order. In the old days, prestige came from conquest or from land, and often inherited land at that. Now mere possession of money brought prestige. This new world was both liberating and threatening. Money changes things and, depending on where you stand, not always for the better.

Petronius, writing a novel in the time of Nero, devotes a chapter of mockery and send-up to the fictional freed slave Trimalchio, despised as vulgar by the elite but having extraordinary wealth from trade. Freed slaves had always had the opportunity to become rich if they had the talent for it, but things were different now. The increase in money supply – and with it the increase in consumer demand, including for imported goods – had increased opportunities: banks could advance loans to anyone they thought could repay, and newly freed slaves could accumulate great sums through trade, financed by bank loans. The scales had shifted.

The characters of the novel wander around the area surrounding what is now Naples. They are young, educated, and on the make, looking for people they can take advantage of. They are sexual adventurers. They get invited to dinner at the house of Trimalchio. They enter his amazing house and at a small dinner party are treated to course after course of the most expensive dishes, as their host works to impress them, flaunting his magnificent wealth and dismissing it as trivial. He is not reluctant to boast of how much he controls, of the great stretches of land he owns. But his young adventurers have, in their minds, advantages over him. Their poverty is outdone by his wealth, but their culture and learning outmatch his. To them he is rich but vulgar, uneducated.

But, vulgar or not, the fictional Trimalchio is rich beyond anything the cultured men could achieve, and his wealth has come from trade. He knows the great profits that can be secured from buying in one place at one price and selling at another for a higher price, and he knows where the differences were. His motto: "I buy well. I sell well." He came from nothing, and is proud of that. He was a slave but has made himself and is willing to take risks.

In the novel he describes how on his first commercial venture he had lost all his capital when the ship carrying the goods he was importing sank. He boasts of his perseverance, of how he was not put off but rather borrowed and, with the help of his wife, restarted his venture. This risk-taking, profit-seeking entrepreneur built more ships, bought goods overseas, a cargo of wine, bacon, beans, perfumes, and slaves. He claims he made a profit of HS10 million or between £50 million and £100 million in our terms, exaggerating in this as in everything else but making a clear point. Trade, for those who are willing to take the risk, can produce fortunes. From trade he moved to property and then into finance, lending to other freedmen.

The fictional Trimalchio represented to Petronius's readers a new world in which an uncultivated man of business could make a fortune that outdid their aristocratic wealth. A new mercantilism was emerging, along with new values, and Trimalchio's values are clear. "Believe me, you have a copper coin, you are worth a copper coin." He says, "What you own is what you are valued at." His was not a refined world. Trimalchio describes the showy and most unrefined monument he has designed to mark his passing and describes it through unrestrained tears. The values of the author Petronius were different: moderate, elegant, refined.

The Golden House

At the end of the fifteenth century, the Golden House of Nero was rediscovered buried under Rome. Artists broke through and came upon an underground cave; inside were exquisite paintings that had retained their freshness from over a thousand years earlier. These images inspired a new style of painting, and once again the old was revived, supplementing the medieval forms that had replaced it. What these artists discovered as they dug deeper into and around the ancient structure was not some building which, like almost all of those in that once-great city, had fallen into disrepair, collapsed or been pillaged when the system collapsed. They were exploring a building that had been obliterated shortly after its completion and buried within the living city, destroyed like the reputation of the man who had built it. They were now exploring a building whose construction and adornments had been magnificent.

The rejected art of the profligate emperor

The Golden House covered a large area of Rome, estimated at between forty and one hundred and twenty hectares. It was built on private lands forcibly acquired from their owners. It dominated the cityscape with its exclusivity. The great palace was a statement of how the constitution threatened to evolve. Here the leading citizen could take land belonging to others and use that land to fulfil his personal dream of what the city should look like and express his personal vision of beauty.

Throughout his reign, Nero lavished money on people and squandered the resources he controlled. Nero completed the port started by Claudius at Rome, but as time went on, he spent increasingly little on infrastructure, which would benefit all and increase the community's prosperity, as Augustus had done. He spent primarily for his personal pleasure and pure extravagance. Capital expenditure fell, but total expenditure did not. Nero also spent most of his money on favourites and courtiers who left nothing behind when their work was done. When Nero died, those who had benefited from his extravagances were ordered to return what he had given them; they were allowed to keep a tenth. However, most of them did not possess even a tenth of what Nero had given them; they had not built up assets from their wealth. Because they were as careless and extravagant as their benefactor, they had nothing to show for all the flow of money, for the HS2.2 billion or between £11 billion and £22 billion in our terms, that Nero had wasted on them. The financial excesses of Nero were thus as damaging as the extreme fiscal prudence of Tiberius had been.

In AD 68, Nero was condemned by the Senate as a public enemy, condemned to suffer the ancient punishment. When he asked what this punishment would be, he was told that he would be stripped and beaten to death. He took his own life before the agents of the Senate could get hold of him. With his death the obliteration of his extravagant house began.

On the death of Nero, the great park that was contained within his Golden House was set to new purposes. The beautiful vista on which he alone, with his guests, looked upon and which was hidden from the great men of Rome whom he did not favour and from all the little people who did not attend him – the beautiful vista with the lovely lake he had created and at the sight of which he once said, "Now I am a man" – was now buried into the foundations of a magnificent amphitheatre, now called the Colosseum. The land upon which only a few people and their attending servants had walked now seated thousands; what had been exclusive became pointedly inclusive.

Some few years later, the transformation of the Golden House was complete when its walls were used as foundations for the great public baths that rose high above the city. Public baths required a small entry fee and were open to all who could afford that. Buried in the foundations of this public enterprise, which sought to benefit all the population both in the enjoyment of its luxuries and the improvement in health that follows from cleanliness, were the beautiful paintings intended for the free enjoyment of a select group who depended on their good standing with an emperor.

The state finances were now being applied in a way that promoted concord, and there was peace again, or such a peace as ever could exist in a world forever threatened along its borders or in its border provinces.

A new crisis

With Nero a new discord had emerged. The state rested on a balance of power between the Senate and the army. No man had been able to hold the highest executive office who did not have both the approval of the Senate and the support of the army. Under Nero there had been a new intellectual flowering, but he had diminished the role of the Senate. A new danger had emerged, and the army in the provinces temporarily became the dominant voice in determining who should hold the highest office. But it could not do that with any stability; within one year after the suicide of Nero, four men held that office as first one and then another won the approval of a fickle and disunited army.

Within one year there were four emperors. The first of these emerged from Spain; Galba was duly confirmed by the Senate and established himself at Rome. He would correct the extravagances of his predecessor. Galba did not, however, understand the subtleties of power, that some things need to be done swiftly and other things more slowly and that the interests of different constituents often need to be balanced. In any case, in the interests of fiscal rectitude, he acted to restrain the costs that might fall on the state treasury and on his own treasury. To that end, he withheld from the Praetorian Guard, whose first charge was the protection of his person, the donative they customarily received on the accession of a new emperor. Without their support, he could not be expected to live long, and he did not. Assassinated, he was replaced with a man chosen by the Praetorian Guard, a man who in his own turn was soon replaced.

The Senate recognised Otho, a fellow senator, as Galba's successor, but the German legions chose Vitellius, who marched on Rome. Facing defeat, Otho stabbed himself to death, his death mourned by the Praetorian Guard who, according to a Roman historian, wept as they carried his body. In Rome, Vitellius spent extravagantly and, running out of money could no longer repay his bankers.

In the East, another general, Vespasian, had himself proclaimed emperor. His army approached Rome and fought that of Vitellius in front of the walls of the city, broke into the city, and continued fighting. The people watched all of this as if it were a show, shouting now for one side and then the other, pointing out the supporters of one side to their enemies on the other side, watching men being dragged out from their hiding places to be slaughtered. The shops were looted, and the streets were piled with bodies in pools of blood. The emperor Vitellius made his way back to his now deserted palace, where he was captured and taken out. He died at the hands of the mob, which had praised him on his

The emperor Vespasian: centralising monetary control

accession and now mocked him as he said, while dying, "Yet I was your emperor."

In AD 69, the Senate recognised Vespasian as the new emperor. With the emergence of Vespasian, the old stability, which had been threatened only for a short time, re-emerged, and order was re-established.

Vespasian was a general who had captured Jerusalem, and he could command the approval of the Senate. Vespasian was a crafty man. Delayed at Alexandria because of the weather and unable to return immediately home to Rome, he was asked to cure a blind man and a lame man. He did not immediately give in to this flattery, this belief in his divine or magical powers; he did not let all of this go to his head. He first arranged that inquiries be made as to the medical conditions of the two wretched souls and, on finding out that the illnesses were temporary, he performed, or feigned, the miraculous cures.

On his death in AD 79, his last words were "Methinks, I am about to become a god." Words with their own humour and from a man who did not take himself too seriously, but also the words of a man who knew the Senate would give him the supreme honour and declare him, on his death, a god, an honour they had withheld from Nero. They did just that, elevating a man of obscure birth to the rank of the gods. They elevated a man whose father had been merely a tax collector in Asia, but who had been at least sufficiently honourable that the taxpayers of Asia erected a statue in the memory of the honest tax collector.

Vespasian had come to power with the support of the legions in the East, proclaimed emperor in Egypt. The accession of Vespasian, and that of Galba and Vitellius, had been proof that emperors could be made elsewhere than in Rome, a most disturbing development. What was good enough for Vespasian was not going to be good enough for others, and he acted to make it difficult for others to repeat his success – to make it difficult for a new rival to emerge from outside Rome.

The reign of Vespasian is marked by very little that could, at first sight, be called achievement. He was, however, remarkable for two things. First, that nothing much happened while he was in charge. His reign was marked by a new peace and stability, and people could get on with things. The Trimalchios could make more money and increase the general prosperity, and the recent disturbances and terrors could fade, become less real, and transform themselves into stories of what must be avoided. And second, he completed the consolidation of the currency. He realised the power of money and how valuable is the right to coin it. Soldiers might find interesting the offer of silver statues and the like as rewards, but a handful of coins was a different matter. The success of Vespasian in the East had depended on the fact that there was a mint there that could be used to manufacture coins. With control over that, he had been able to change silver into coin and ensure that his soldiers were paid. He had controlled their pay; the central authorities had not. In addressing this political problem of his, he inadvertently solved a weakness that existed in the monetary system devised by Augustus, a weakness of which Vespasian was perhaps unaware. In doing so, Vespasian unknowingly increased his power and that of the Roman state.

The weakness of the Roman money system

Currencies such as the Roman currency, which use coins made of valuable metal and are exchanged in fixed and universally accepted ratios, have an inherent weakness. In the Roman currency one gold coin, an aureus, was worth twenty-five silver coins, twenty-five denarii. However, both the gold and the silver coins had a worth of their own, the value of their metal content. They were not coins such as those we use today, the fifty-pence piece in the United Kingdom or the ten-cent piece in the United States, whose metal content is worth much less than the face value of the coin. It makes no economic sense to melt down the fifty-pence piece or the ten-cent piece to extract the metal in those coins. Sometimes, however, it made economic sense to melt down Roman coins or the coins of most currencies used in the world until well into the twentieth century. These currencies had a technical weakness that could be exploited for profit.

If the price of gold increased, then the gold aureus became, for some people, more valuable as a source of gold than as a coin for buying large-value items. A manufacturer of jewellery looking to get gold to make new bracelets, for example, could find it cheaper to melt down gold coins rather than to buy gold. A speculator could find it profitable to exchange his silver coins for gold coins, melt those down for sale to some trader or manufacturer who needed gold, and then take the proceeds in silver coins. The silver coins were now more valuable as coins than as metal because they could be exchanged for gold coins at a favourable rate. All of this is harmful to the currency. Gold coins that are needed so that people can buy and sell valuable assets are being destroyed, and the supply of money is being reduced. The gold disappears from the monetary system where it facilitated commerce and sits inertly as plates on tables or jewellery on wrists, for example. If the price of gold falls and the price of silver rises, then the pressure is on the silver coins.

There is a limitation to how far this exploitation can go, however. There is a limit to the demand for new gold to make ornaments, and there is a demand for coins to use in transactions. Presenting a gold ingot in payment for a plot of land is not the same as handing over the same weight in gold coins. The weakness, however, becomes close to fatal when two different currencies, both based on gold and silver, are used in neighbouring territories.

Exploiting the weakness is a technical matter, but small fortunes could be made by those who understood the opportunity. For example, suppose the coins exchange at twenty silver coins for one gold coin in one territory and twenty-five to one in the other. Suppose the gold coins in both territories are of the same weight and the silver coins are also of the same weight. In this case it makes sense for the speculator to get gold coins in the first territory, melt them down, offer the gold metal to the mint in the second territory, and take the proceeds as silver coins. So long as the mints continue to accept bullion, the speculator makes money. This was a problem for world currencies until the nineteenth century.

For example, towards the end of the eighteenth century, Great Britain experienced a currency crisis as money left the country or coins were melted down. Money had been leaving the country because people had seen an opportunity to profit from exploiting the currency. France, Germany, and the Netherlands had different currencies, with different gold and silver coins of different weights. There was always a profit to be made, sometimes by using silver coins to buy gold coins and sometimes the other way around. The pressure was particularly acute because of the easy access between England and Holland, which operated two separate currencies.

The problem became so acute that there were insufficient numbers of coins for merchants and others to do business; retail and other transactions became difficult, to the extent that in some towns local businessmen produced their own tokens for use in trade, illegally creating their own currency.

Any and all ways in which money could be made from the fact that the prices of gold and silver fluctuated and that coins could easily be melted down were there to be exploited for profit. When the price of silver dropped, then large amounts of silver coins, shillings, were presented to merchants who, because the shilling was legal tender, were compelled to accept the coins in exchange for more valuable goods, or else find ways to avoid the sale. Gold coins that had become worn with use and contained less precious metal than new coins could be dumped on merchants. All of this was damaging to commerce.

The problem of a metal currency was first explicitly solved in 1816 when the United Kingdom enacted legislation to stabilise its currency. The first measure that was enacted was simple in its genius. The mint would always buy silver shillings for more than their silver content. It now no longer made sense to melt a shilling for its silver. Indeed, a worn-out silver coin was as valuable as a newly minted one. It also made economic sense for the mint; after all, it costs money to mint coins. Private arbitrage opportunities had been shut off.

The second measure was to limit the extent to which the silver coinage was legal tender. This rule removed the risk that coins could be acquired cheaply when the price of silver fell and then dumped on merchants. It also tended to limit hoarding.

The effect of these two rules was to generate a stable currency free from arbitrage difficulties and was, as William Scott remarked in 1910, "one of the chief causes of England's long continued dominance in the field of international finance".

It was these two rules, together with a rule introduced in 1774 that made gold coins legal tender in unlimited amounts, provided the gold coins were of full weight, that made for a stable currency and paved the way for the creation of fiat money. When in 1920 the silver content of the shilling was reduced by fifty percent, the debasement had no inflationary effect and did not disturb confidence in the coinage. The shilling had by then become a universally desirable commodity, a necessary condition for coinage. These developments never happened in the Roman world, but an approach was taken which had the same effect, or at least for a period of one hundred and fifty years.

A powerful currency

Vespasian completed a project that had been started before Augustus and had proceeded in small steps but never finished. He finished the unification of the currency. With that, he achieved a quiet transformation that was enormously to the benefit of commerce and the general well-being of his world. All rival currencies, with the exception of that used in Egypt, had been eliminated – and even that was controlled. Cities were allowed to produce copper coins that might have local emblems, but the coins must be produced to Roman standards of weight and size.

Coins were made in the mints by melting metals to form small discs. These were then struck by dies to create an image on one side, and the discs were then turned over and a different image was struck on the other side. These coins were struck from metal mined, as for example in the silver mines of Spain or from metals handed over as tribute. Enormous numbers of these coins were struck each year in mints, which were set up across the empire. Augustus, for example, established mints in Spain near the mines there and in Lyon in Gaul to coin the bullion being supplied as tribute, the regular taxes paid by the territory that had been conquered by his adoptive father.

Vespasian closed these and other local mints, and from now silver and gold coins, with the exception of Egyptian silver coins, could be minted only in Rome, in mints controlled by Vespasian and his successors. He centralised the capacity to turn precious metals into money. It would no longer be possible for generals in the further reaches of the Empire to seize the local mints, take possession of the dies, and then turn local treasure into the coins that the soldiers were accustomed to receive as pay. The ability of speculators to make profits was also severely curtailed.

For long periods, the Roman imperial coinage was a stable currency, did not collapse, and indeed continued to be used despite being debased. Control of the currency by restricting minting rights within the empire, together with the need for coin to pay taxes, as well as the commercial need for coin, which provided demand for the currency, all acted against the pressures towards destruction of the currency.

The spreading of the currency and the universal demand for it had other advantages. The universality of the currency gave it a stability that the world currency was not to see again until monetary reforms in early nineteenth-century United Kingdom produced a new global currency, and it gave the central authorities a new economic power.

Then and now, control of the currency is a source of economic power. In 2018, for example, the United States President issued a proclamation that forbade the participation in the United States financial system by individuals or companies who traded with Iran. The purpose of this proclamation was to depress the economy of Iran by restricting trade with it and to impoverish that country. Public companies value their ability to transact through the United States financial system and, faced with the choice of losing Iranian business or loss of access to the United States financial system, they chose to lose the former. The power that the United States exercised in this case was not military, nor was it the brute power of withholding loans or grants. Nor, indeed, was it the withdrawal of its own goods and services from the Iranian market. It was the simple exclusion of companies from the financial system of the United States.

To all intents and purposes, the United States dollar is the dominant currency in the world today, which gives the United States a power comparable to its military power. From the time of Vespasian, the Roman state controlled what was, to all intents and purposes, a dominant currency then and exercised a similar power. The success of this world currency enabled the next phase of development: the growth of towns and cities and the creation of an urban power-house.

Chapter 5
Cities

My grandparents, who were farmers in Ireland, needed no money for milk, eggs, bacon, and most of the fruit and vegetables they consumed. Nor did they need it to feed their horse. The milk they needed came from the cows that grazed their land and that were milked early in the morning and in the evening before tea. Eggs were laid by hens that roamed the farmyard. They were locked into the henhouse at night to protect them from foxes. As a small boy I found and brought one of these eggs in and showed it proudly to my grandmother. She smiled at me and said that she had left that egg in the barn on the straw so that the hen would sit on it. It would then turn into a little chick, like those outside in the yard.

The house was heated from fireplaces in each room, which burned wood fallen from trees in the fields. Ducks and pigs provided meat, and hay taken from the fields fed the horses. A sack of flour stood in the kitchen, and from that, with butter and milk, pastry was made, which, with apples taken from the orchard became never-to-be-forgotten apple tarts. The flour and the sugar were bought in the town, as were other supplies, but most of what they needed came from their land and their own work. Bad weather meant that the surplus was reduced; it was not a disaster.

The people they knew in the local town needed money for almost everything they consumed. While some would keep a few chickens in the yard at the back of their house, almost all the food they consumed was bought in shops, not grown by themselves on their own land. Their work was not largely devoted to the production of what they themselves consumed but to the production of what was consumed by others or to the rendering of services that were useful to others. The shopkeeper bought goods at one price, stored and displayed them, and hoped to sell them for a higher price. The dressmaker bought cloth from him and turned out dresses to the shopkeeper's order or to the order of clients who visited her. What all of them needed from their customers was money. There were no services that the blacksmith who made horseshoes could offer the shopkeeper who had no horse. The coins, however, that the blacksmith received from the farmer whose horse he had shod were good for purchase in the shopkeeper's store.

The town was a garrison town, and its barracks were connected by straight roads to the villages beyond the town and near the great landowners' houses, roads built so that soldiers could move out quickly, escaping the ambushes that the older, meandering paths had made easy. These straight roads were financed and built by landowners for their protection from attack by the locals. The soldiers protected the town and the surrounding country from insurrection. The notes and coins distributed to the army as pay circulated out into the town from those soldiers who lived in the barracks and those who lived in the army cottages on either side of the main road. That money in turn made the traders, and those whose services they used, wealthy, and it funded the import of goods, which tradespeople sold at a profit to their fellow towns-people and to the soldiers. As the businesses of the traders prospered, there were new employment opportunities, which drew people to the town, looking for work. Without money, none of this would have been possible.

By the end of the reign of Vespasian, in AD 79, a universal currency had been created, which was recognised throughout the vast area governed from Rome. It was as widely recognised and trusted across that area as the legal tender of any country now is recognised by a small child. The universal trust in this currency greatly facilitated commerce. A man entering a town anywhere in this vast area with some silver denarii on him and perhaps a gold aureus or two had the wherewithal to transact business, to feed himself, and to find accommodation. His coins would not be refused as foreign, strange, or dubious. They were familiar. The migrant arriving in a town or city knew the price of his labour in the place from which he came and could negotiate around that for coins needed to procure lodging and food.

Work in the cities

Roman towns and cities had long offered opportunities. Located in the walls that were built later around the city of Rome in the middle of the third century, a time when the stable order of the Roman world was threatened, are what survives of a great monument erected by a freedman, a memorial to himself and to his wife. Just as the fictional former slave Trimalchio, who had also designed a great funerary monument, had attained great riches, so had this real former slave. It is a monument, erected not long before the reign of Augustus, to a husband and wife who ran a baking business.

Making money from food production

The frieze along the top illustrates the business of baking. The monument is large, some ten metres high, and the couple who made it were wealthy. Great wealth could come from baking, much as great wealth has come from food production in our time, in the fortunes of families descended from the original Mr Heinz and the

87

original Mr Kellogg. The money came from the same source: the paying customers.

The husband who erected this monument was a freedman, a former slave who had started out with nothing beyond what his master had given him along with such sum of money as he had been allowed to accumulate during the time of his slavery. His wealth did not come from any great inheritance but from what he had built up over time out of his skills and his work. He had this monument erected so that after his death he and his wife would be remembered. The memorial is also a public statement of what could be achieved by a man on his own, starting out with very little.

Eurysaces, however, did not become wealthy just because he and his wife were good bakers or because they had one shop where they sold bread they had baked themselves. There is not enough money in a business like that to pay for the great memorial Eurysaces erected. They needed other abilities as well, such as the ability to organise production and distribution, and then sell what they produced. They needed to be able to manage a supply chain so that grain was always available to the bakeries, and they needed to be able to negotiate with their suppliers. Those qualities, beyond their expertise in their craft, were much the same as needed today by anyone engaged in business.

Eurysaces the husband and Atistia the wife

The man who had previously owned Eurysaces profited from all of this as well. Roman inheritance laws required former slaves to leave part of their estate to their erstwhile owner and, in any case, the owner could reach whatever agreement he liked with his soon-to-be-freed slave. The slave owner did not lose a valuable asset when he freed this man; he may have acquired a share in a new profitable business.

The city of Rome, like other cities of the empire, was a mass of all sorts of people working in various trades. There was great choice for the customer. There were the makers of felt footwear and the makers of women's shoes. The shopper went to those makers of the exact type of shoe she wanted. There were tailors, jewellers, metalsmiths, spinners, weavers, dyers. There were butchers and there were bakers. There were as many occupations and trades as in London in the eighteenth century or later, and as many opportunities for employment and apprenticeship.

There were dealers who connected producers and customers, both wholesale and retail. One man was a dealer in cloaks and another a dealer in oil from Baetica, in southern Spain. There were dealers in books, in metal, in marble, in slaves, in meat, in fish, or whatever else you might want to buy. All of these dealers could see the great memorial that one man had previously set up to celebrate himself, his trade, and the great wealth he had generated by pulling himself up by his own bootstraps. They could see many other memorials around the towns and cities set up proudly to commemorate men in all these and many other occupations. Those surviving memorials make it possible for archaeologists to compile the long lists of occupations that existed in the towns and cities of the Roman Empire, occupations such as shoemaker, clothes folder, carpenter, mosaic maker, wool weigher, butcher, baker, dealer in cloaks, dealer in perfume, dealer in oil, dealer in books, dealer in marble, architect, doctor, hairdresser, bodyguard, cook, comic actor, financial agent, administrator, secretary, and many others, all recorded on monuments set up to commemorate the lives of those inhabitants of Roman towns and cities.

Even in these early centuries we find a high degree of specialisation, a basic requirement for increased productivity. In Rome, for example, some craftsmen made only the eyes of statues. They used imported ivory and bone, coloured stones, glass, and other materials. The eye craftsman shaped the ivory to be the right size for the socket. He got the colour of the eye right. It was a fine craft.

Specialisation: making eyes for statues

A maker of eyes for statues developed relationships with dealers who sourced the ivory and other material he needed, and he developed relationships with the local sculptors and the dealers who bought the eyes he made. All the time statues were being erected in Rome: statues of the new emperor, the cult statues in the new temples or statues of people like Eurysaces who wanted to commemorate themselves. But Rome was only one market for the eye maker. The product of his workshop could find its way to anywhere in the empire, to the distant town of London, say, not through any planning on his part but through a series of transactions between dealers, each interested in making the profit that comes from buying at one price and selling at a higher price.

With the large market available to him, it was possible for a man to concentrate on the business of making eyes for statues, to make nothing else. With each day in which he made more eyes, he learned how to do things a bit better: how ivory responds when you cut it just so, how to make the glass fit better. These lessons settled into his fingers and his memory, and, over time, he produced more eyes of increasingly fine quality. Thus he expanded his business.

A young man coming by chance to his workshop – a young man arriving from some distant town, with nothing but hope and his youth and a few denarii – might become an apprentice, learn the trade, and help his master in his craft and business. They both depended on the city to provide them with food, clothing, footwear, and the rest of what they needed, all of which could be sourced only by means of the silver denarii – from the city and beyond – that they received from the sale of their product.

Workshops clustered in the city of Rome as elsewhere. Areas of the city were devoted to one business or another. The production of a silver vessel could be carried out by a succession of different individuals who specialised in different aspects of the manufacture and carried out their business in separate workshops. All these people depended on one another and on the dealers who imported the silver metal as well as the dealers who took the finished silver vessels off their hands. Just like the man who made eyes for statues, they could become even more expert at what they did. It was a massive system of individual production units, all integrated with one another.

Another requirement for great commercial success is the availability of customers. The United States provided those to the original Mr Heinz and Mr Kellogg, and Rome, with its one million plus inhabitants, provided that to Eurysaces the baker. A baker sitting in Rome could see more customers in a week than his counterpart in a small village might see in a lifetime. The customers of these dealers and manufacturers were not just the wealthy senators and the rest of the elite. The tradesmen were customers for one another. The butcher dealt with the tailor. Money flowed throughout this complex of enterprises. As the city grew and the great infrastructure projects were completed, providing more water to the inhabitants and better access of all sorts, the population grew – the customer base increased. The conditions were just right for a spiral of wealth creation.

Competition developed within a trade, customers having the option to choose from among multiple craftsmen. The woman passing the workshops in the streets where shoes were made could choose between the different types of shoe and also judge the craftsman by the quality of what he produced. Another factor in her decision, of course, was the price to be paid on each item.

Sometimes, however, it is good for business people to manage how they compete with others in the same trade as themselves. The New York Stock Exchange is the largest stock exchange in the world. Its foundation rests on an agreement made between two dozen businessmen in the late eighteenth century. The agreement consists of one sentence only. The men agreed that they would not buy or sell stock for a commission of less than 0.25 percent and that they would give preference to one another in their dealing. The men who set up this exchange had no power to compel others to join, no power to prohibit others from dealing in stocks, and no power to prevent others from forming such associations. They continued to compete against one another, and some did well while others did badly in that competition. They undertook, however, to restrict their competition in the one area where unrestrained competition would have left them all worse off, which was the commission they charged their customers. By giving preference to one another they also made it difficult for others to enter and undercut them. Any other stockbroker looking to get stock for a client could not easily source it from this club. The largest stock exchange in the world today was built on a one-sentence agreement. The businessmen of Rome had the same acumen as those of eighteenth-century New York.

Associations which had legal form and were known as "collegia" were found in Rome and across the empire. Different trades grouped together, such as wine importers or dealers in grain. In the harbour town of Ostia outside Rome are the remains of a structure, now known as the Square of the Corporations, which had separate areas for the different dealers, who sat together and worked, as did the New York stockbrokers, to serve their individual and collective interests. When men of business in Roman towns and cities formed these associations, they did it not just to regulate their affairs but also for other mutual benefits. They provided insurance to cover the funeral expenses of one another and in that regard were similar to the mutual insurance societies of nineteenth-century England. They were also social. It was enjoyable then, as it is now, for people who trade in the same area to meet and chat, sometimes about how to keep new competition out of the market.

There were other opportunities to associate. Buried beneath the Basilica of San Clemente in Rome is another, earlier church, and below that lies a temple of Mithras. Through these layers of history we come to a space in which businessmen and soldiers once gathered.

They worshipped the god Mithras in the same way he was worshipped in London, and afterwards they sat together and socialised. Some of them, the soldiers, had travelled to be there, and some of those had been to the eastern territories or to Africa or to London and had stories to tell of what happened there. Others, such as a slave recently freed and trying to develop a baking business, or a maker of eyes for statues, had nothing in common as far as their craft was concerned but much in common as concerned sourcing materials, selling, and making deals. Soldiers told stories of distant markets, and the maker of eyes for statues might wonder whether the eyes he had crafted had made it to those faraway places.

All these associations were different from the medieval guilds, which survive in the modern livery companies of London, for example. If in medieval London you wanted to be a baker, then you had to join the Worshipful Company of Bakers as an apprentice. These guilds of medieval England were established by Royal Charter, and the rules that governed them were approved by the state. They were exclusive in a way that the Roman associations were not. No man could make bread for sale in medieval London who did not belong to the Worshipful Company of Bakers. They could also set the rules that governed how bread was baked. They could constrain innovation and anything else that challenged their position. The Worshipful Company of Bakers, for example, operated a state-sanctioned court in which the judge and jury were all senior members of the company. They enforced the penalties against those whom they found guilty, including pulling down the oven of the miscreant or forcing him to swear never again to work as a baker.

In the time of the Roman Empire this compulsion did not exist, and it was possible to challenge the established business order. It was not necessarily easy. The members of the collegia could act in

93

their own self-interest and try to keep competition out, but the state placed no restrictions on the trade. The path to wealth of Eurysaces and Atistia, had they lived in medieval London, might have been different, or it might have been blocked altogether. They might have been poorer and the citizens less well supplied with good bread at a reasonable price.

Migration and urban growth

These centres of urban wealth creation became population magnets. They drew people in with the prospect of making a new life, of making a fortune, just as they were to do later in medieval Europe. In the time of the Roman Empire, however, it was easier to move to the towns and cities, and it was easier for the towns and cities to grow.

Schoolchildren are told the legend of Dick Whittington. A long time ago there was a poor orphan boy. Alone in the world, he heard that the streets of London were paved with gold, and so he travelled there in the hope of making his fortune by digging in the streets. He was disappointed when he arrived and saw nothing like he had expected. His luck was in, however, and a merchant took pity on him and gave him a job in the basement of his house as a kitchen boy. At night Dick Whittington slept in the attic of the house, gnawed at by rats while he slept, until he found a cat to hunt down and kill them.

The merchant Dick worked for, about to set off on a trading venture, offered each member of his household the opportunity to make some money. He would sell whatever they gave him, and so Dick Whittington handed over his cat.

Now at night, the rats returned, and he decided to leave. But as he stood outside the town, the bells of London called him back. "Turn again, Dick Whittington, three times Lord Mayor of London." He returned and learned that his master had got a great price for the cat, which had hunted down rats in a distant kingdom.

The legend is based on a true story, which has been embellished, of course, but there actually was a boy named Richard Whittington, and he did succeed in life. There was gold in London, but it did not lie on the streets for picking up. Hard and intelligent work brought gold, and position. Richard Whittington first became Lord Mayor in 1397 in the Guildhall where his successors are still elected. He was knighted, created Sir Richard Whittington. His accumulated wealth, generated from trade, was sufficient for him to set up a charitable foundation in his will that continues to this day and provides accommodation and support for those in need.

When Richard Whittington was a boy, not everybody could move freely from land to town, although that started to change in his lifetime. Many were tied to the land, bound in service to their feudal masters, as people had been for centuries. They lived in a form of slavery that was pervasive across Europe and beyond and that lasted, in the case of Russia, well into the nineteenth century. Roman slaves similarly had no voluntary right of movement although they could be moved from the land to the city if it suited their masters' interests. Even Richard Whittington's mobility was limited. He could move from the countryside to the town and settle there but could not move beyond England with anything like the ease with which he could move within England.

Migration has always been a significant factor in the formation of great cities. The city of New York in the nineteenth and twentieth centuries grew at a rate that could not possibly have happened through births within the existing population. The City of London in the nineteenth century also grew spectacularly. There, too, growth required migration from farms and villages, and from overseas, as labourers left the land to labour in the workshops of the city.

Roman towns could grow in a way not possible for European towns of the early Middle Ages, because of freedom of movement. A young man sitting in the Roman town of London could hear stories about Rome, find out how to get there, and, if he was a Roman citizen, journey along roads kept safe by an army that recognised his rights as a citizen. He could carry currency that was trusted and useful at all the places he might stop as he travelled. If he had learned Latin, he could make himself understood as he moved along in the western part of the empire especially; he was more likely to succeed by speaking Greek in the eastern part.

His medieval counterpart could make that journey only with

great difficulty. For that young man to reach a distant city of opportunity he would have to cross several kingdoms, none of which he had a right to enter, with nothing to offer in exchange for food and board other than a currency they did not recognise and no hope of making himself understood in the many different languages that people spoke. The likelihood is that anywhere along the way this stranger (obviously an outsider because of the way he dressed) wandering in a foreign country and unable to speak the language would be set upon, robbed, and left for dead. For the young man of medieval times, the roads to overseas cities of opportunity were effectively blocked. There were exceptions. Merchants, for example, travelled for trade, and some churchmen could travel long distances, finding shelter along the way with fellow churchmen, in monasteries for example, but for nearly everyone in medieval Europe these were impossible adventures.

St Paul, by contrast, freely travelled through the Middle East, through Greece, and on to Rome. The landmass of the Roman Empire in his time was about half that of the United States today: it encompassed Egypt, North Africa, parts of the Middle East, the Balkans, all of southern Europe, parts of northern Europe, and large parts of Great Britain.

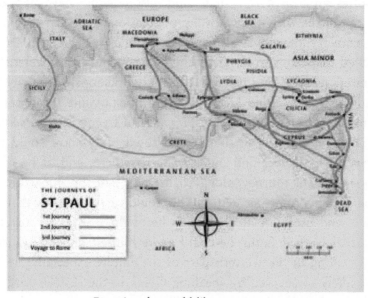

Roaming the world like never again

St Paul could travel across that area and settle where he liked with greater freedom than is possible even today. He needed neither passport nor visa. Cities such as Rome and Antioch, for example, and towns across the empire could draw on talent and labour located anywhere in that great landmass. The new migrants were a pool of labour that Eurysaces could draw on, as could the maker of eyes for statues. One needed someone to labour in his bakeries; the other needed someone creative and dexterous.

As people migrated from the land to the cities and towns, a structural change began to happen. Those who lived on the land produced most of the food they needed, like my grandparents in Ireland. Those who migrated to the towns no longer produced it but still needed food. In a few cities the authorities distributed free grain to parts of the male population, but it was never more than a man needed to feed himself. It was not enough to feed his wife and children. Those who found work had money to spend, and the first call on their resources was to feed themselves and their families. The migration into the towns created an increased urban demand for food and brought to the rural landowner new opportunities for profit. The urban market for their product was growing.

Eviction for profit

In the eighteenth century, a process of land transformation in Great Britain, which had started in the fifteenth century, was nearing completion. Land in the time of Richard Whittington was not a personal possession a man could buy or sell at will. It was held as a grant from a feudal overlord in return for services rendered to him. Land was also worked as common land, with many different people grazing their animals on the same patch of land. There remained much common land in the seventeenth and eighteenth centuries until Parliament enacted enclosure laws, which enabled owners to take control of common land. With time the English system of land ownership changed and approached nearer to what prevailed in Roman times, when land was owned outright by individuals who worked it for their own benefit or rented it out. In addition, across Great Britain, especially in the eighteenth century, landlords acted to consolidate holdings. Leases were not renewed, and land was cleared of tenants.

The process produced much misery. Families were forced off the land on which their people had lived for generations and which they had known since childhood and had watched change through the seasons of the year. They left for the towns and cities to find new homes and new work. For most of them their skills were related to field work, and there was no demand for such skills in the towns where they settled. Many of them brought with them only their brute labour and others only the ability to learn. Some received help from neighbours or family who had arrived earlier.

What drove all this change was the opportunity for profit that was opening up for landlords; growing towns and cities were increasing the urban demand for food, and that was an incentive for landlords to dispossess tenants. They could meet the increased urban demand for surplus food by evicting some of those who worked on their land and making the remaining labourers work harder. Many people were dispossessed. They worked in the towns to buy food produced on the land they had left, further increasing the urban demand for food from the rural estates.

The land consolidation and the removal of people from the land that happened in Great Britain in the seventeenth and eighteenth centuries had happened before in Rome during the first century BC. In the second and first centuries BC, the elite acquired and consolidated landholdings using the proceeds of war, displacing the existing rural population and replacing that labour with the slave labour also acquired through war. The great numbers of slaves that Julius Caesar had placed on the market had been transported across the empire, and many of them ended up on farms. Enriched men bought up land from farmers who had inherited land, buying it in small patches and consolidating them. Land consolidation during Roman times happened for the same reasons it happened in eighteenth-century England: the profits that could be made from selling food to a growing urban population.

This forced migration was not always from a rural idyll to an urban hell. Life on the land had not always been a pleasure. On small plots of land, life is a misery compounded by hope dashed by disappointment. In a good year, when there is enough rain for the crop to grow and no downpours that beat the wheat to the ground and make it unharvestable, when the sun shines brightly enough but not so fiercely as to scorch the ground, then in that good year there is plenty. On a small plot of land, however, if only some of the conditions needed for a good harvest are not met, then when the crop fails there is deprivation. For the owner of broad acres there is always enough. In good years he has a large surplus and in others just enough and he can draw on his accumulated savings. For the small holders, however, it is either survival or starvation.

Some land structures create poverty

Many of those who lived on small holdings produced no surplus, even in good years, after they had consumed what they needed to stay alive. In very good years there was something left over to trade but in most years scarcely enough to survive on. A family of seven people living on a small holding and working that land was, most of the time, idle and unproductive. In the spring it does not take long to sow the field, and in autumn it does not take long to harvest the crop. In between there is nothing much to do, perhaps some rough work to be done in repairing shoes or making clothes. They were working land that needed no more than one able-bodied man and not even he was required full time. It was for many an existence in which a change in the weather could destroy their livelihood and bring misery. It was also for many intensely boring, beyond the amusements of storytelling and songs.

A landscape covered in small holdings like this produces no surplus. As these units were consolidated and as fewer people lived on the same land, there was more surplus food, because the smaller number of people spent more of their time working and less time idle, and not as much of the food produced on the land was consumed there.

With the consolidation of land holdings in the Roman Republic, profits increased, as they would later in eighteenth-century England. By the time of Augustus, the same land was worked by fewer people, it was worked more efficiently, and there was more surplus at season's end. It was this surplus that fed the urban population. With this ownership change and a focus on profits, agricultural strategies changed. An owner looked now to consider which markets might buy what he produced. He could apply a different set of production strategies: set the land all to wheat or to wheat and vegetables or to that and pasture. There was an industrialisation of production. Fine villas were built out of the proceeds of these profits, on pleasant estates farmed for the direct benefit of the owner by freemen and slaves or rented out.

However, a new misery and a new cruel efficiency were introduced to the Roman landscape. Farms were created which were worked entirely by slaves, manacled and shackled at night, fed only enough to be alive and strong enough to do the work they were set and with no means for enjoying life. Offspring were bred from them to replace them in due course. The hope that by hard work or diligence they might be released was for them an empty hope. Theirs was not the position of Eurysaces the baker or of the household slaves who worked in the fine villas in the country around them. Their purchase price and the minimum costs of their maintenance were reckoned out with pitiless accuracy, and the profits generated were calculated and compared with the return required on the land.

Mass producing cities

To those who came to the towns of the Roman Empire – whether voluntarily or through displacement – and who thrived, life was good. Much as life was good in the nineteenth century for some of those poor Irish emigrants and their children who, reaching New York, settled, found work, and made their way in the New World. Those who were fortunate had the opportunity to prosper financially but also politically. Descendants of some such emigrants, moving from poverty in Ireland, became President, and many others reached positions of high standing throughout the political life of the new country their people had come to. It was much the same with those who came to the towns of the Roman Empire from the first century AD onwards.

The towns of the Roman Empire governed themselves in ways borrowed from the city of Rome, which offered the successful, the energetic, and the ambitious controlled access to the governing councils. Town councils were run in a manner similar to that of the Senate of Rome. Leaders were appointed with executive authority, just as in the old days of Rome the consuls had been the leading executive authority. As with Rome, there was a career structure men followed in the towns if they wanted to be leaders. Sometimes military service was followed in due course by a year in the management of the city infrastructure, another year in city finance, yet another in the administration of justice. Those who reached the top had experience of what made a town work. Although towns were similar in structure and functioning, each shaped its own constitution. The essential feature was the same: the governing system was open to new entrants and, while the incumbents could resist, there were limitations to how far they could resist.

Membership of the local governing body was a high honour and a position men fought for; the respect attached to that position brought with it special seats in the amphitheatre and general recognition in the community. There was the prospect of progressing to yet greater things in the imperial capital for a man or for his offspring.

Local councils in the provinces were important for central government because they collected the taxes due to the centre, the tribute that was assessed for their area, which they levied as they saw fit among the citizenry of the town and the surrounding country. The councils ran the local bureaucracy and it was to them, and the army, that the governor of the province looked when he sought to implement central policy.

They also raised local taxes, and in their meetings, projects were discussed, such as the erection of new temples or the adornment of the town or the resolution of a problem at their port. Central control was exercised over their budgets. New taxes and new public works required approval from Rome. The new projects brought employment to contractors, suppliers, and common labourers, just as they did in Rome. Those who had travelled to Rome or other towns and cities saw what was done in those places and took ideas back with them to their own towns. The towns vied with each other, in competition to excel.

It was ever thus. When we think of the Australian city of Sydney, most of us think of either the opera house built on its harbour or the great bridge that spans that harbour. These structures speak to cultural values and architectural and engineering achievement. They were erected because they served functions: a place where performances can be held, infrastructure that imposes connectivity and so improves the local economy. But they are also wonderful civic expressions of identity.

The town of Pula, located in what is now Croatia, lies on a bay. What survives of Roman Pula is a wonderful amphitheatre, a triumphal arch, some temples, and much more besides. The Pula Arena, which has a capacity considerably greater than that of the Opera House in Sydney, is visible as you approach from the sea. It's magnificent now and was, in its day, as impressive as the Opera House at Sydney is today.

The same civic pride prompted both buildings, but they were designed for different performances. In one case, theatre and music, of death acted out in *Don Giovanni* or enchantment in *Sleeping*

A small town amphitheatre

Beauty. In the other, gladiators fought, often to a real death, animals were slaughtered, or criminals brought to the beasts.

The amphitheatre, which is now used for theatre, music, and light shows, was not invented in Pula. The concept originated elsewhere and was copied in other places until at last the men who ran the council of Pula decided that they wanted one too. It was completed before the emperor Vespasian started to build the Colosseum at Rome. Not all good ideas originated in Rome, and Rome was capable of learning from other cities.

There were many towns such as Pula across the great landmass of the Roman Empire. In AD 79, during the reign of the emperor Titus, the volcano Vesuvius erupted and buried two such towns: Pompeii and Herculaneum. Towns such as Pompeii were unexceptional for their time. Their public buildings offered their inhabitants many opportunities to live socially. They were furnished with theatres, gymnasia, markets, and law courts open to the public.

The towns and cities of the Middle Ages had magnificent cathedrals. These soared higher than anything that was created in the towns of the Roman Empire, their towers pointing heavenwards. The coloured stained-glass windows, narrow and tall along the side walls, magnificent rose windows, often at the west end, let light into the interior, which cast changing patterns of colour where the light fell. The tones of Latin chant filled the space – in a language not spoken or understood by most people who came inside the cathedral. Some of these structures were surrounded on the outside by hideous gargoyles, which drained the water off the roof, rain dripping through the eyes of devils' stone heads. It was otherworldly, beautiful, and sublime.

Taken all together, however, there was far more for the citizen of Pompeii to do with his time, far more opportunity to be social than for his medieval counterpart. There were opportunities for the actor in the theatre, the athlete in the gymnasium, the haggler in the market, and the customer in the brothel and the bar. There were opportunities to be entertained and to learn. It was not a dull time.

The towns of the Roman Empire expanded, adding new forums and temples, some financed by the towns themselves, and other temples and buildings erected by private individuals – to honour an emperor, for example, or to otherwise mark themselves and their families, much as wealthy men and women endow buildings in universities today.

Towns had long been established in the eastern part of the empire, but in the west and in North Africa and elsewhere, new towns were introduced by the Romans and spread through the area they governed. It was not difficult to fund their establishment, and there were many who profited by the work. The remains of these towns are to be found everywhere, preserved as ruins in Libya or Lebanon or worked into the walls and churches of Rome or freestanding in a town in Croatia.

Transport and urban growth

There was, however, a limit to how large these towns could be.

Every morning, after he had milked the cows by hand, my grandfather took the milk to the local creamery on a horse-drawn cart. As a small child I sometimes sat beside him as he drove along, watching him nudge the horse with a word or stir of the reins. Churns unloaded, and milk poured out at the creamery; there was time to chat with neighbours, all of whom had come similarly with carts and on the same business. There was a car outside the house, one of the few in the area for a long time, and that was used for other things – for Mass on Sunday, for example. My grandfather continued to take milk to the creamery on horse-drawn dray, and so did most of the men in the area for a long while. But eventually the car replaced the horse, and once a few people had changed, everyone changed. When my grandfather used the cart, he used a system that, in its essence, had not changed since Roman times or indeed since a long time before that. He travelled no further from the place where he lived than his counterpart outside Pula or Pompeii had done.

Going to market

In *his* grandfather's time there had been a difference, though, because there had been no creamery, because there was no railway connecting the local town to the big cities. The milk that my grandfather brought to the creamery and which was made into butter was surplus destined to be consumed in distant towns and cities. And these would be reached by train.

The building of the railway that passed through the local town transformed life for the local farmers. No longer were their milk products consumed within a few miles of their farms. Although, like his predecessors, my grandfather still used the horse dray, the milk he produced could be consumed a hundred miles away. It made sense to put more work into the land, to raise more cattle and buy more land because he could now reach new markets, far from the local town.

The train also changed the city. The great train stations of London are located well within the current metropolitan area, but when some of them were built, they were at the edge of the city. At that time, the land just outside London was used for market gardens and produced the fruit and vegetables that Londoners of the nineteenth century ate, perishable food that could not be transported over long distances on slow-moving vehicles. When the train started to be introduced, the land used for market gardens could be built over with new houses because the food that had grown there could now be brought in from far away. Developers who bought up the market gardens and land around the small villages outside London made fortunes. Farmers who could now service new markets also had their share of new profits. The building of these new train stations enabled the city to expand in a way it could not have done before, because until then its size was limited by the amount of food that could be brought in every day on animal-drawn transport, and some canals.

It was the railways that enabled cities to grow during the nineteenth century. All overland transport before had been based on animal energy, brute beast or human. Travel at walking speed, the speed at which loads are carried, is about four miles an hour, and the maximum distance that can reasonably be covered in a day is about thirty miles. Men who need to return to where they live and beasts that need to return to where they are stabled can manage a return journey of about fifteen miles out and back and that, until the nineteenth century, was the maximum size of the hinterland of towns and villages. The construction of canals in eighteenth-century England made transport of heavy loads inland over long distances possible, but even these used animals to draw barges and did not travel long distances in one day. With the invention of the railway, the hinterland of towns and cities expanded to a hundred miles or more.

The idea that makes the steam engine possible is this. If you heat water in a container with a small number of exits, then, as the pressure inside the container forces the steam out, motion can be created. The energy released by burning the wood or coal can be used to make things move. This technology existed in ancient times. Hero of Alexandria, who was alive during the reign of Vespasian, described how to make one.

An idea long known but not commercialised

The difference now is that the energy source is not muscle power but wood, coal, and anything combustible. Machines can be constructed that go faster than animals, can travel without the need for rest, and can pull heavier loads. The many incremental steps that take these ideas to commercial exploitation never happened in the Roman world.

The urbanisation levels achieved by the Romans were at the maximum that could be achieved until the building of the railways. Rome, however, failed to develop the new technology.

Cities and wealth creation

The largest towns in England in the fourteenth century outside London were York and Bristol, and both were about the size of Pompeii. It was not until the eighteenth century that England had provincial towns much larger than Pompeii. In the time of the Roman Empire, however, a town such as Pompeii was unexceptional. Towns of twice its size were common.

The largest city in England was London, which did not exceed a population of one million until the early nineteenth century, a size that Rome had reached close to two thousand years earlier. The patterns were much the same across Europe. The Roman cities of Alexandria in Egypt, Antioch in the Eastern Mediterranean, and Carthage in North Africa had populations greater than any city of

107

Europe in the seventeenth century. It was not until the middle of the nineteenth century that the city of New York had a population larger than Rome had had at its height.

The commercial and residential buildings of New York and London in the nineteenth century were no higher than those of Rome of the first century, and those Roman stone and brick buildings surpassed anything that was used for similar purposes in medieval Europe.

The following graph shows the populations of the cities of Rome and London at different dates.

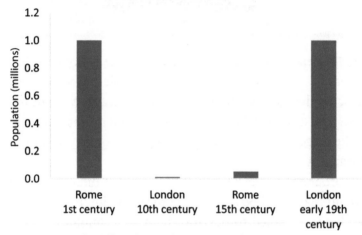

The fall and rise of European urbanization

The population of Rome had dwindled well before the Middle Ages. By the eighteenth century, London, which had been an insignificant town in the Roman Empire, had grown to a population of one million.

The Roman Empire was highly urbanised. Between the Roman Empire at its height and the emergence of the new world capital of London in the eighteenth century, urbanisation collapsed. This led to a collapse in wealth creation and caused a great impoverishment.

Higher levels of urbanisation are associated with higher GDP. The following graph illustrates the modern relationship between GDP and urbanisation. Each dot represents a country. The horizontal axis shows the percentage of the country's population that lives in towns or cities, and the vertical axis shows the GDP per capita of the country. The line shows the relationship between urbanisation and GDP. In general, the greater the number of people living in towns or cities, the wealthier the country.

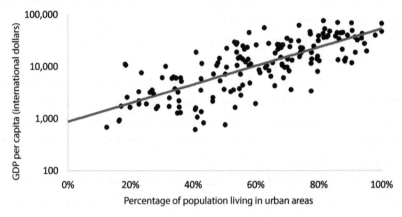

If more people live in cities, then the country is richer

The countries of the world, each represented by a dot in the above graph, differ enormously – in climate, history, social organisation, law. They range from countries that have the most wretched living conditions to countries whose inhabitants have wealth beyond what has ever been achieved since people first walked the earth. They include countries of exceptional inequality whose rulers extract billions and live in palaces and in which the bulk of the population has as its primary and endless task finding daily food. Some countries govern themselves with an equality and respect for all, which is also exceptional in historic terms. Some countries have a benign climate, and life can be lived comfortably in houses open to the elements. In others, cold and rain drive people indoors. Each of these countries is represented in the above graph by one dot. The countries represented by a dot in the higher part of the graph are richer than those shown in the lower half. What is evident is that, despite all the diversity in the world, countries that have higher urbanisation tend to have higher per capita income.

The relationship flows from the fact that the principal product of the countryside is food, whereas people in towns and cities are necessarily involved in other areas of production. Migration from the land increases productivity.

First, as labour migrated from the land in England in the eighteenth century and in Rome in the second and first centuries BC, those who remained on the land and worked there became more productive. Large landholdings were farmed by fewer people, and those people spent less of their time idle. As farms became consolidated, landowners moved to the production of higher-value food, meat in addition to grain.

Secondly, those who migrated to the towns needed to work in order to survive. This was additional production. They worked as labourers in the construction projects of the city or in the bakeries of Eurysaces. These people were paid about the same amount as those who laboured on the land.

Thirdly, some of those who migrated to the towns acquired new skills. The young man who was taken on by the maker of eyes for statues was one such. Such workers were paid more than labourers.

These factors – increases in agricultural and urban productivity caused by urban migration – explain what we see in the above graph, which relates the average income per capita and urbanisation in the countries of the world today.

The urbanisation that was possible in the time of the Roman Empire depended on freedom of movement, private land ownership – which allowed land consolidation – free entry into trades, and a universal currency.

We can illustrate the effect that urbanisation has on income by considering a hypothetical pre-industrial economy in which all the population live on the land and are almost all engaged in manual labour, largely food production and without the benefit of any machinery and with only limited tools. People in such an economy are not very productive and for long periods of time are unoccupied. Let us say that the population of this economy is fifty million, the magnitude of the population of the Roman Empire in the first few centuries AD. The total income of such a hypothetical economy is about £75 billion a year in our terms. This is point **A** on the graph below. (The calculations and assumptions are set out in the notes to this chapter.)

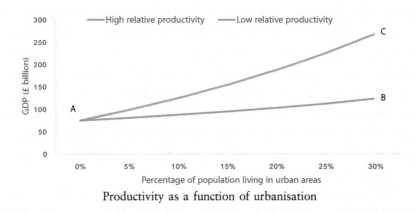

Productivity as a function of urbanisation

Now, if towns are established and people start to move towards those towns, we go from point **A** towards point **B.** In this case it is assumed that many of those now working in the towns are untrained manual labour with no particular skills and that urban productivity is higher but not much higher than rural productivity. At point **B,** just under a third of the population is now living in towns, and the rest of the population continues to live on the land, which was about the mix of people in towns and on the land when the Roman economy was at its height. The same amount of food is produced by those 35 million people on the land as was produced by the 50 million people who lived there before. The rural workers have become more productive. There is also the additional production of the 15 million now in the towns. These together increase total income to about £120 billion.

Now if those in the towns specialise and are more productive, then income moves towards point **C.** At points **B** and **C,** the numbers of workers living in the country and in the towns and cities is the same, and the same amount of food is produced and consumed. What changes is that the 15 million people living in the towns and cities become more productive. Urban life has changed. There are more people involved in specialised parts of production; more and finer silver pieces are produced, for example. The production of hardware, plumbing hardware, for example, has become more specialised, more ornate, and finer fountains are produced. Labourers continue to work on the building sites, continue to tote loads around the city, but there are more and more apprentices learning fine crafts, more and more workshops. All of this additional production creates additional jobs and additional income, increased spending power, money to spend on the goods and services that others produce. The higher productivity increases the total income. In this example it increases from £120 billion to £270 billion. The more productive urban workers now earn much more than rural labourers, and this attracts more labourers to the city, increasing urbanisation further. This increase in total income also increases the potential tax revenues of the state.

What is needed for all this to function is a currency that allows people in the towns and cities to exchange the output of their specialised labour for something everyone will accept: money. If that currency starts to fail, then urban life becomes more difficult. This happened in eighteenth-century England when money was leaving the country as speculators looked to profit from the valuable metal in the English coins. Commerce became difficult, and those difficulties continued until the authorities found a way to stabilise the currency. It has happened elsewhere and at other times. Towns and cities of this size need a universally accepted currency to function, and without it most of the economic gains of urbanisation disappear, in this case about £200 billion of additional income per annum.

Trade is also important for this level of wealth creation. The urban craftsmen can become more specialised, can spend their time on highly specific work, such as exclusively making eyes for statues, for example, if there is a large number of customers available to them. These customers become available if there is extensive trade. The customers of such a worker are then not just the buyers in the worker's town but also in a much wider world, every town and city in the Roman Empire and beyond. These transformations allowed the Roman Empire to flourish in a way no other empire had before.

Chapter 6
Prosperity

In the middle of the second century AD a Greek orator visiting Rome said:

> All men sing of and will sing of this city . . . where lies the common trading centre of mankind and the common market of all the produce of the earth . . . Here is brought from every land and sea all the crops of the seasons and the produce of each land, river, lake, as well as of the arts of the Greeks and the barbarians, so that if someone should wish to view all these things, he must either see them by travelling over the whole world or be in this city . . . there will always be here an abundance of all that grows and is manufactured among each people.
>
> So many merchant ships arrive here, conveying every kind of goods from every people every hour and every day, so that the city is like a factory common to the whole earth. It is possible to see so many cargoes from India and even from Arabia Felix . . . there can be seen clothing from Babylon and ornaments from the Barbarian world beyond . . . Your farmlands are Egypt, Sicily and all of Africa which is cultivated. The arrivals and departures of the ships never stop . . .
>
> Whatever one does not see here, is not a thing which has existed, or exists . . .

113

It was not just Rome; what came into Rome, came from somewhere. What left Rome, went somewhere. The prosperity this orator observed was as much a marvellous human creation as the Parthenon of Athens. It had been created partly as a matter of government policy, partly by men and women individually setting up and running their own businesses.

This speech was given in AD 155. Had that orator come to Rome one hundred years earlier and looked at the activity in its ports, he would have seen nothing then on the scale of what he saw now, and he might have been impressed by the military power of this city or the past glories of its people. It would have been like someone from London coming to New York in the early nineteenth century, impressed but not too much.

Internal peace

When Vespasian died in AD 79, he was succeeded first by one of his sons and then the other. Chance of birth, and not election or any other process, would determine who served as principal citizen of Rome. Of Vespasian's two sons, one was a man of ability and the other a disaster.

Titus, his first son, had been successful in war. Since the settlement of Augustus, the empire had stayed more or less within the bounds Augustus had set, but there had been unrest from time to time in the border provinces and threats of incursion from beyond the borders. The security of the state and the protection of its territory had been then, as it is today, a permanent concern.

In AD 66 the province of Judea had turned troublesome, had rebelled and not for the first time. The authorities at Rome determined that the pacification of Judaea could no longer be left with its governor. The army was dispatched to subdue Judaea, a campaign which Titus completed.

Thus, Rome sacked the ancient city of Jerusalem in AD 70. The centuries-old temple was desecrated and destroyed, leaving only a wall standing, the Wailing Wall, against which the descendants of those who once worshipped there still mourn its irreplaceable loss. The treasures of the temple were looted and taken to Rome. The triumphal arch of Titus, which was erected in Rome to mark this, stands to this day. For the educational benefit of those who lived in the city or who came there as travellers from all across the Roman territory, the arch shows depictions of the great treasures of Jerusalem's temple being carried into Rome.

Bringing the treasures of Jerusalem into Rome

The lesson of the arch: if you threatened the peace of the empire, all that you held most dear would be destroyed or taken from you. This message was widely promulgated. The bronze coin of Vespasian shown in Chapter 4 commemorates this event; anyone throughout the empire buying bread with such a coin or getting such a coin in their change was reminded of the cost of insurrection.

Titus succeeded his father on his death in AD 79 but did not himself survive long. On Titus's death from fever in AD 81, his brother Domitian became emperor and brought back the fiscal policies of Nero. Like his father, who had erected buildings such as the Colosseum, which served the public, Domitian built a stadium for athletic contests but, like Nero, Domitian erected palaces in the city for his own enjoyment. He lavished the revenues of the state on these palaces rather than on infrastructure. He also increased the pay of the army by one third, the first change in the remuneration of the soldiers since Julius Caesar had regularised the army pay over one hundred years earlier.

The reign of Domitian lasted fifteen years. He was removed by assassination in AD 96. The emperor was in place for life; there was no limit to his term of office, no date by which he must resubmit himself to the process that had led to his entry into office. The only routes by which he might leave office were resignation or death, and since Domitian would not go voluntarily, he would have to go by death. The news of his death was received with indifference by the people and with joy by the Senate, whom he had terrorised.

The essential legacy of Vespasian was now evident in what did *not* happen. When Nero had died, it had been possible for generals outside Rome to compete for the position of emperor, using the power they had through the command of their legions. This was no longer possible. If they attempted insurrection against the state to further their ambitions, then the state would cut off the supply of coins to the soldiers, whose anger would turn against their general. There was gold and silver to be looted from the local temples or the local rich, but the mints that turned those metals into coins were centrally controlled. The army took the news of Domitian's death badly, but there was no insurrection.

The succession after Domitian was peaceful. The Senate – the leading citizens of the empire – selected from amongst themselves a new leader for the state: Nerva, an old man of no particular distinction other than that he had survived in the service of Nero, Vespasian, and Domitian. There was another advantage of choosing Nerva. He was childless and could not establish a personal dynasty. However, if an emperor had no heirs, then waiting for him to die before choosing a successor could add uncertainty to the process. But Nerva adopted a son, designated him as his successor, and began to share some of his power with him. The successor to Nerva was a senator chosen on his abilities and on his acceptability to the Senate, the body that, in due course, would confirm his elevation to the rank of emperor, and who commanded the respect of the army. The basis on which power would be transferred was now established, the same basis that had been used by Augustus, who had been succeeded by his adopted son, Tiberius.

Trajan: expanding the economy

A new order had been built, and with this new order came a new peace, one that was to last almost one hundred years. The man whom Nerva chose as his successor was Trajan and, when in later years, after Trajan's death, someone was to be praised as an exceptional man, that man was first compared to Augustus and then to Trajan. The internal peace that followed the elevation of Trajan brought prosperity, just as the peace of Augustus had done more than a hundred years earlier.

The world flourished now for almost a hundred years until a new and most crippling disorder entered. It flourished as many countries in our world have since the end of the last world war. In both cases, the political stability and certainty – which allowed change to happen and enabled trade to flourish – also made it possible for people in widely scattered parts of the world to use their abilities and resources and to exchange the product of their work across the world with one another. Where they can do this, trade flourishes.

The Forum of Trajan

Trajan began a new public building programme in the city of Rome. Large areas of the city were levelled, the slopes of one of the hills of Rome were excavated, and a new public space was laid out. In the centre of this Forum stands a column that tells the story of

Trajan's conquest of Dacia, in carvings that wind their way up and around the column.

Trajan's Column

The Dacians, who lived in what is now Romania, had never been subdued, and their country had never been settled by the Roman people. Their land lay just over the border of the Roman Empire, and from it they had crossed the Danube at will, harried the peoples and towns of the Roman province of Moesia, in the Balkans, and then, again at will, retreated back into their territory across the broad waters of that river, which for them acted as a moat, protecting them against the mighty empire.

In AD 105, Trajan marched on Dacia, bringing with him soldiers disciplined and trained in centuries-old routines. They were trained to fight but brought other skills as well. Some were accountants in the camp, and others were engineers. Just as the US Army Corp of Engineers builds the dams for the United States, so these soldiers were used in the infrastructure projects of the empire. They slowly and systematically built a great bridge across the Danube. The moat of the Dacians protected them no longer, and Trajan marched into their territory, slaughtered many, and subdued the rest.

The art on the ancient column of Trajan at Rome celebrates war, victory, and brutal success. The soldiers display the severed heads of their enemy. They hack at their enemy. The bodies of the Dacians lie dead on the ground or drowned in the river that once protected them. The viewer of this column is meant to be overawed and to understand the power of the Roman state. The Romans walking past were to feel a sense of destiny, their special place in the world. There was also security. Those who, for example, bought land in the border provinces, land they would farm and whose produce they would trade, knew that their investment would be protected against loss from rebellion and invasion, and that encouraged trade.

In the centre of London is a square somewhat similar to the Forum of Trajan. This public square is surrounded by monumental buildings, and a large column surmounted by a statue celebrates a military victory. It was laid out in the first half of the nineteenth century, just as the population of London was beginning to match that of Rome in the time of Trajan. In 1805, Admiral Lord Nelson defeated the French and Spanish fleets at the battle of Trafalgar and prevented Napoleon from gaining control of the seas and threatening the maritime trade on which Great Britain depended. Trafalgar Square, laid out by a grateful nation, commemorates that victory. The base of the column has reliefs showing scenes from that and other battles: the death of the victorious admiral, the defeat of the enemy but no bloody decapitation.

Many businesses depended on Nelson's success. Silver plates are on display to this day in the Lloyd's of London building; they were prizes that the insurance business awarded to naval commanders who were successful in battle; Lord Nelson was one of the recipients. His victories had kept the seas open for British ships trading around the world, and these ships were insured by Lloyd's of London. It was more than patriotism that motivated these men of business.

The Forum of Trajan was somewhat different from Trafalgar Square. Trajan's Forum was a crowded and busy space, where news travelled quickly. Daily the great men of Rome came down to the Forum – businessmen and politicians, their importance indicated by the size of the crowd of clients who followed them. Their modern equivalents – government ministers, members of Parliament, and chief executives – are hardly ever seen walking in Trafalgar Square, and no one goes there in the hope of seeing them. There was a different energy in Trajan's Forum. At times of high drama, the atmosphere of a football stadium or a mass political rally filled the space. On a quieter day, there was the mumbled hubbub of many conversations. It was street theatre.

Information flows

News from the city of Rome and the world outside flooded into Trajan's Forum and the Forum of Augustus and the other meeting places of the city. You could see and feel what was happening, in the excitement or dullness of the crowd. You could feel the mood of the day, how things were turning against some senator or another. You could hear stories about what the emperor had done – get all the latest rumours.

News in cities like Rome could travel like wildfire in a forest. If in one hour you tell ten people a bit of news, and each of those tells another ten people in the next hour, then in two hours the news has gone to more than one hundred people. In six hours, it has gone to a million people. Within a few hours, news arriving in the Forum of Trajan could be known throughout this city of one million people.

Successful businesses rely on information, just as they rely on relationships. Eurysaces the baker and his wife were long dead by the time Trajan's Forum was constructed. If the business they had set up were still in operation, then the Forum was an important place for the owners to be seen. Their business depended on a supply of grain, and what was happening in the world mattered. News of any crop failures in Egypt or unrest in Britain, of an unusually good harvest in Sicily, the bankruptcy of a grain supplier, rumours about the solvency of the banker with whom they had placed large sums of money on deposit, bad weather preventing ships from docking – all this was interesting or important, and astute business people would know what to make of it. They would understand what news affected them, what information they could ignore and how to react.

Information did not just circulate in the towns and cities of the Roman Empire. Business, political, and administrative information flowed out and back, through a network of roads. Roads stretched out from Rome. While news in the town circulated quickly, it flowed more slowly through this outer network. A message from a governor in what is now Turkey took roughly ten days to reach Rome, about the same length of time it took a letter from London to arrive in New York in the late nineteenth century.

These highways were connected to municipal roads built by the towns to allow access for their people and the army. These municipal roads were in turn connected to smaller roads built by landowners so that the traffic of goods and people could move from their estates and into the towns, just as the landowners near the town where my grandparents lived in Ireland had financed the construction of roads.

All of this was mapped out, itineraries and routes available. Thus, if you wanted to go from one town, London, say, to another, Rome perhaps, the towns you needed to visit on each step of the journey were named and the distances between them shown. Setting out from London was an adventure but one that could be undertaken with knowledge of the steps along the way.

The road system was used for moving the army through the territories controlled by the Romans. It was also used by the imperial postal system, which carried messages around these territories. The postal system was used for governmental business, but time-limited permits were sometimes given out to private individuals, which allowed them to send letters through the system.

Along these roads, the imperial messengers hurried by horse, carrying with them messages from everywhere to everywhere, messages from the governors of provinces to one another, messages from governors intended for the office of the emperor in Rome. The imperial messenger was not to know what great matters of state were contained in the letters he carried, what events might turn on their safe receipt, but he was well aware of the importance of what he carried. The smooth running of the state depended on him. All made way for him. Every five to ten miles along the network of Roman roads was a posting house with fresh horses for him to use, maintained by the state.

Information highways

A collection of letters sent through this system at the beginning of the second century AD survives. There are letters between the emperor Trajan and the senator Pliny, whom he had sent to be governor in Bithynia, in modern-day Turkey; the sender and recipient were about one thousand miles apart. Their correspondence was no different from that of the chief executive sitting in the head office of a modern company corresponding with the heads of overseas branches and subsidiaries.

The style of the correspondence between the two men – members of the Senate who knew each other – is friendly, professional, and secure. Trajan wants to follow precedent; thus, in answer to some questions, the state archives are consulted to ascertain what was done in a similar circumstance in the time of Pompey, for example, a century earlier. The established ways of doing things are to be followed wherever possible, and the decisions of predecessors are to be respected. Trajan tells Pliny in one of them that what must matter to them in the government of the province of Bithynia is the public interest and only that.

The letters deal with the normal matters of government: finance, law and order, public works. Pliny on arrival sets out on a review of the revenue and expenditure of the province, ferreting out any public money being used illegally or private individuals holding on to public funds. Building projects must be cost-effective, paid for out of the normal surplus revenues of the province and not to be funded from raising the level of taxation. There is concern in their correspondence about new associations of people being set up; these can turn quickly enough into political groups and create disorder. Pliny seeks guidance on what to do about the Christians, and in his reply, Trajan sets out the policy to be applied. First of all, there is to be no active search for Christians. Secondly, all anonymous accusations are to be ignored. Thirdly, if someone is charged with being a Christian and the charge is proved, they are to be punished. However, any charged Christian who offers prayers to the Roman gods is to be pardoned.

Information did not just travel out from Rome to the cities and towns of the provinces and back. It swirled around in pools in those cities and towns, in the Square of the Corporations in the port town of Ostia outside Rome, for example, where traders in different commodities did business.

The information that flowed into the ports of Rome with passengers arriving on ships, that came into the city in the messages carried from governors to the imperial administrators, or the gossip that the imperial messenger carried with him, picked up in the Forum or elsewhere, might be relevant to the prices that imports would fetch or where they could be taken. A dealer with ownership of grain in the granaries at Ostia being the first to hear of a glut of wheat in Egypt might unload his stock as might a dealer in timber hearing of the imminent cancellation of building projects in the city. Just as in the Forum there was an excitement here in learning what was going on all over their world, in the news that came in on the ships and that was shared in the shipping offices of the town and in its public spaces.

Maritime peace

The bulk of long-distance trade in goods in the world today is maritime, as it was in the time of the Roman Empire. Today large ships carry goods to major ports such as the Port of Rotterdam, goods which are then either taken by road or river deep into continental Europe or are transhipped, leaving Rotterdam for other ports. This vast shipping network depends on the maritime peace that prevails across much of the world's seas today. Fear of predation from pirates or seizure of vessels in hostile acts of war at any stage of the sea voyage of these ships reduces trade. Were there no peace or at least workable agreements and treaties concerning the oceans, fewer ships carrying goods would leave their home ports. The manufacturers of these goods would have fewer customers in Europe, stock would be unsold, insurance premiums would take up more of their profits, and businesses would shrink. Fewer crew would be found to man ships carrying clothing manufactured in China, say, into continental Europe. Trade in the time of the Roman Empire similarly depended on peace and security.

Among the men whom the Romans considered a model of their values, a man against whom they measured themselves and one another was Cato the Elder, who lived until the middle of the second century BC. He had been through all the stages of the political progression, having served in the army, in the administration of the city, of justice, and in the Senate. He had reached the highest office of the state. He had been elected as censor; his had been the job of deciding, from time to time, whether those serving as senators were fit to continue in that role, judging whether their wealth still met the minimum threshold and whether they remained of good repute. Through Roman history he remained a model of severity, of an austerity that was valued.

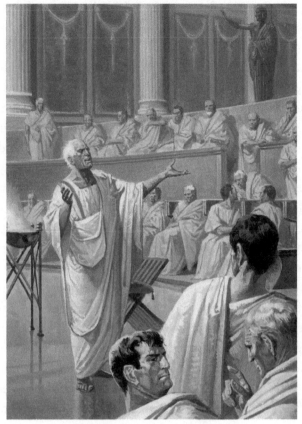

Cato: destroying the competition

His speeches to the senate ended with the words "Carthago delenda est." Time and time again he finished his contributions with the exhortation that Carthage must be destroyed. Destroyed it was indeed. Rome's superiority lay in the army. Carthage had been its rival at sea. Earlier, Rome had defeated Carthage on land, it had captured Carthaginian ships and copied them. Then in 146 BC, Rome defeated Carthage on both sea and land. The ancient city was captured, after long years of war, and levelled. In time, a new Carthage was built, but it was part of the world controlled from Rome. In destroying the old Carthage and building a new one, Rome destroyed its main rival. It not only eliminated the only other superpower, but it also gained control of the Mediterranean. Much as the insurance underwriters at Lloyd's were grateful to Admiral Lord Nelson for a naval victory that left control of the seas with

London, so were the Roman men of business grateful for Rome's control of the seas. There were, however, other dangers that needed to be eliminated.

Until the middle of the first century BC, fleets of pirate ships based themselves around the Mediterranean, raiding coastal towns, enslaving those it captured, and attacking ships in transit across the sea, as they had done for centuries. They came into Ostia, through which Rome imported much of what it needed, and attacked that too. This made the risk to trade severe and the city's supply lines insecure. The difficulty in dealing with this problem was not logistical but political. Those political difficulties were solved by the plebeian tribune Gabinius in 67 BC. The law he proposed and which the plebeian assembly enacted gave extraordinary powers – but for the limited period of three years only – to one man: the former consul Pompey, an associate of Gabinius. Fearful of what a powerful Pompey might do, the Senate had resisted these measures, but they could resist no more. Pompey was given the fullest authority to act as he saw fit on the Mediterranean. No limit was set on the state funds he could draw down for this purpose. Fifteen senators were named as his deputies. Pompey was successful, and the Mediterranean became a Roman lake policed by an imperial navy. There were no safe bases for pirates anymore, and no maritime rival.

Infrastructure

The Port of Rotterdam has expanded considerably in recent times as did the port system around Rome in the first century AD. Rome has no natural harbour. The principal landing places for goods destined for Rome, during the Republic, were Ostia, on the mouth of the Tiber, and Puteoli, in the Bay of Naples. Ostia was a way station, a place where ships stopped and then unloaded onto smaller boats, which then made their way up the river to the quays at Rome. The port of Puteoli was about one hundred miles from Rome. Goods loading there were taken overland to Rome. It was all quite inefficient and easily clogged by congestion and delay.

By the time of Augustus, Ostia had substantial unloading, loading, and storage facilities but limited protection for ships from storms. In the first century AD a harbour near Rome was constructed for the first time, begun by Claudius and completed under Nero. The harbour, Portus, was artificial; it was not an enlargement of a bay or inlet or any other natural feature that protects ships at anchor from wind and storm. New seawalls were constructed from concrete, which had been designed to set under water and which was one of the few Roman innovations at that time. New storage houses and granaries were built to receive imported goods.

From the death of Nero until the accession of Trajan there was no new building work in the ports around Rome. Then Trajan built a second harbour at Portus and expanded the port capacity around Rome.

The next graphic shows the change in the capacity of the ports around Rome from the time of the Republic to the end of the reign of Trajan. Ports provide landing areas and wharves where goods can be loaded and unloaded. The measure used on the vertical scale is wharf length. If you double the length of the wharf, then you double the amount of goods that can be carried in and out daily.

The port built under Claudius in the middle of the first century AD more than doubled the import and export capacity around Rome. By the end of the reign of Trajan in AD 117, the volume of goods that Rome could take in and send out was more than four times what it had been in the time of Augustus a century before. This increase in capacity had taken place in a period of roughly fifty years, but there would be no further addition to the port capacity around Rome until modern times.

The capacity of these state-sponsored ports with the deeper harbours allowed bigger as well as more ships to come close to Rome. It made sense for private businesses to invest in larger ships.

Other infrastructure was built to make these ports efficient centres for distribution and redistribution. Canals were built to take goods straight into Rome. The more storage capacity there was near the unloading docks, the quicker ships could be unloaded, and so more warehouses were built. Goods taken off ships could be taken straight to warehouses rather than remaining on board until the next transport vehicles arrived. For almost a hundred years after the last

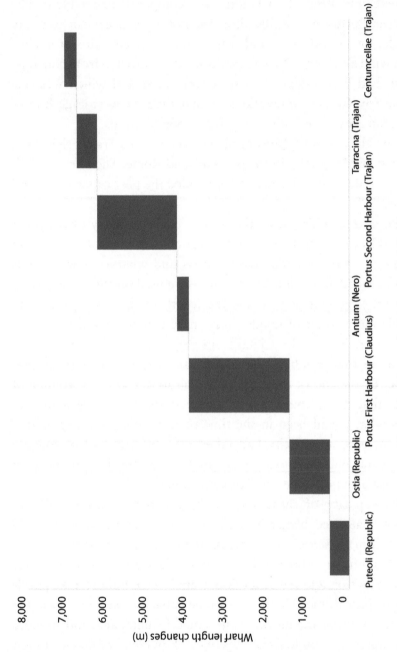

Increasing the port capacity around Rome

enlargement of these ports was completed, towards the end of the first century AD, storage capacity continued to expand.

The new ports served not only as gateways for goods in and out of Rome. Like Rotterdam today, they were also transhipment areas. Goods were taken to the warehouses and stored, the owners provided with documentary proof of their ownership. You could sell goods you owned in the warehouse to someone else by contract without having to move the goods, just as today's traders buy and sell grain without ever seeing or touching it, and ownership of the commodity moves from here to there while the commodity stays in the warehouse. What mattered, then as now, was information and how it was used.

There was a policy to increase capacity across the empire, not just in Rome. This policy facilitated trade. For example, an exchange of letters between Pliny and the office of Trajan at Rome described the difficulties the inhabitants of a town in Bithynia were having in exporting goods. That town, Nicomedia, lay about twelve miles from a lake across which goods could be transported – goods such as marble, timber, grain, and other products. Taking these materials across the lake was easy and cheap, and trade between the towns near the shores of the lake was good. But it was difficult to get goods from there to the sea because goods had to be transported overland to the sea by road, which was difficult and expensive. This restriction limited trade. If the lake could be connected to the sea by a canal, then the transport could happen by boat, which would open up the towns to new markets across the Mediterranean world and bring them new wealth.

There was no shortage of labour in the area to carry out the work. However, there was a lack of technical expertise to build a canal. Trajan responded by commissioning a survey of the lake: its size and how it was fed. He placed Pliny in contact with someone who could provide an engineer.

There was another motivation for Pliny besides the improvement in the local economy. He had seen the remains of an earlier attempt at constructing a canal, which had been undertaken by one of the kings who ruled in this region before the Romans came. That canal had never been completed. The Roman canal was to be as much a monument to Roman superiority as the column that stood in Trajan's Forum. Furthermore, the canal enhanced trade. The resources of the region, such as timber, could now be sold into towns and cities around the Mediterranean and not just around that lake. There were new markets for landowners who grew grain. More money flowed into towns such as Nicomedia.

The expansion in port capacity at Rome under Trajan was mirrored across the Mediterranean. For example, starting in the first century AD there was a growth in harbour capacity along the coast of North Africa, financed partly by private individuals and partly by municipalities as they worked to increase the exports of fish, olive oil, wine, and grain produced in that region. The main port along the North African coast, Carthage, when it was enlarged, was as big as Portus at Rome after Trajan's expansion.

Containerisation is one of the factors leading to the rise of China as a trading nation today. The cost of shipping from China to Europe on container ships is now a minor additional cost, and the goods can be sold cheaply and profitably in Europe, and in large volumes. The increase in the port capacity of the Roman world had a similar but less dramatic effect. While the expansion of port capacity because of containerisation has been about eightfold, that of the first century AD was about fourfold.

There was money in all of this for the state, the municipalities, and the harbour authorities. Customs duties were levied on goods imported into the empire. Within the empire were customs zones, and customs duties were levied on movement between those zones. The more things moved, the more money the state made. Harbour duties were payable by ships docking, and the use of the warehouses was not free. All these entities provided employment too. There were jobs for the managers and staff of the warehouses and for dockers lifting goods on and off ships.

Progress

If one such docker who worked on the docks of Portus in Trajan's time had been transported to the sixteenth-century ports of London or Rotterdam, he would have noticed some differences from what he was accustomed to at Portus. The men around him in London or Rotterdam would dress differently and speak a language unfamiliar to him. In his time a lot of goods were carried in amphora, the Roman shipping container, wine and grain, for example, and he would see in the sixteenth century more barrels and sacks than he was used to. However, much of what he saw in the sixteenth century would be completely familiar to him. The ships entering and leaving were driven by wind, and they were docked in the same way. The loading and unloading of goods was done by gangs of men. It was hard labour, and he would have recognised the work as the same he had carried out. It was slow. The loading of ships took many days to do as men ran up and down narrow gangplanks. Ships waited for long periods out in the harbour while other ships were unloaded.

The amphora: a Roman shipping container

What would have struck him most, however, was the size of the ships. They were much smaller than he was used to. Large ships coming into Rome on the main shipping routes, from Alexandria in Egypt, for example, or sailing across the ocean from India to the Red Sea, carried cargoes of between two hundred and four hundred tonnes. Hardly any of the ships coming into London in the sixteenth century were able to carry cargoes weighing even two hundred tonnes.

Had he returned at the beginning of the nineteenth century, our friend from Trajan's Rome would have seen a more familiar picture. Now the ships were larger and not much different in size from what he was used to seeing in the Rome of his day.

First-century Rome or early nineteenth-century London?

Returning again, about one hundred years later, at the beginning of the twentieth century, and looking out at the ships coming into the harbour, our friend would have been astonished. Some of these ships were beyond anything he had ever seen, with no sails, smoke coming out of large pipe stacks and unimaginably large. What might have amazed him most, though, is if he had turned around and looked at what was happening on the dock. Seeing the London dockers running up and down gangplanks, unloading sacks and hurrying to obey their overseers, he would again be back in a world familiar to him. Hardly any of that had changed, even by the beginning of the twentieth century. There were bigger and better cranes, but it was all much the same. He could stand in a queue in the morning for work with the other dockers and be as useful as any of them.

If our friend came back now and visited either of the ports of London or Rotterdam, he would see a world wholly unfamiliar to him. The quays are now almost empty of people. There is no job for him in this world.

The goods carried on these ships arrive in uniform containers; there are no sacks or barrels. Now goods are moved smoothly and quickly off ships. A twenty-tonne container can be moved in two hours, substantially faster than the contents could be moved by a crew of men running back and forth and trying not to get in one another's way. As a consequence, the time that a ship needs to spend at the docks has dropped dramatically. It is this level of speed and efficiency that has increased the capacity of the world's large ports by a factor of eight.

Specialisation

With the increase in connectivity and the higher levels of urbanisation, changes started to happen in the Roman world. The level of wealth of the ordinary citizen increased. Goods previously reserved for the rich now were available to the general population. The rich sought out finer versions for themselves, and more high-quality goods were produced. The level of production increased, making more work available. The bored idleness of the peasant sitting on a farm with nothing to do was replaced by a new creativity.

More and larger ships now docked in the enlarged ports around Rome, and so a greater quantity and variety of goods could be taken in and out. It became much easier to trade, and it became easier for businesses to develop. The production of glassware, for example, expanded. Flowing into the new ports at Rome came ships carrying blocks of glass made on the Eastern Mediterranean coast, to be transformed into run-of-the-mill glass cups and bottles or luxurious glassware. Timber arrived for the furnaces to melt the glass blocks so that glassblowers could shape the molten glass. Iron was brought in to be made into the blowpipes they used. Flowing out from the new ports at Rome went packing cases full of these manufactured goods destined for everywhere in the Roman Empire and beyond, to East Africa, India, the Arabian coast, Scandinavia, and north central Europe.

Grain came in from North Africa in great quantities as well as from those parts of the world which had long fed Rome: Sicily and Egypt. Landowners near Carthage served the same market as those located on the Nile, and the grain supplies were now more certain.

Trade flourished across the now peaceful world, and with it came new wealth. The landowners of North Africa, with access to the wide market located on the Mediterranean basin, became wealthier. The enlarged and newly created ports in their part of the world meant that more and larger ships could dock there also and be loaded with their grain. It paid for them to increase the productivity of their land, to buy new land and bring it into cultivation. They did not need to know where their grain was ultimately destined to go or whose hunger it would abate or what food it would be transformed into or where. What mattered to them was the price at which they sold their grain to the merchant and the costs that they had incurred in producing that grain. New money flowed into Carthage as the increased harvests of grain flowed out, and there was more money to spend in Carthage and elsewhere – the gold aureus and the silver denarius that were accepted and trusted throughout their world.

Roman soldiers and administrators arriving in the towns and cities in North Africa brought with them their possessions, including the glassware they used. The local landowners saw goods that were better than anything they had or that their parents had had before them. They wanted to know how they could get something as good or, to be frank, even better and show off their wealth. The common tableware could be made locally, but luxury glass goods were sourced from abroad, much as purchase orders for quality cloth or fine tailored suits are still sent to Italy. Orders flowed to Italy and other places through a network of dealers, orders for new pieces made of glass.

Glassblowers working around Rome filled these orders. The glassblowers – those crea-tive, skilled men – located their workshops near each other, looking at the work of those beside them, copying new ideas and ways of

Roman fine glassware:
a delicate survival

134

doing things, making everything better. There was creativity in producing something exceptional, fine, and beautiful. There was enjoyment too in this creativity, the satisfaction of looking at their accomplishments and of knowing that what they produced was wanted by others, and the pure simple enjoyment of exercising a beautiful skill.

The creativity was not just in producing luxury glassware. It also required creativity to figure out how to produce standard vessels more cheaply and quickly. All that creativity, whether of ideas for a new shape or ideas for a more efficient process, contributed to the glassblowers' profits. The coins they got, some of which came from the North African landowners' profits, paid for the bread they bought, which was made from wheat, some of which perhaps came from North Africa.

As the production and export of grain increased in North Africa, land in Italy and elsewhere that had previously been set to grain was turned over to pasture, to be grazed by sheep and cattle. The poor man's diet began to be more like that of the rich man, and meat was less of a rarity for him than it had been for his parents. What was unknown to them had become normal for him. He could now buy glassware of a type that his parents had never owned, and his budget extended to food that they had hardly ever eaten.

As the demand for glassware increased along with the wealth and creativity of the glassblowers, so the demand for the raw glass increased. All that raw glass had been produced exclusively in the area around Sidon in the Eastern Mediterranean because it was there that the compound could be found that made it possible to melt the sand, which is the basic component of glass.

Sidon had long been a centre for glass production and was known for that in the time of Homer. It was only around the time of Augustus, however, that the art of glass blowing had been invented and the old and inefficient ways of making glassware had been replaced by a new, more flexible technique which, because it could produce objects with thinner walls, not only produced more elegant vessels but ones that needed less glass and were cheaper to make. Production costs fell, and profits rose.

The glassblowers of Sidon migrated, some to the areas around

Rome, They went voluntarily to be near their customers or they migrated as slaves to generate profits for their owners. The work at Sidon and the profits at Sidon were now largely in the production of blocks of glass. By the middle of the second century AD, raw glass was also being produced in Gaul and Spain.

Innovation

The Roman mentality had in the past not placed a premium on innovation. Custom and precedent were valued over new ideas and practices. Indeed the phrase for revolution, with all the sense of destruction and chaos that it carries, was *res novae*, "new things". The Romans happily borrowed from others and took competitive pride in making what they copied better than it had been when in the hands of those from whom they had copied it. The sword they used was based on what the people of Spain had used before they were conquered. The Greeks had been their undoubted superiors in the art of oratory but not anymore. Something, however, of a new spirit emerged in the first century AD; an innovative spirit entered. The Romans borrowed and improved on the technology of glassmaking. But they also invented. They invented furnaces to make the process yet more efficient and flexible. The art of glassmaking now reached a new height and, until the nineteenth century, all that the world was to know of this art had been invented in the first century AD. Production levels increased to new heights in the first century and stayed broadly at that level in the second century.

The Roman mentality in the past had also had an aversion to luxury; it associated that with degeneracy. They looked back with fondness to a simpler, and therefore better, time. Seneca, writing under Nero, remembered Scipio Africanus, who had defeated the Carthaginian general Hannibal, a successful campaign which had given him the addition of Africanus to his name. The baths that Scipio used were small and let in hardly any light; people of Seneca's time would have turned their noses up at those baths because they had become accustomed to better fixtures. The glass blocks that arrived in Rome were now being turned into windows – another innovation. Windows were made out of glass, and the baths that were being built were monumental. High walls were punctured by spaces, which were filled by these glass panes, which now let in light and also kept the heat in. A new luxury was available to all who sat in the steam rooms of these airy buildings, such as the baths of Trajan, which rose above the buried ruins of Nero's Golden House.

Investment and Risk

All of this activity – in the ports at Rome and elsewhere across their world, the securing of peace, the building of infrastructure and ships, and the making and selling of goods – required money. Some of this was state money, collected in taxes, but most of it was private money laid out in the expectation of profit. Glassworkers in the workshops around Rome needed money to finance the purchase of the furnaces they used, money to pay the rent on their workshops, and money to buy glass. Some of this could come from savings, the accumulated profits generated by past sales. Borrowing was another source of funds. For those who had funds to lay out, all this new activity represented new ways in which they could invest, lay money out for profit. There was nothing new about the desire of the rich Roman citizen to make money or the legal mechanisms by which he could protect his investment. What was new was the scale of the profit opportunity.

The elimination of the Carthaginians as a superpower in the Mediterranean had meant that Roman ships travelling across the Mediterranean would not be threatened with attack from Carthaginian ships, but it also meant that Roman traders had eliminated their major competitor. The Carthaginians were traders. Markets previously served by the Carthaginians were now open to Roman traders. Cato, the man who in the Senate had ended his speeches with the exhortation that Carthage must be destroyed, took advantage.

Money mattered to Cato. He was scientific in his approach to the maximisation of agricultural profits. Trade, however, was where the money was. He formed a *societas*, a type of company, with fifty members and as many ships. The fifty ships that made up the *societas* formed by Cato were a large fleet; in the early part of the seventeenth century that was about the number of ships that the East India Company, then one of the largest trading companies in the world, sent out to the East. Cato's model was to lend to the members of that company, who without his finance had no business, have their assets as his security, take a small equity stake, install his man as a manager, and then let his partners do all the work and take most of the risk.

The profit opportunities of trade are different from those of craftsmen such as a glassblower or a baker, all of whom make objects to be sold. Trade is a strategic game. A trader can, for example, try to set himself up in a port as the dominant buyer and take over or eliminate other buyers in that market. He can shut down sellers by refusing to buy. He can then acquire his own monopoly in that port and then may have a monopoly in the port to which he takes his goods. The profits from such ventures and from such strategies have built great fortunes, such as that of the Rockefellers. We don't know the strategies that Cato's trading company employed, but the profits he accrued were large. The abilities of a man whose political skills had carried him to the top of his society and whose military skills were excellent could as well be applied profitably to business and could make money beyond the capability of the finest craftsman.

The legal structure that Cato used, the *societas*, was a well-established structure used for many business ventures. Some were formed to enter into contracts with the state for military supplies or for the collection of indirect taxes or for the removal of urban waste or for running mining operations. They were also used for trading ventures, as in Cato's case.

These corporations were like modern companies. The members, like modern shareholders, appointed a representative, effectively a managing director, who did business on behalf of the company and could bind the company in agreements. The assets of the company were separate from those of the members. They often had management structures with executive officers and record-keeping. The representative had the right to sue on behalf of the corporation.

Amounts due to the corporation were due to it and not to the individual members. Amounts owed by the corporation were owed by it and not by the individual members. These structures were effectively limited liability companies.

The Romans had other arrangements like the partnership structures used now by professional services firms, such as accountants and architects, and by bankers such as, until recently, Goldman Sachs. A legal agreement sets out the terms on which the various partners participate. Partners can leave, on terms set out by the group, and receive their share of the venture, and new partners can enter, but the overall structure continues. Funds can be accumulated within the partnership as long-term capital to grow the business and take risks. This system can accommodate partners who might need the money now as well as a business that needs the assurance that capital invested in a venture will not be withdrawn at short notice.

The first of these arrangements, the *societas*, has the particular advantage that it separates risk from the investors. For example, few investors will be found who will hand over £1,000,000 to an enterprise where, if things go badly, they will be asked to hand over more money to pay for losses over which they have no control. That can happen in a partnership, but at least in a partnership the partners know each other or have a good knowledge of the day-to-day business of the partnership and the risks involved. The partners know what might cause such losses, usually notice when it starts to happen, and try and put a stop to it. What a *societas* did was allow Roman investors to hand over their equivalent of £1,000,000 knowing that they would get their share of the profits, they might lose all of their investment, but they could not be forced to pay up more than they had invested. The structure made it easier for the entrepreneur to raise funds, build up a new business, and add to his wealth. It made it easier for investors to access new sources of investment return without risking personal ruin. This legal structure, the *societas*, facilitates economic growth. It disappeared with the collapse of the Roman legal order on which it depended and did not re-emerge until the very beginning of the seventeenth century, when it again facilitated economic growth.

Similar company structures, for example, were used for trade with the East Indies and for the settlement of what became the United States.

Both of these structures, the *societas* and the partnership, allow for permanent capital. The business owns its own assets and can use them for the long term without its managers having to worry that one of the passive owners of the business might turn up tomorrow and ask for his money back, forcing the sale of assets tied up in the business ventures. That ability to plan and invest for the future, as well as the freedom to manage a business without daily interference, facilitates long-term growth. Profits are made, a proportion of the profit is distributed to the owners, and the rest is retained within the business, allowing it to grow.

Time makes money, in the right circumstances. Suppose a company is set up with initial capital of £1,000,000 in our money terms, a trading company which buys goods in India and transports them for sale in Rome. The cargo might be spices and the company one that operated in the second century or in the seventeenth century. If the business pays a two percent dividend and grows at five percent per year, then the owners will receive £20,000 income in the first year. However, after one hundred years, the shares will be worth £130 million, and the then owners will receive £2,600,000 in dividends each year.

All of this requires the right circumstances. It requires a stable currency, which allows large transactions to be conducted across great distances. It also requires a well-developed and administered legal system and a stable political environment so that the company can enforce its ownership of assets. Stolen goods can be recovered. Theft is punished, and the government does not expropriate. These conditions, and an adequate transport infrastructure, are factors that encourage trade. If these conditions exist for a reasonable period of time, then substantial growth in volumes of trade can occur. These conditions were optimal in the second century AD.

Chapter 7

Life

Trade in the Roman Empire flourished and that brought prosperity. It had other benefits. A newborn infant placed in the hands of a well-to-do citizen of the Roman Empire would be expected to live longer than a newborn infant placed in the arms of a well-to-do family in medieval Europe. It was only by the middle of the eighteenth century that a child in Europe could have the prospects of life of his predecessors in Rome, some one and a half thousand years before.

> Incipe, parve puer, risu cognoscere matrem
> matri longa decem tulerunt fastidia menses
> Incipe, parve puer, cui non risere parentes
> nec deus hunc mensa, dea non dignata cubili est

> Begin, little boy, to recognise your mother with your
>   smile
> ten months brought her long sickness
> begin, little boy
> no god or goddess has ever thought
> a child on whom his parents have not smiled
> worthy of food or rest

Our basic needs in life are for safety, nourishing food to eat, and clean water to drink. The infant boy, in the above passage from

141

the *Eclogues* of Virgil, who recognises his mother in her smiles, is in a part of the world that was safe, after the ending of the civil wars under Augustus, and in a part of the world in which people were well nourished. By the time of Trajan, with the new peace and the increased prosperity, these benefits were spread throughout the world ruled by Rome, benefits which were lost by the Middle Ages.

Food

In the 1950s, a Dutch professor, Slicher van Bath, set himself the task of finding all records of historical grain yields going back as far as medieval times. He had access to medieval manuscripts such as those of monasteries and to later records of European aristocratic estates. He compiled lists of these thousands of figures and separated them into the different grain types. In the introduction to his book, he notes that the purpose of his work was to provide material that might be useful someday. I found a copy of his book in the Institute of Historical Research in London. It is seldom consulted, and hardly any reference is made to it in any publication. But it is an immensely helpful piece of work because of what van Bath's figures reveal, and because understanding what was happening in Europe in medieval and later times helps us better appreciate the Roman achievement.

Each of these figures that Slicher van Bath recorded represented the performance of a monastery or estate in one particular year. The servants of the abbot who ran the monastery or of the lord of the estate counted the sacks of grain being taken into the fields to be sown in the spring; months later at harvest time, they counted the sacks of grain being carried in. The yield at harvest for every sack of grain planted depended on the weather at that time and place and reflected how diligently the ground was tilled and weeded, and how carefully the crop was gathered in.

From more than 1,500 individual wheat yields we can construct graphs that trace the changes over time in what was happening in Europe. The figures shown in this graph are the numbers of kilograms of wheat a field measuring one hectare produced in the years

142

from 1200 to 1750. One line on the graph shows productivity of an average field in France, and another line shows productivity of an average field in England. Over that period of several centuries, the two fields produced increasingly higher yields. There is, however, a difference in the stories of the two countries. At the end of the period, the English field produced three times as much food as it had produced at the beginning of the period. However, between 1300 and 1750, the amount of grain produced from the field in France hardly changed. In one country we see progressive improvement and in the other stagnation.

The long-term increase in agricultural productivity changed what it was like to live in England and changed how the country looked. We may imagine a man who for some service or another was granted lands, lands which his family was to hold for centuries after that. Let us suppose that at the beginning of this story it was only a small estate that could support the man, his family, a few servants, and no more. As time passed, and if their land became more productive, as the average field in England did, then more food was produced, and more people could be fed from this estate. Men could be employed in the quarrying of stone and the building of a more magnificent manor house. Men could be employed in the draining of marshes, the clearing of woodland, and the creation of more agricultural land. As their land became more productive in grain, some of the land could be used as pasture, and cattle and sheep could be raised, thus providing a richer diet.

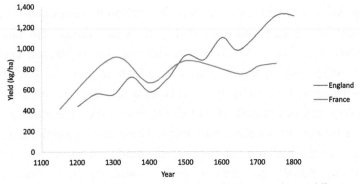

Agricultural productivity in France and England since the Middle Ages

Through this period, urbanisation increased in England, and as the nearby town grew, new markets opened for this family, opportunities to exchange their surplus for money and to acquire the means to buy goods from that town, goods made there or imported from elsewhere. If the estate continued to be well managed through the generations, then it became possible for its owners to buy neighbouring lands that were forced onto the market by mismanagement or sold for some other reason.

Through this long period, the wealth of this family increased, and their land changed in appearance as they managed it differently, reclaimed waste land, cleared forests, set more of their holding to pasture, and consolidated neighbouring estates into their property. Their connection to the world around them changed. The local town, and the urban centres beyond that, became important to them as buyers of their produce and as markets that could supply them. The continuing stability in that world mattered to them more as time went on.

The agricultural improvement that happened in England in the late medieval ages did not happen in France during that same period. England did not suddenly acquire some secret that it was able to conceal from France, some new technology that could not be copied, for example. Technological changes during that period were limited. But, in significant aspects, some of the ways in which people organised themselves in England were beginning to resemble the old Roman ways.

At the very beginning of this period, life in England and France was much the same. They were both feudal worlds, each ruled by kings who were absolute monarchs although dependent on the support of the rich and powerful in their kingdoms, and ultimate owners of all the land. By the middle of the eighteenth century, these were very different places in which to live. In England, a constitutional monarchy had evolved, and rights to own private property had developed, as had the rights of the individual. France had remained an absolute monarchy. The constitutional changes in Great Britain had not, in themselves, made the country's systems more like Rome's, but they made it possible again for individuals to do what they had been able to do in Roman times.

We now can extend this survey back further in time, adding other data on crop yields. The following graph shows agricultural productivity from the Stone Age in Europe to eighteenth-century Europe. The numbers indicate kilograms of wheat produced from a field measuring one hectare. This graph tells a story of economic growth and decline and then, after a period of about one thousand and five hundred years, a recovery.

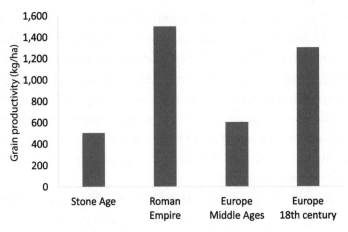

The rise and fall, and rise again, of agricultural productivity

Social and cultural change

The period spanning imperial Rome through medieval times and into the middle of the eighteenth century was not a time of significant technological change. It was, however, a period of profound social and cultural change.

The world fragmented after the collapse of the economy of the Roman Empire in the middle of the third century AD, creating much instability. Small kingdoms formed in what had been provinces of the empire and warred with one another. Peoples who had lived together under a common rule and whose energies had been spent on bettering themselves and enjoying the fruit of their labours had to turn those energies towards defending themselves from one another. There was a decrease in exchange and in trade. Material culture became simpler. The people who lived in medieval Europe no longer had easy access to a range of goods, which had been common in the time of the Roman Empire. The world was a poorer place, and it was not just the poor whose circumstances were reduced. The rich were poorer too.

Europe then faced broad cultural changes such as the Reformation. The powerful medieval church had stressed the rejection of wealth and pleasure and had been suspicious of the intellectual, of those who challenged the accepted world view, of private rather than collective activity.

All of this changed as the eighteenth century approached and the world recovered and was somewhat restored to conditions of the former Roman Empire. Post Reformation, large parts of Europe shifted – partly in reaction to the Reformation – and became less self-denying and communal and more self-loving and individualistic. These changes in values moved the world into an atmosphere and state of functioning much more like what people experienced during the great days of Rome. But such changes happened much earlier in England than in France.

Let us take a closer look at what was happening in medieval times, because this will help us understand why people in the Roman world produced so much more food from the same land.

Rights of medieval man

The illustrations, taken from the Luttrell Psalter, made in the first half of the fourteenth century in England, a few decades before Richard Whittington was born, show workers in the fields during the spring, ploughing the land and sowing seed. One of the men chases birds away with a sling, another beats their horse with a stick.

The land in this painting is from the artist's imagination but reflects the reality of the time: people working the land. This world is quite different from ours. The rights that these people had and the rights that their masters had were different from ours. For example, were we to stand somewhere in front of such a place and ask one another, "Who owns this land?" we would expect a clear answer because, to us today, ownership is clear. But to the people represented in this painting, the question of ownership would be

146

Sewing and ploughing the land in fourteenth-century England

meaningless. If you or I own a plot of land, we can use it more or less as we wish; there will probably be some planning restrictions on what we can build on the land, but beyond that it is up to us what we do with our property. We can, for example, sell it whenever we want, to whomever we like, at whatever price we set with our buyer. Hardly ever will we need anyone's permission to carry out this sale. However, the land we are looking at in this painting cannot be sold at will by anybody, and it belongs, in our sense, to nobody in particular.

Land in medieval Europe when the Luttrell Psalter was produced was not private property. Large holdings of land were allocated by the ruler to men loyal to him, in return for services to him: armed service in his campaign and the provision of men and materials. Those lords allocated lands further down to men and women such as portrayed in this painting, again in return for services and produce: working so many days a year for their master, for no money payment but because they were obliged to. So long as the lord of this manor provides his king with loyal service and the peasants under that lord provide him with the allotted days of service, all may stay as it is. But neither the lord of the manor nor the people working for him can sell the land.

There were further restrictions. The illustration above is also taken from a fourteenth-century psalter produced in Lincolnshire, England. The people in the image are entitled to live on this land, as are their children. They are not employees who were selected for the tasks at hand. It is almost impossible to evict them and replace them by more diligent workers, but neither can they leave. Their rights are even more limited than that. If they are wronged in some way, then the court to which they take their grievance is the manorial court of the man for whom they are working.

Large parts of the land of Europe at the time was also church property held by abbots of monasteries or heads of other religious organisations. The men who led these organisations reached their position as they progressed through the religious world and survived its politics. These men of the church were responsible for the management of large estates. They were not men of business; in fact, many of them had taken vows of poverty.

Here was an inflexible world in which it was difficult for conditions to improve. The men working the fields in the illustrations in the Luttrell Psalter are perhaps in these fields as part of the day's service they owe their master, sent there to sow his crop. They are not paid for this and thus have no incentive to work well or carefully, beyond the need to avoid punishment and the hope of finding favour with their master. If the diligent worker is more careful than his neighbour and nobody notices, so what? They have both put in the service required. If the diligent man discovers a more efficient way to work – again, so what? Will it really benefit him? More than likely, his efficiency will result in his doing more of the work. There is no small patch of land he can call his own property, which he can improve for his own benefit. If he does increase the land's value through his hard and thoughtful work, he cannot sell it or bequeath it to anyone. The worker does what he must do; perhaps he works harder if an overseer is present. But overall, people do their work but do not work any faster or better than is absolutely necessary; they have to show up but do the minimum required.

Restrictions applied also to those higher up in the social hierarchy.

The man for whom these people were obliged to work so many days each year might accumulate funds from the sale of the surplus food produced for him, but what could he do with those funds? There was little scope for him to invest and grow his funds. It was difficult to use these coins to buy land, manage the new asset, improve the land, and expand his holdings as his later counterpart in England was able to do. There was not much he could do with his money besides spend it, hold it, or give it away. What he often did do was commission religious works, such as wonderfully illuminated prayer books, and set aside money to pay for priests to pray for his soul daily, forever.

Roman land ownership

In the Roman world, property rights were a different matter from what they were in Europe during the fourteenth century.

On the 19 January AD 103, Reburrus, a man born in Spain whose father was called Severus, was given the military diploma shown on the next page, found in Cheshire in England many centuries after it was written. It is a legal document, witnessed by seven men. It documents that all soldiers serving in certain divisions of the Roman army in Britain who had completed twenty-five years of service were given Roman citizenship for themselves and their descendants and that Reburrus is one of those granted this privilege. The document is a certification of citizenship: a copy of what is in the state records. It declares that the names of all those who received this grant are recorded on a wall behind the temple of Augustus at Rome. This grant of citizenship was unexceptional and what a serving soldier expected to earn.

This document confirms the soldier's status, which gives him certain rights. He has the right to participate in political life, to vote and, if qualified, to stand for election. He has the right to enter contracts and to sue in the courts.

Many of these diplomas survive as records of what was considered a great achievement and a source of pride for men of whom little is known beyond their names and the bare details of their military service. A man such as the soldier who received this diploma

The soldier's reward: Roman citizenship and property rights

could present it to the authorities of any town, have it scrutinised, watch officials check that it was all in order, and then be told that his name would be recorded as a Roman citizen in their archives. Local men of business had walked the political path and become town councillors, leading men in this world, and on achieving status in this town had been awarded full Roman citizenship. The name of the veteran granted citizenship stood beside theirs in the records of this municipality. The soldier, however, could boast that his name was inscribed on a wall near a temple in the great city of Rome.

The veteran ended his service with something else besides. Since the time of Augustus, he had received on retirement a bounty of HS12,000, which amounts to 120 gold aurei, or between £60,000 and £120,000 in our terms. If he had been frugal and saved from the salary paid to him, then he had more. With this, he could buy land, a small estate, sufficient land to support his family and, in a good year, generate a surplus. The freedom of movement that this man possessed was beyond what his counterpart would have in medieval Europe. The medieval-period lords of the manors in Europe would never enjoy the freedom to own land outright – a right that a Roman soldier expected after his allotted years of military service.

A returning veteran came back with even more than citizenship and a pension. He had seen the world, been to places far different from his birthplace. He returned with skills, whatever he had learned in the military camps, where he might have functioned as blacksmith, carpenter, cook, or accountant. If farming were not to his taste, then perhaps he could set up an enterprise.

Medieval Europe celebrated poverty and religion. Wonderful cathedrals were built from which little streets ran out, lined with houses built of wood, not stone. The world of the Roman veteran was one of private property, and your rank in that world depended directly on how much you owned. Every so many years, the censors, the highest magistrates in the Roman world, assessed each man's estate; all his holdings were valued, and they placed him into a category corresponding to that valuation. A senator, a man in the first class, who had managed his wealth poorly or just simply been profligate, might fall one notch from the highest wealth category and no longer be qualified to serve in the Senate, with all the personal shame that would bring. A retired soldier had enough to make it to the fifth class, the lowest category above the landless proletarii, and if he managed his assets well, might progress up the scale and, in time, exceed the social prestige of men from families that had been at a higher social status than his when first he left town to serve in the army. All of these, if they and their families cared for their status in this world, were motivated to manage their wealth, to preserve and increase its capital value in ways not possible a few centuries later.

In Rome, land was owned by women as well as by men. Terentia, the wife of Cicero, who died about a hundred and fifty years before the veteran Reburrus was born, was a wealthy landowner in her own right. She owned farmland, which she had received from her father, and rented out properties in the city. Her wealth helped her husband progress in his political career. She ran her estate independently of him and reckoned how to make the most of what she had and enjoyed property rights well beyond what women in most Western European countries enjoyed prior to the nineteenth century. Wealth creation and property management were not exclusively men's prerogatives.

Property was essential to the Roman way of life, and wills were important means of preserving a person's reputation. A man could leave the ownership of land to one person while giving the right to use it to another for the duration of that person's life. Or he might leave some relative a fixed pension for life. All of these were to be valued, and the Roman valuation system was sophisticated. It was a flexible system, and it encouraged people to be productive.

Invention, discovery, and copying

The workers shown in the Luttrell Psalter are harvesting a crop, cutting down stalks, which will then be gathered, taken in, and threshed, and the grain ground down to make flour. Each of those stalks came from a seed, and what transformed that seed so that it produced many more seeds was its absorption of elements from the air and soil. The rain that fell and the air around the seed provided the carbon, hydrogen, and oxygen that made the carbohydrate that nourished the people who ate the bread produced from the grain.

Energy needed for this growth comes from the sun. All of this is provided without any work on the part of the people in the field and is outside their control. When the weather is good, neither too wet nor too dry, a good crop can be produced.

Other elements are needed for this transformation of one seed into many, and nitrogen is the principal of these other elements. It is present in the atmosphere from which this plant absorbs its carbon. The plant cannot, however, absorb nitrogen from the atmosphere and must take it from the soil. Land rich in nitrogen will produce a good crop, but as the years pass and the nitrogen is depleted, the fertility of the land will decline. Rain, dust, birds, weeds, and the seeds bring traces of that element to the soil, but humans have devised ways to supplement the nitrogen in the form of fertiliser. Even when chemical elements such as nitrogen were unknown, farmers had discovered how to nourish the soil for higher food production.

It is not just the addition of fertiliser that helps the seed produce more. It is also the work done in the fields when the crop is growing that matters, how carefully and diligently the field is tended. Between the time the seed is planted and when the crop is harvested, weeds come up in the fields, and these weeds compete with the crop for the nutrients in the soil. The weeds also absorb water that might otherwise have been absorbed by the crop, and they can block the light that the growing crop needs. All of this serves to reduce the yield from the crop unless workers go into the fields and regularly bend down, pull these weeds up, and come back again and again to do this hard and back-breaking work. The yield produced reflects this hard work, or the lack of it.

In medieval times the amount of new grain each seed produced was on average not much different from what is produced by grain in the wild when no human ingenuity is applied to enriching the soil and regularly removing weeds. This is illustrated in the graph on page 145. Men and women such as those represented in the Luttrell Psalter went out in the spring, ploughed the land, and sowed seeds. They gathered the crop during the harvest and did not do much beyond that. A more scientific and motivated approach would have produced a better result.

The works of some Roman writers survive from the late third century BC and later who occupied themselves with how to maximise the return from agricultural land. These were men such as Varro, Cato the Elder, who had been keen that Carthage be destroyed, and Columella; often they were called the "agronomists". They noticed that different results were produced from different fields at different times and that changing methods could produce better results. Following the same process year after year was not always effective, and so farmers should learn and improve. Varro describes a rich experimental approach for knowledge development:

In fact nature gave us two ways to develop agriculture, namely experimentation and imitation. The original farmers established many practices by trial and error and their descendants by imitating them, for the most part. We ought to apply a combination of these methods, imitating other people and ways in order to generate experiments to test certain hypotheses, not in a random way but systematically.

The approach was trial and error: for example, plough the land differently – more deeply or less deeply – and see what happens. Weed the land several times and see whether this makes a difference. People like Varro also looked at what other people were doing; if they could find a better way, then they happily copied that. They would not simply take their world as it was; they expected to improve it, and they didn't care whose idea worked.

The books that these men produced set out the results of their work. They give detailed instructions on how much seed should be sown in land of a certain quality, how the land should be ploughed, and how the crops should be cultivated. They did not evolve a chemical theory of elements such as nitrogen, oxygen, carbon, and hydrogen, but they did develop their own scientific understanding of what worked. They did not know that the nitrogen that wheat cannot absorb from the air but can absorb from the ground can be added to the soil by other plants, mainly legumes such as clover, beans, and lentils, which can absorb nitrogen from the air. They learned by trial and error that rotating crops produced better yields over the long term. They learned that land can be replenished by setting it to pasture for a year and allowing the livestock to manure it. They did not need any scientific theory of chemical elements or a periodic table to produce the commercial benefits of increased yields. They came to similar results through systematic observation, trial and error, and collation of results. Their approach was, in any case, the approach later used by scientists starting in the seventeenth century, to construct new bodies of experimental knowledge, which in time became the foundation of our sciences.

This knowledge mattered even to those who had no interest in the pure joy of discovery because in the Roman world personal wealth mattered. The wealth of Terentia, for example, depended on the productivity of her country estates as well as on the regular payment of the rents on her flats in the city. Agricultural productivity would have mattered to Reburrus too, if he had invested his money in land in Cheshire, for example.

This scientific approach was a great help to landowners of every class. They did not need to read these books themselves; the knowledge had been generated, and the results were evident: a careful and scientific use of the land would lead to higher food production. Some farmers were willing to learn from the works of the agronomists, and others could learn by copying. Increasing urbanisation of the Roman world brought its own benefits: the greater demand for food created more opportunities to make money. Terentia and any other member of the elite or any members of the lowest class who owned land were incentivised to produce more food to feed the growing cities and to get in return, gold aurei, silver denarii, or increases in their bank balances.

The profit calculations could be ruthless. In the second century BC, Cato had been merciless in his desire for the destruction of Carthage and was just as merciless in maximising the profits from his estates. The more grain he produced from the same land, the better the profits. What also mattered was the costs that went into production; the lower they were, the greater the profit. He reckoned out the bare minimum of food the slaves needed to do the work demanded of them – how much more was needed for those set to the laborious tasks and how much less was needed for those whose work was lighter, and that minimum was what they got. Food produced on his estate that would fetch a good price in the market was sold for profit, and the slaves could eat the poorer stuff. Not all were as ruthless as Cato, but for slaves owned by such men life was a hopeless imprisonment, unbearably worse than the life of a medieval serf.

We can be as scientific and as efficient as we like, but not everything lies within our control. The amount of food the land produces depends on the weather as well as on the hard work and the good farming practices of the people who tend it. Weather conditions can vary dramatically from one year to the next. Conditions in the United Kingdom in 2012, for example, were such that crop yields fell by one third to a half, and much of what was produced was useless for milling or malting. We do not, however, suffer food shortages today when such conditions occur because ours is a connected world. The shortfall is made up partly from grain reserves but, especially when the failure of the harvest is severe, mostly from grain imported from elsewhere in the world.

By the time of Trajan, it was much easier for grain to be imported and exported. The flow of information around the Roman world, the increased shipping fleet, the enlarged ports, and the desire of landowners and traders to make profits, all worked together to bring grain from parts of the empire that had produced bumper crops to those where crops had failed. Food shortages became a rarity.

Land which, because of competition from suppliers in distant parts of the empire such as North Africa, no longer produced grain for nearby towns could be used for pasture or market gardens. The food supply was not only secure but also more varied.

Water

Towns and cities depend on a regular supply of clean drinking water, and failure to provide that can lead to disease. For example, in the middle of the nineteenth century, a doctor, John Snow, seeing outbreaks of cholera in Soho in London, noticed that those who were falling sick had all used a pump in what is now Broadwick Street. In those days, disease was believed to be carried in bad air or to be the result of the sinful behaviour of those who fell sick. The doctor had the pump handle removed; with people of the area no longer able to access the infected water, the cholera outbreak subsided. Waste matter from the houses of that neighbourhood had leaked from cesspools and contaminated the ground water. The poor, dependent on the well, had been drinking the contaminated water. It would be some time before causes of disease were better understood, before people knew the importance of clean water. It would be some time before London acquired the dependable and readily available supply of clean water and the efficient drainage that Rome had managed almost two thousand years before.

Water was carried into the towns and cities of the Roman Empire along aqueducts, flowing gently and steadily, gravity providing the energy that carried this pure clean water from lakes or mountain rivers miles away. Water flowed into the city of Rome, into public fountains, to the public baths, and from there through the sewers, flushing the waste of the city through drains into the river, which carried that waste to the sea. All of this – the aqueducts, the sewers

156

London children dying because of dirty water

– had been built by private contractors paid out of public funds. It was not, however, only gravity and public private partnership that kept this system functioning. Somewhere, anywhere along the length of the aqueduct, a brick might crack, water enter the crack, freeze, expand and widen the gap, a leak develop, water start to escape, and the flow into the fountains some miles away start to weaken. In time, no water would be flowing into the baths, and the unflushed drains would begin to stink.

A young man intent on a political career, of a good family personal reputation and the money to back him had a chance of making it to the top. Reputation, connections, and money would, however, never be enough to carry him there. Having completed his time in the army and acquitted himself well, he might stand for one of the lowest-ranking magistracies, that of aedile, and if successful might be given responsibility for the maintenance of the aqueducts. Failure to maintain the smooth running of the water into the city and then attempting to stand for next highest magistracy when his opponents could mock him for the few days when the water in this or that fountain slowed to a trickle, was not going to help his career. Those who aspired in this competitive world to the highest office had to know how to keep the water flowing smoothly and had to make sure it happened.

The supply of clean water to the ancient city of Rome was better than it was for much of nineteenth-century London. Sanitary conditions were also better. The poor, or anyone who wanted, could use public latrines, and usually for free. The water supply maintained by young aristocrats carried the waste away for the convenience of the poor and the health of all. If the drains were blocked or the flow of water that flushed waste away reduced and the poor sat in the stench, then they knew who was responsible and who should fix the problem.

Aristocrats working for the convenience of the public

The illustration shows public latrines at Ostia, the port town near Rome. Those seated here sat in a room into which clean water flowed, first into a wall-mounted basin near the entrance where they could wash their hands as they left, then into channels along the floor by their feet and from there into the latrines to flush the waste away. It was healthy living.

The rich, if they chose, could have wonderful seats made for them, such as this lavatory seat, now on display in the Vatican. It once stood in the Lateran Palace when this object designed for the sanitary convenience of a member of the Roman elite was grand enough to serve as a ceremonial throne for a medieval pope.

An aristocratic convenience

The network of drains through which the water flowed into the Tiber had been built over centuries. Part of that network survives in the city of Rome and continues to carry water to the river. The Roman historian Livy, in writing of the early history of Rome, puts words of complaint into the mouths of the citizens. Why should they be put to the task of building drains when they could be out fighting wars? What they built, however, and what their successors improved on and expanded made life in the city more pleasant and healthier, and it saved lives.

How long we live

We can see how the length of life has changed over the centuries by looking at the experience of the British peerage – those who were barons, viscounts, earls, or dukes in the years after 1550. The estimation of past life expectancies for the British peerage over that period of several centuries is made possible by careful record-keeping; the details of the birth of an heir to a title were essential to the succession to that title, and the details of the death of a holder were just as important. From this information it is possible to work out how long members of the British peerage lived several centuries ago.

The following graph shows how life expectancy changed over the last almost four hundred years for that elite population. The horizontal axis shows calendar year, and the vertical axis shows the life expectancy of those born into the peerage in that year. The life expectancy shown for 1550 is about thirty-five years. This was the life expectancy at birth for the elite, those with the best access to food, housing, warmth, and clothing. The rest of the population had more limited access to such necessities, and we can assume that their life expectancy was even lower.

The hundred-year period between 1550 and 1650 was a dismal time. Children born then to the elite lived shorter lives than their parents did. This was a miserable time for the general population as well, and plague contributed significantly to their suffering. The news of the devastation happening in Europe arrived in England before the ships carrying the disease did. There was little that people could do, beyond quarantining the sick; they knew nothing of the causes of the disease, what made it spread, or how to stop it. They prayed and waited, and the disease came on infected ships, swept through the country, and each outbreak was gone as suddenly as it came.

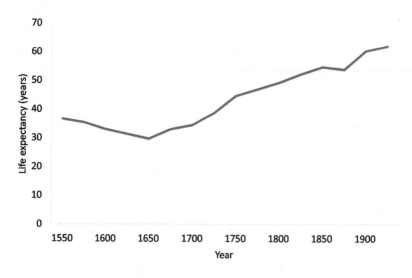

Life expectancy of the British peerage

Between 1544 and 1666 there were eight crises in England when deaths increased because of plague, on its own or in combination with other diseases. Such times were full of horror caused by the news of the unstoppable approach of the plague and then the scourge itself: fearsome to see, with dead bodies piled up.

But the horror of the plague hid something more dreadful. On those eight occasions when the plague came and quickly left, the number of extra deaths was never more than one tenth of the deaths that normally occurred in the country each year. Even that probably overstated the horror of the plague. When the disaster hit, almost all deaths would be attributed to the one undisputed event – the plague. Those already weakened by hunger or old age were included in the count. The plague was visible and memorable, but most people died at a relatively early age due to causes unnamed and unrecognised.

Poor diet, scarcity of food, and dirty water never caused such scenes as the plague, but they took away more lives. Sometimes even the price of food caused deaths – on a scale similar to deaths during the plague years – and there were three such crises in the period 1544 to 1666. When people could not afford food, they died. Even today, how long a person is expected to live depends, all else being equal, on their wealth, which guarantees access to good and nutritious food and what the body needs to stay robust enough to fight infection. Wealth also provides security, removes the anxious concern for tomorrow's food, removes the worry of how to heat the house in the winter, to keep out the cold, the rain, and wind.

The sixteenth and early seventeenth centuries, when the children of the elite lived shorter lives than their parents, was a time of disruption, destruction, and chaos. Beautiful religious works of art, loved for generations, were destroyed; great tracts of land were seized and redistributed; followers of one religion were persecuted, then the tables turned and followers of another religion were persecuted; civil war broke out between one faction and another; and a king was executed. Those who could avoid, or survive, all this, who could protect their wealth and continue to farm their land, could live much as before. For the rest, life was uncertain. A year or two when their fields remained unploughed, when food was scarce or they could not afford it, made all the difference. When peace returned, their bodies were weakened and less able to withstand the cold and infections. When the peace came, it would be their children who benefited.

From the late seventeenth century onwards, those born into the British elite lived longer than their parents had done. Through most of that period, there were no medical advances that might account for the change, no new drugs or treatments such as antibiotics.

What did change over that period were the conditions in which people lived. The world became more peaceful and ordered. There were wars beyond their borders, other countries suffered revolutions and invasions, but Britain was at peace with itself if not with its neighbours, and the constitutional changes that did take place were brought about with hardly any violence. Property rights were secure, as were the supply chains that brought food from the estates into towns and cities. More and better food was produced. The wealth of the population increased. The quality of life improved, and the risk of death from infection reduced in a population where hunger, with its debilitating effects on the body, was rarer. By 1925 the lifespan of a member of the British elite had doubled.

By the time of Trajan, the Roman world was a world at peace. The internal armed conflicts, the civil wars, had become matters of history, not the experience of people of his time. The borders of their world were kept secure, and at the heart of their government there was stability, too. Clean water was plentiful, and those who had money enjoyed quality and variety of food. They gave as little thought to what might be in the markets as we do to what might be in our shops. If it was there yesterday, then it will be there today, and we can turn our minds to other things.

There are no surviving lists of birth and death dates of the Roman elite, but we can estimate how long they lived. They commemorated their dead and erected monuments to mark the lives of their parents, children, husbands and wives; these monuments provide some evidence of lifespans. They lived longer and better lives than those who lived in Europe during the Middle Ages, and their quality of life was not exceeded until around the middle of the eighteenth century, and in some places not until long after that.

All of this depended on cooperation between the municipal and state authorities, who commissioned and financed works, such as the ports, and the contractors who made profits from building those works. It depended on the private estates from which food was produced for the enrichment of their owners. Without the enlarged ports, the import and export of food would not have been possible to the extent that it was. Without the aqueducts and the drains, clean water and hygiene would not have been possible to the extent that they were.

So long as the money system remained secure and property rights were respected, private individuals continued to invest in trade and manufacturing and in farms, and food and goods were produced for sale locally or in distant markets. The aqueducts and ports needed maintenance, and as long as young aspiring politicians had incentives to take charge of and maintain this infrastructure, then the basic necessities of life were available, at least to those with access to money.

The long life expectancy that all of this produced provided opportunities to learn and become more productive. With a short life expectancy, it does not make much sense to spend the first twenty years of life acquiring knowledge and training, when the young could be put to work in the fields. A longer life expectancy allowed the young to spend more time becoming skilled, taking up apprenticeships, paid little initially but then becoming more productive and better paid.

However, life was different for those who had no money, and for the sick who could not find work. Although there was great social mobility and people could better themselves, it remained a competitive world. For those who could not compete and who had no one to help them, there was little hope beyond what emerged about one hundred years before the death of Trajan in the troublesome province of Judaea.

> Blessed are the poor in spirit, for theirs is the kingdom
>   of heaven
> Blessed are those who mourn, for they shall be
>   comforted
> Blessed are they that are persecuted for the sake of
>   righteousness, for theirs is the kingdom of heaven

These words came from a new religion – which Trajan had acted to discourage – that preached gentle words of hope. It welcomed the excluded and those who did not prosper. It offered them even more than that. There was a life after this, they were told, a blessed life where the poor, the bereft, and the persecuted would live forever. This new religion would long outlive the religion of Mithras, which had also emerged from the East and at about the same time. But not all the words of this new Christian religion were gentle.

But woe betide the rich, for you have already received your comfort

And:

I have come to turn a man against his father, a daughter against her mother and a daughter-in-law against her mother-in-law.

It was a world of inequality, and there was a harshness in it, and discontent.

Chapter 8
Chaos

The peace

After the second world war, the Soviet Union ruled from Moscow a territory encompassing most of the land that had constituted the Russian Empire: Russia itself, the Ukraine, Kazakhstan, Armenia, and so on. For the Soviets, the recent memory of the invasion deep into its territory from an army marching out of Europe was alive, as was the memory of Napoleon's invading army, which, over a hundred years earlier, had reached as far as Moscow. The Soviet Union protected itself by bringing under its control countries along its borders: Poland, Hungary, Czechoslovakia, Lithuania, Latvia, and others. These countries were annexed or compelled to enter alliance with the Soviets, and attempts at rebellion were crushed with military force. They were required to follow the same economic, social, and political systems as those run from Moscow. Migrants from the Russian heartland settled in some of these countries, seeing themselves as Russian first and Latvian, for example, second. The schoolchildren of these border countries learned Russian and, in time, fluency in that language was widespread across the lands under the sway of Moscow. In fact, competence in that language was a prerequisite for economic and political progress. The Soviet Union was now protected by a surrounding cordon of countries; any invading army must cross them first. Moreover, these countries were populated by people whose culture was increasingly aligned to that of Moscow and whose loyalties lay more and more with the empire for which they were the buffer.

In broad outline, this was the same approach the Romans had taken to defend their empire, and it was extended by Trajan during the period when he was the leading citizen, from AD 98 to AD 117. The threats to the empire lay across the Danube and along the Rhine and in the east, in the desert lands, the remnants of the old Persian Empire. For example, Trajan's successful campaign against Dacia had been matched by others into what is now Armenia. Lands that would later become part of the buffer zone protecting Russia protected the Roman heartland in Trajan's time.

Some of those who had lived in the countries Trajan invaded, the new provinces he established, were enslaved or pushed out; those who remained lived under a different order, that of Rome, and they lived a Roman life, not the tribal life of their ancestors. The army camps developed into urban settlements, fed by the surrounding country, which now used Roman agriculture and Roman law. New self-sufficient provinces exported grain and offered opportunities to those who wished to adopt Roman ways, live under its laws, and become wealthy.

The wars to establish these new buffers were expensive, adding to the normal cost of the army in armour, replacements, and engineering works. The Romans financed that additional cost, however, through the sale, as slaves, of those captured and the loot that became available, such as the gold of Dacia. The new provinces offered opportunities to those who lived across the empire. A young man in Italy, for example, might leave for Dacia and find work there in one of the new towns or on new agricultural estates. The new wealth of those whose grain fed these towns, or which was exported, needed outlets, and now there were new customers for dealers and manufacturers in places such as Alexandria or for olive growers in Spain, much as the bloc around the Soviet Union was later to provide markets for its products. This strategy financed itself and was not a drain on the Roman exchequer.

Trajan died in AD 117 in the eastern part of the empire, without a publicly recognised heir. The man who had added so much to the infrastructure of the empire, had so facilitated the growth in trade and the enrichment of the population through its own endeavours, who had secured the borders against external threats, and who was later remembered, along with Augustus, as the best who had ruled over them, died without having publicly named a successor. Perhaps this was wise – and his way of managing rivalry while there was so much else for him to do. Perhaps he hoped to live longer and deal with that part of the state's business later. In any event, letters were sent to the Senate at Rome signed by his wife, Plotina, which declared his adoption of Hadrian as his successor. On the authority of these letters, the Senate approved Hadrian as the new emperor. It could have disputed the nomination, and there were some who suggested that Plotina and Hadrian had concocted it, but the Senate did not dispute the choice of heir. Perhaps it was satisfied that all was in order. Perhaps the execution by Hadrian of four of the members of that body who opposed him made a difference. But, in any case, the transition was smooth, and the balance on which the state depended – the balance between the emperor, the Senate, and the army – was maintained.

Those other constituencies – the people of Rome and the people of Italy and the provinces, those constituencies that were seldom active agents for change but whose dissatisfaction could upend things – all these were content as well. It might have worked out better in the long run if the Senate had had a more decisive role. If there had not been the suspicion of a process being manipulated, perhaps there would in later years have been a better counterbalance to the strong man and his ambitions.

A period of peace followed, but it was a strange peace. The activity of Trajan's time was replaced with a quietness. In the areas such as Dacia, into which Trajan had marched, conquered, and subdued the populations, a new defensive strategy was applied. When Hadrian took power, he ended the ongoing wars already in progress and did not start any new external wars but put down revolts in the empire when they occurred, in Judaea, for example. He built the wall in northern Britain named after him, and some years later his appointed successor, Antoninus, built another defensive wall further north.

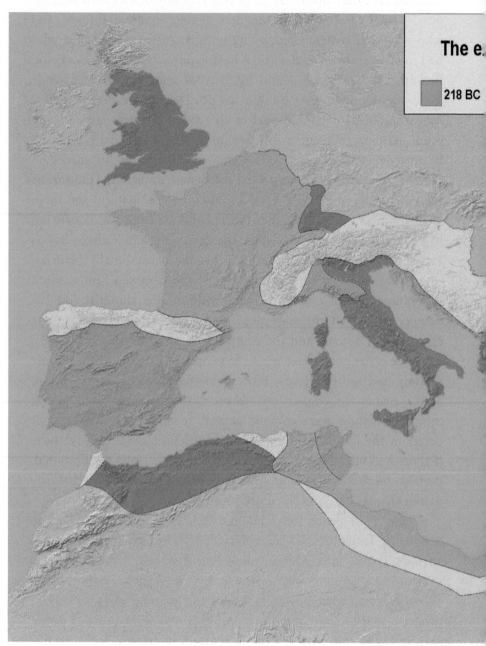

The e.

218 BC

Long centuries of expansi

ent of the Roman Republic and Roman Empire in

| | 133 BC | | 44 BC | | AD 14 | | after AD 14 | | AD 115-117 |

rinding to a halt

Changes in military strategy: standing behind walls

Hadrian maintained the discipline and training of the army, but it was an army training in the camps, not the battlefield. The legions could claim that they had stopped this or that incursion, this or that insurrection, but they could never add to their battle honours a list of new territories that they, not their predecessors, had seized. Along with Hadrian's non-war strategy, he paid money to those who threatened the empire, money to keep them quiet. Perhaps these signs and the walls built in northern Britain suggested to those who lived across the frontier of the empire that it was not so much to be feared as before. It was a change of strategy and expensive too: the gains from earlier campaigns, which had helped finance the military machine, were there no longer.

Trading continued across the peaceful Mediterranean. For example, distant towns such as Londinium still had goods for sale that had been produced thousands of miles away in North Africa or Egypt. Towns and cities continued to thrive, and their infrastructure was maintained: water flowed in the fountains, the baths were heated and clean, there was food in the markets. The ports were still amazing theatres of activity, commerce, and wealth. The building works continued under Hadrian and his successor, Antoninus Pius. They built new harbours and aqueducts. Production of goods continued as before.

Trouble along the borders

Antoninus Pius was succeeded in AD 161 by Marcus Aurelius and in the capital of the empire, a new column was later erected, taller than the one Trajan erected to mark his victories. Winding around it were stories told in carvings, of victory in war. The column of Marcus Aurelius commemorates a victory, just as the column of Trajan commemorates a victory. It is, however, different.

Torching huts

This is not the Dacian war, in which aggressors who had dared to trouble the empire have been taught a lesson, where war brought in gold and slaves. No new territory came to Rome because of the victory of Marcus Aurelius. Their territory had been defended from invasion, and that was about it. Their victory in one case had depended on a miraculous change in the weather, not on their superiority, and that was the new story they had to tell themselves.

The Roman Empire had faced disaster in the east in AD 161, the year in which Marcus Aurelius became emperor. The trouble came from the Parthian empire, which covered all of modern-day Iran and much of modern-day Iraq. The king of Parthia entered and took control of Armenia, a territory that had been conquered by Trajan but relegated to a client state by Hadrian.

The Roman governor of the neighbouring province of Cappadocia responded by entering Armenia but met with catastrophic defeat

171

and humiliation. Within three days the men of his legion had been slaughtered and he had committed suicide.

The Romans reduced the military manpower protecting the northern border of their empire, from the Danube, and sent those soldiers to the East. The Armenian capital was retaken, and in AD 165 the Romans pushed into the Parthian empire as far as modern-day Baghdad, restoring peace for a few decades. The soldiers, however, had been drawn deep into the territory of the Parthians, supply lines had failed, and food had run short. When the legion returned to the Danube, it was weakened by hunger and carrying infectious disease.

At the same time, the Romans faced disaster along the northern borders of the empire. Starting in AD 162, encouraged perhaps by the Roman strategy of non-engagement and the withdrawal of men to put down the troubles in the east, invaders repeatedly crossed the Rhine and Danube and were repeatedly repulsed. The difficulties were made worse by disease brought back by the soldiers returning from the east, and many died in an epidemic during the winter of AD 168. One year later, for the first time in almost three hundred years, enemy soldiers made it into Italy, destroying as they went. Again, they were repulsed. This pattern of invasion and pushback continued through the reign of Marcus Aurelius.

The column erected at Rome in commemoration of Marcus Aurelius celebrates his victories in Armenia and Parthia and along the borders of the rivers Rhine and Danube, but what it shows is not inspiring. The image from the column is a scene of soldiers torching huts. These people who fought against the Romans and threatened Rome's security did not have the economic might of the Roman Empire, its superbly maintained currency, its great material culture. They are shown as living in huts not houses, huts that the Romans burnt as the women fled taking their children, looking back on their menfolk being killed.

The peace established by Trajan along the borders was gone, threatened by peoples the Romans had controlled before. Within the heart of the empire, however, around the Mediterranean, the world was still undisturbed. Trade continued peacefully between the ports near Rome and those in North Africa and elsewhere, but the mood had changed.

Internal instability

Not only were there tensions along the borders of the empire but also instability was filtering into the top of the political system. When Marcus Aurelius was dying in AD 180, he surrounded himself with his advisers and then gave into their charge his son and heir Commodus, who he said needed their guidance because of his age and lack of experience. For much of the reign of his son, these men stood as his counsellors. They stood in that position by the authority of his father and for no other reason.

What Marcus Aurelius had done was place the interests of his son above the interests of the state he had led. This son of his was not competent for the role. Commodus was far younger than any man who had ever been allowed to be consul in the time of the Republic. He was eighteen years old, the youngest man since Nero to be emperor. Whatever talents he had, whatever beliefs and loyalties, whatever competence he had acquired, had not been tested.

This eighteen-year-old was now the chief executive of the state, with all the power of his predecessors. He had, for example, the power to enter treaties with other states. He could summon the Senate, present proposals to it which, if he secured a majority of their votes, became law. He could present candidates to them for their confirmation as magistrates. The executive powers, the policy-making powers of Trajan, for example, were now his. The empire Trajan and his office had managed carefully through a stream of letters sent to his fellow senators governing the provinces – letters of instruction, advice, letters of a man who understood how it all worked and who cared for precedent – that empire was now in the hands of Commodus, who did not.

Commodus was emperor for no other reason than being the son of an emperor. There had been no consideration of others who might have been better suited, who might have a subtler under-standing of the constitution of this world, stronger claims to military competence, or any of the other attributes that made a

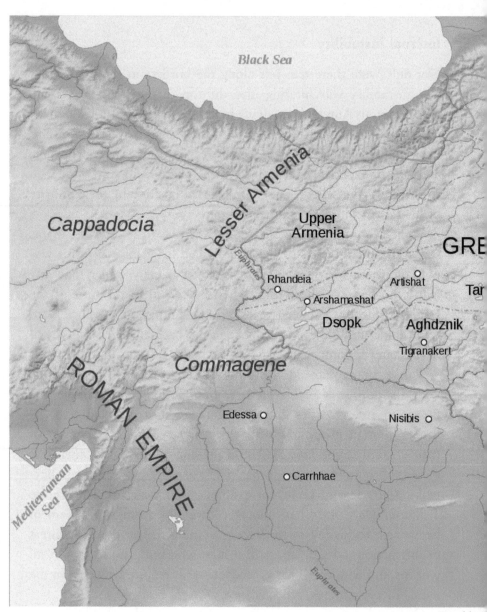

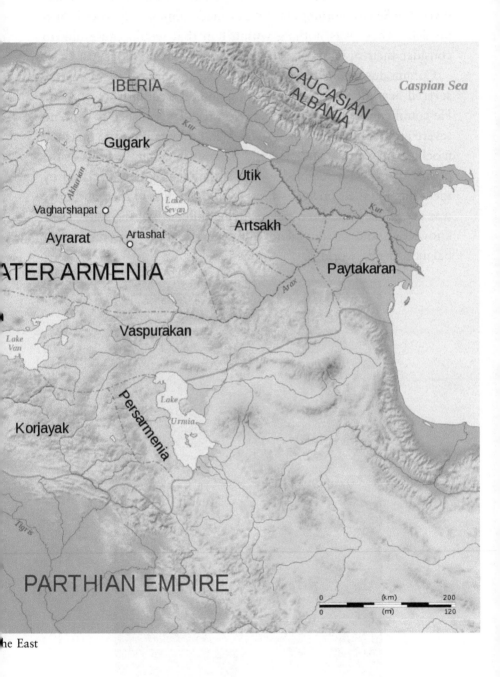

the East

man fit to lead this world. More to the point, however, Commodus owed the Senate nothing. It had not made him, and he owed them no debt. There was nothing within him that would cause him to consider their opinion or be restrained by that opinion.

Commodus mocked the senators in the amphitheatre, waving the severed head of an ostrich, that long-necked bird, in front of them. He could cut off their heads too. No rage was returned to him, no severe and threatening disapproval. What they returned to this man mocking them was concealed and nervous laughter. In front of the people of Rome, assembled in this amphitheatre, they declared by their inaction their powerlessness. With that, most of their authority was gone. They had been the steadying influence of the state. Their knowledge and wisdom had for generations kept a restraining balance in this world.

The emperor who mocked the Senate and dressed absurdly

Absurdities now crept in. The emperor renamed each of the months after himself or his attributes. He dressed as Hercules, abandoning the ancient and solemn dignity the emperors had used to portray themselves. This was another Nero but an unrestrained one. The man who had crept away in the face of the Senate's resolution that he be killed, who had crept away to take his own life, had never been given the highest honour possible for an emperor after his death. The Senate never declared Nero a god, and no altars were set up at which he could be worshipped, no temples were built to honour a deified Nero and to house his statue. They declared him instead to be an enemy of the state. That power of the Senate, which mattered to anyone who cared for their legacy, was now lost. Now Commodus declared himself a god, on his own authority.

At the heart of the settlement established by Augustus had been a balance among the power and authority of the chief executive, the Senate, and the army. So long as that balance was maintained, there was stability in the system. There were tensions, conspiracies, jealousies, officials who sought position and wealth, who schemed against rivals, but the system held together. Now the authority of the Senate was largely gone.

Disorder crept into the world, and this disorder became the new normality. Food shortages started to happen. Cleander, a senior official under Commodus, bought up the corn supply of Rome, brought in by private enterprise, and then withheld it. His plan was to shut off the distribution, starve the city, and then use the grain to buy the loyalty of the citizens. A fire raged through the city, as it had during the reign of Nero, and destroyed some of the most beautiful temples, but the fire brigade failed to control it. Disease swept the city of Rome. Perhaps the maintenance of the aqueducts was failing, and clean drinking water was not readily available, or sanitation was not what it used to be. Perhaps disease was coming into this once-clean city because public order was failing, as it would in our own modern cities if drains were not maintained and waste piled up in the streets.

Now there were revolts in Britain, Germany, and Africa. A peaceful world was becoming disturbed. A disciplined army and a contented population were now becoming restive. Commodus had increased taxes and planned to confiscate the wealth of the rich to pay for the army. The administrative system that normally collected taxes, peacefully, and paid for the army that kept the peace was being burdened beyond its capacity to deliver.

The Roman people had faced disruption before, in the time of Augustus two centuries before and of Nero and then of Domitian one century before, and they had recovered. It is possible to recover from some failures, but some decisions cannot be reversed and are fatal. Sometime before AD 192, very likely during the reign of Commodus, a decision was taken to increase the amounts that the soldiers received as net pay. This was an enormous imposition on the resources of the state, and it could not be reversed without the risk of revolt. To understand what happened we need to look at how soldiers were paid.

Army pay

Regularly and routinely, masses of documents were produced in the Roman Empire. These included census records, confirmations of citizenship, accounts of private estates, accounts of cities and towns, records of bankers and traders. Letters public and private were sent here and there throughout the empire. Hardly any of that mass of documents survives. But a few do.

Outside the town of Oxyrhynchus in Egypt was a rubbish dump, and there the citizens of that town dumped papyrus documents over a period of centuries. The documents they left there would not normally survive, but they did thanks to the dry sands of Egypt. They are the ordinary documents of everyday life and include the pay accounts of individual soldiers.

Pay accounts drawn up in AD 81 for two soldiers were found by archaeologists in this rubbish dump. One of these soldiers was Quintus Iulius Procolus, from Damascus, and the other was Caius Valerius Germanus, from Tyre, both serving in this town in Egypt. Their pay accounts were credited with their salary and then deductions were made for food, clothes, arms, and the like, and most of the soldiers' pay went to those deductions. For example, out of each HS100 the soldier got to keep less than HS30, as shown in the illustration below.

What the soldier was left with after deductions

The system had been in operation for generations before either of those two soldiers had joined the army and was to operate for generations after they left. The amount left over for the ordinary soldier was less than the amount deducted for food. It was something to spend in the neighbouring town, to save, or to send home. There was the retirement lump sum to look forward to, but serving in the army, provided that discipline was maintained, was not a way to get rich quick.

The money that flowed into an army camp went mainly to men who were not soldiers. Those who supplied food and clothes to the camps together got twice as much as the soldiers. The same system used by Augustus and the Senate in the building and refurbishment of temples in Rome was used at army camps throughout the empire. Contracts were put out to tender to supply grain or clothing. Needs were specified, contracts were awarded, and there was law then as now to protect the aggrieved when the terms of the contract were broken. Networks of dealers and suppliers produced whatever was needed and got their remuneration. It was a machine. And it was a business.

The amounts deducted from the soldiers' pay were notional and did not consistently match the actual costs of, say, food that month. Costs are variable, and it would be unhelpful to have to explain to a soldier why more was being deducted this month than last month. In any case, supplying the necessities was a business that was run from within each camp: camp officials negotiated contracts for the food, clothing, and whatever else was needed. Profits or losses accrued as prices varied, as the amounts charged for supplies were more or less than the amounts deducted, and as the camp officials negotiated well or badly. The profit-and-loss ratios of camps could be compared and questions could be asked if there appeared to be problems.

Other, slightly later pay accounts than these also survive. Some date to AD 84, when Domitian was in power. He had raised the soldier's pay average by one third, but the deductions from the soldier's pay had also increased by a third. Where before the soldier kept HS30 out of every HS100 he was paid, there was now an extra HS10 for him. It was an increase of thirty percent in the net pay to the soldier but a modest increase of only ten percent in the total cost of the army.

Other, later papyri tell a different story. The accounts that survive from the end of the second century and from the beginning of the third century follow a simpler format. The pay deposited has increased significantly, and there are no deductions in these accounts for food, clothing, and so forth. The only deduction shown is for tax. The soldiers' monthly supplies were now paid for by the state and not by the soldiers. This change happened at some stage before AD 192, the earliest date associated with the new format, and was a substantial increase in soldiers' remuneration. Soldiers who previously had little to spend in the local markets now had three times as much money to spend as before. The soldiers now had the wherewithal to spend money and find other things to do with their time. They might even grow bold enough to ask for further increases in pay.

There is no record of who made this decision, but it was unwise. It severely damaged the state's finances. And, of course, the concession could never be reversed; new funds would have to be found from somewhere to replace the deductions previously made from soldiers' accounts – the equivalent of two thirds of the cost of the army. A wise ruler would not have done this. A Senate with authority would not have permitted it.

The sale of the office

Commodus was assassinated in AD 192, the first emperor to have been assassinated since Domitian almost one hundred years earlier. He was not taken out of this world through Senate resolution or suicide. A petty conspiracy ended his existence. The chaos that followed the death of Nero rose up again. There was no man whose succession had been agreed upon before the demise of the old ruler, a man accepted by the Senate, the army, and the people. The head of the Praetorian Guard, that elite unit that Augustus had established and that camped close to the capital, went with one of Commodus's officials to the old senator Pertinax, the last survivor of the counsellors whom Marcus Aurelius had appointed to guide his son. Pertinax, thinking that these men who came to visit him at night had come to kill him too, prepared himself for death and let them in. They asked him to become the next emperor. He attempted to refuse the privilege, but his visitors praised him for his reputation in the Senate and the regard with which he was held by the people of Rome. He consented.

The news of the death of the tyrant and the nomination of Pertinax spread through the city of Rome. He was acclaimed by the people of Rome. The Senate listened to the modest speech of this honoured member of their ancient assembly and acclaimed him too. In the face of this support, the army at Rome acquiesced but did so reluctantly. They consented but not for long. They had become used to life under the tyrant who had preceded this old man Pertinax, used to the new liberty to insult the people and to pillage.

The new emperor set about restoring order. He removed the onerous taxes that had been imposed by his predecessor, the new customs tariffs. He prohibited the soldiers from mistreating the citizenry. But poor Pertinax lasted only three months from that night when he had accepted the throne. Soldiers from the Praetorian Guard, which had reluctantly accepted him, rushed his palace. He refused to flee but instead went out to address them. He told them that he, an old man, was not afraid to die but that he had nothing to do with the plot to kill Commodus and that it was their duty to protect him. Some turned away and left. Others turned on him and killed him.

Now it was the turn of the Praetorian Guard to mock the Senate and the people of Rome. They put the position of emperor up for auction. They had done away with the last one, and the next could pay for the privilege of living as emperor. Julianus won the auction and got the prize. But it was money that won him the position of leading citizen, not personal authority or achievement – and the people scorned him. Worse still for him, the sums of money he had promised the soldiers in the auction for emperor were beyond his own resources and beyond anything he could raise from his friends, and so he lost the support of the Praetorian Guard. He was done away with too, on the orders of the Senate, who elected Septimius Severus as emperor, a general now marching on Rome.

Camped outside the city of Rome, Septimius Severus tricked the Praetorian Guard to come out unarmed and greet him. They did, in all their finery, with gold rings on their fingers, proof of their changed status since the accession of Commodus and the money they now garnered. He spared the fools and sent them into exile rather than slaughtering them in front of the city.

Septimius Severus: doubling the pay of the army

Civil war – worse in its violence than any civil war between Pompey and Caesar or Mark Antony and Augustus – continued to consume the empire as Septimius Severus worked to eliminate another rival, the general Niger. When Septimius Severus finally emerged as unchallenged emperor, it was the start of a military dictatorship. He had cleared the barracks at Rome of the old Praetorian Guard, and now he built the barracks to be twice its old size and filled it with his own men. And he went further. He doubled the pay of the army.

An inscription with a dedication to Septimius Severus survives from Lambaesis in North Africa. The inscription does not mark any specific great victory in which Septimius Severus had led them as general against some enemy, a new honour to be added to the proud battle honours of their legion, or their part in the glorious story of the Roman army. The head of the legion's administration and his deputy, the actuarius, set up this inscription in gratitude to Septimius Severus for doubling their pay.

Septimius had appeased the army and bought its loyalty but had fatally undermined its discipline. He had unsettled the minds of soldiers who for generations had seen pay come as predictably as all the other routines of camp life, a predictability needed by men who in military engagement exposed themselves to death and faced the greatest uncertainty of all. Now pay could increase substantially at the whim of the emperor, and the army could be bought. Worse still, the emperor had become the army's hostage.

When in 211 AD, at the end of his reign, the emperor Septimius Severus lay dying on campaign in northern Britain near York, he gave instructions to his son and co-heir, the ill-tempered Caracalla, that he look after the army above all else. "Be harmonious, enrich the soldiers and scorn all other men." This Caracalla did, but he first got rid of his brother, co-heir.

Caracalla: looking after the soldiers above all else

In AD 212 Caracalla increased the pay of the army by fifty percent and went further than that. He increased the lump sum paid to the soldiers at the end of their service by two thirds. Until then there had been no appreciable increase for two centuries, and inflation over that period had been negligible. Caracalla went even further. He now increased the size of the army. From 300,000 soldiers, its approximate strength since the time of Augustus, it grew to 415,000 soldiers, and almost all the new soldiers were auxiliaries, men who were not Roman citizens.

The prospect of improvement in status matters, then and now. It incentivised new recruits to the army, and it incentivises new recruits to professional service firms today.

If, say, you have just left university and you have started work as a trainee lawyer, accountant, actuary, or architect, you have most likely joined a partnership. The senior individuals in those organisations are partners, and you sit at the bottom of a pyramid. The partners have rights and status that you do not have. They, however, need you to get their work done, and you will work long hours and do the excellent work they require. In time, if your work is good enough and if you survive the years needed, you, too, will be elected to partnership. That privileged status is part of what motivates you. Before Caracalla, about half the army comprised auxiliaries, men who were not Roman citizens, who served separately from those who were, and who were commanded by Roman citizens. At the end of their service, they, like the veteran Reburrus from Spain, who settled in Britain, were awarded Roman citizenship, a reward they greatly anticipated, along with their retirement lump sum. Caracalla removed that motivation. He gave citizenship to everyone in the empire.

In Alexandria, Caracalla, offended at some slight, assembled the youth of that ancient city, the second of the empire. Isolated and surrounded by soldiers, they were slaughtered and then buried in pits, some still alive and dragging their executioners down with them to be buried too. Such a mass slaughter in a law-abiding city of the empire, the capital of one of its richest provinces, all on the whim of one man, had never been seen before. The law that had maintained peace and sustained commerce was now replaced with the whims of a dictator. The certainty that comes from knowing the consequences of lawful and unlawful actions was replaced with the uncertainty of reading the mind of a capricious man.

The problem of increasing current expenditure

The total increase in the annual cost of the army under Caracalla was over £8 billion per annum in our terms. The total amount that had been spent by Augustus during his entire reign on the restoration of Rome and on new building works there was just less than £10 billion, again in our terms. Just over one year's worth of the additional amount being handed over to the soldiers would have paid for all the work undertaken and supplies needed by contractors, architects, engineers, and labourers in the restoration of the city of Rome, in the building of aqueducts, roads, public spaces, and temples. All that work had added to the beauty of the city and had enhanced the life of those who lived there. It had provided clean water needed for healthy lives, assembly places for doing business. There had been improvement in social life and a new amazement and vigour in a renewed city. New employment had been given to many, and the chance to acquire new skills as they worked on these projects, skills that could be used elsewhere. And these works lasted well beyond the lifetime of those who had built them; their labour was what provided water in fountains and seats in theatres for the enjoyment of those born generations after they were gone. The roads they repaired were walked on and the public spaces they built were used generations after them by people who built ports, which supplied generations after they, too, were gone. Each generation added to the work of its predecessors, and the wealth of the world grew.

Instead of all this, vast sums of money were now given to men who were already being paid and who did no extra work for this additional reward. Paying this money to them did not increase their economic activity, did not generate additional goods and services, did not build something for the future. It did, however, fuel demand. The substantial increases in the amount of money available to the soldiers gave them a purchasing power beyond that of most people

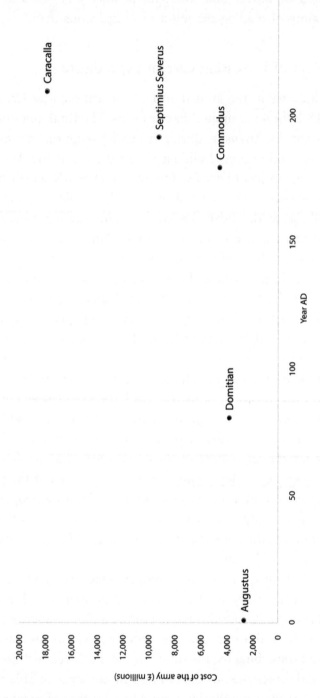

The cost of the army under Caracalla was about ten times higher than under Augustus.

who went to the markets near the camp where they lived. Their silver and gold coins distributed to them in ever increasing quantities chased luxury items and work-a-day items that were now produced in such ever-increasing quantities. Merchants responded to the increased demand for their products by increasing prices. What the soldiers bought, others could not afford.

As prices increased, the soldiers needed more gold and silver to get what they expected to get. They had by now learned how to get that additional gold and silver – and it was not by working more. They increased their money by demanding more. The world in which those contractors who did the best work got the jobs was being replaced by one in which a particular constituency, one representing about one percent of the population, demanded and got what it wanted without working for it.

The increases in army pay were increases in current expenditure; once given, they had to be paid in each subsequent year. There is a great difference between capital expenditure with its one-off commitment, such as building a new temple, and current expenditure with long-term commitments, such as increasing the amount spent every year on the army. If you undertake to give someone an amount of money equal to your monthly income to pay for a one-off purchase, that is all well and good. If you have the spare cash, then all is well. If not, perhaps you can economise in the months after that or sell something to get the funds. But if you contract to pay them more than your month's salary each and every month, then you have a problem. You have nothing left over for your normal living costs, and you do not have the funds to meet this obligation anyway.

The annual cost of the army, the largest item of state expenditure, was now ten times what it had been. This was beyond the revenues of the state but had to be paid. There was no going back. When Macrinus, Caracalla's successor, attempted to rein in the cost by removing the increase from new recruits but leaving pay at Caracalla's rate for the rest, he was assassinated. In any case, the normal tax revenues of the state could not pay for any of this additional expenditure. Indeed, when Caracalla first gave this salary increase, he sent the soldiers into the temples and the treasury for the money. Pay which had been met through a smoothly administered tax system was now replaced by state-sponsored looting. Other things had to give. Now the property of the wealthy would have to be targeted, not just as part of political revenge but as essential to paying the army.

Cutbacks were introduced to fund the additional sums being made over to the army, and construction projects were limited. Caracalla built enormous baths at Rome, but by AD 250 construction throughout the empire had declined dramatically; not just state construction but all construction effectively stopped. Even the memorial inscriptions which for centuries had been set up by those who mourned, such as the widower for his wife, were now scarcely any longer being designed, carved, and erected. Most of that activity had stopped.

It was not just new buildings that were not going up. The old buildings were suffering too. Buildings and other structures need to be maintained. Aqueducts that are not regularly checked and repaired spring leaks and stop functioning. Roofs lose tiles and, if nothing is done, the rain comes in, more tiles fall off, whatever they cover becomes unusable, and the home is no longer habitable. The harbours and ports on which this world depended for its trade, on which it depended for its food, supplying surplus grain to places where the harvest had failed, needed maintenance. Warehouses must stay secure and watertight or goods are stolen or grain rots. All such maintenance costs money, and, during this period of economic imbalance, there was no money left over. Other problems were emerging.

The silver mines

Until the middle of the second century BC, there had been two superpowers in the Mediterranean: the Roman and the Carthaginian. Their conflict lasted centuries and only finally ended in 146 BC with the annihilation by the Romans of their rival. Along the way, Rome had won partial victories. In 201 BC it gained the Iberian Peninsula, an asset to be of lasting benefit for close to four hundred years. The Iberian Peninsula is rich in minerals, gold and silver for

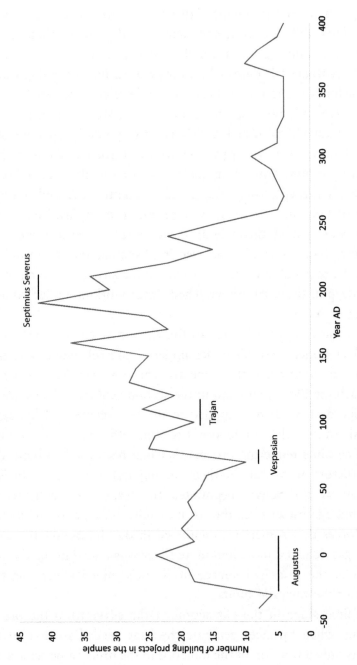

The rise and fall of the Roman construction industry

those who have the technical and organisational capabilities to extract it.

The Romans never commercialised the power that comes from steam. They did, however, commercialise the power that comes from water falling a distance, the same power that is used in modern hydroelectric dams where the great rushing of falling water turns turbines and that motion generates electricity. Outside Roman towns were mill houses, arrays of wheels. Water carried in on industrial aqueducts turned wheels as it fell, potential energy being changed into kinetic energy. The wheels turned millstones that ground grain into flour. As grain was carried to these complexes, the wheels turned slowly and steadily, unattended, and a day's supply of flour for the towns was produced each day. That technology was copied throughout the empire wherever there was commercial advantage. It was used in Hispania, and on an industrial scale, to grind and crush ore containing silver, ore taken from mines deep in the earth by wretched slaves working underground, hacking at rocks.

From the time of Tiberius, in the early first century AD, gold and silver mines were all under imperial control, but it was not the state that extracted those metals. The same ruthless efficiency that Cato the Elder (who had in the second century BC so wanted Carthage destroyed) had applied to the management of his agricultural estates, that same profit-seeking efficiency, was applied here. The same tendering process that had been used to build the infrastructure was used in their mining industry. State officials overseen by the Senate negotiated the terms, and contractors competed against one another to maximise their gains, managing work forces that sometimes numbered in the thousands. It was a way to get rich, and more and more silver was mined in the Iberian Peninsula, the principal source of Rome's mined silver, for the benefit of the imperial mints.

The final stage in the extraction of the silver from the ore is smelting, when furnaces generate the heat needed so that silver, which is only a fraction of the minerals in the ore, can be separated out. Lead is one of the most significant by-products of this process. For every gram of silver, you get three hundred grams of lead.

Part of the lead extracted in those furnaces escaped into the atmosphere, and part of that was then deposited in Greenland, in the rain that fell there adding year by year to the ice sheet. Analysis of the lead content of samples extracted from the Greenland ice sheet can be used, with other archaeological evidence, to generate a history of lead – and therefore silver – production. The rate at which silver was extracted from the earth increased massively while the Iberian Peninsula was under Roman control, then declined around AD 170 to AD 180 when control of that peninsula was lost to invasion from Africa during the reign of Marcus Aurelius; the Roman mining technology was not equalled again until the nineteenth century.

The silver from these mines was converted into coins in the imperial mints. The silver denarius, the basic coin of the Romans, was introduced when they captured Hispania and commercialised the mining operations there. So long as they had this flow of silver from the mines, they could maintain a currency in which the coins had a good silver content. There were other silver mines, in Britain, for example, and there were gold mines, in Dacia, for example, but Spain was the principal source of mined silver. There were other but less reliable sources. In the sack of Jerusalem in AD 70, the conquest of Dacia in AD 106, and the capture of the royal treasures of the Parthians in AD 190, the Romans acquired booty that could be melted down and the metals sent to the mint to be coined. That source of metal was unpredictable, requiring aggressive war and victory, and was not a match for the steady supply of metals coming from the silver mines of Hispania, produced by men motivated by commercial profit rather than war.

Unlike governments today, which can create money out of thin air, the Romans needed metals, and with the incursions into the Iberian Peninsula from North Africa in the last years of the reign of Marcus Aurelius, the Romans lost the steady source of those metals. They lost a source of gold and silver they had possessed in the four centuries after their defeat of Carthage in the second Punic war. The army, whose principal charge was to protect their borders, had failed them. This had cost them dearly. Yet, soon after that defeat the army would see its pay increased under Commodus.

The collapse of the currency

While the empire had been run peacefully, it paid for what it spent out of the tax revenues it collected and the silver and gold mined on its behalf and coined in the Imperial mints. As each emperor succeeded the next, he issued coins that had his own image and whatever message he wanted to send out: the story of the capture of Judaea, for example. New coins could also be issued by melting down old coins paid into the treasury as taxes. Coins, however, abrade and become worn down with use, and if the new coins were to be high quality, then gold or silver from melted-down treasures or from the mines needed to be added. That metal was becoming more and more difficult to source.

There had always been a temptation to cheat, to debase the coins and issue coins that looked as good as those issued in the past but that contained less silver or gold and more base metal. In this way, more coins could be issued for the same amount of silver, leaving more money for the central authorities to spend. The temptation became harder to resist when expenditure rose and the state needed more money than it received through regular tax revenues.

The following graph shows how the amount of silver in one denarius varied over time. The vertical axis shows the grams of silver in a denarius and the horizontal axis is time.

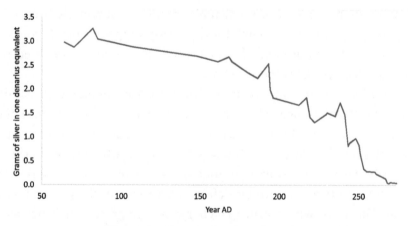

Change in silver content in a denarius

Since the denarius had been introduced, there had been a steady decline in the amount of silver per coin. From about AD 160 the silver content of the denarius reduced at a faster rate until by AD 260 there was hardly any silver in the coins at all. The supply of metals to maintain the quality of the currency was now severely reduced, and there was an ever-increasing need for coins to pay the soldiers.

The Roman world had long been one of price stability. Prices had varied year on year. The price of wheat, for example, had varied up or down in different localities as the harvest was good or poor in that area. But long-term prices had been broadly stable. Until the reign of Septimius Severus, the price paid for bread, or wine, or anything else was, on average, more or less the same as it had been during the reign of Augustus. There had been some inflationary increases before his reign but nothing of any significance or comparable to what followed the accession of Septimius Severus. This was a longer period of price stability than any modern economy has experienced. Now, from the end of the second century AD inflation began to disrupt the economy. The enormous amount paid to the soldiers and the debasing of the denarius all acted to push up prices.

Around the beginning of the first century AD, the Romans had invented the first money system in which gold and silver coins were exchanged in fixed and universally accepted amounts, and this had been enormously to their commercial advantage. However, from about the time of the emperor Philip the Arab, who ruled from AD 244 to AD 249, there was no longer a fixed rate between the two coins. This mattered. If you go to a shop with a ten-pound note to buy something priced at two pounds, then you expect to get eight pound coins in change. That exchange rate between the piece of paper and the pieces of metal is not questioned by you or the shopkeeper. You do not expect to be offered only six pound coins in exchange. If something is priced at ten pounds and you come along with ten one-pound coins, you expect to be able to buy the item. You do not expect to be told that only a ten-pound note will be accepted. If, however, the relative values of notes and coins might change with no warning, you would no longer know what you could afford. More of your time would be spent negotiating and haggling in the shops – not over goods but over how much change you should be getting.

Life in the towns and cities depended on a stable monetary system. The maker of fine glassware, for example, needed so many gold coins to pay the rent on his workshop and to pay for his raw materials, and the tools of his trade. He needed silver coins to pay for the bread he ate every day, and his wine. He looked to get good coins from his customers, good silver coins he could exchange for gold coins. But from about AD 250 the maker of fine glassware might look at the silver coins he had collected and not know whether he had enough for his rent or tomorrow's bread. The difficulties confronting a maker of fine glassware because of the collapse of the currency also confronted his suppliers and customers. Whether because of these difficulties in doing business or because of the political instability and disruption to trade, the production of fine glassware, which had increased so substantially in the first century AD, declined in the third century AD.

A further disruption was taking place. The civil war in AD 193 that followed the death of Commodus led to a reversal of the currency reform put in place by Vespasian (see Chapter 4). Vespasian had consolidated the mints. He had closed all mints producing silver and gold coins except for the imperial mint at Rome. He had done this to make it difficult for rival claimants to finance insurrection by seizing a mint and using it to produce coins from confiscated metals. This had the effect of concentrating demand for precious metals for coinage at Rome, making that one mint the principal buyer of precious metals. This had stabilised the currency by reducing dramatically the threat to the commerce when coins are melted down for their metal content.

This reform was now reversed. During the civil war of AD 193, a new mint was opened in what is now Turkey and used by both Niger and Septimius Severus, rival claimants for the position of emperor. More mints were opened through the third century AD, in what is now northern Italy and also France, Serbia, Bulgaria, Croatia, Turkey and elsewhere. All this was a threat to commerce, but it was also a threat to public order. The controllers of these mints had a demand for precious metals with which to make coins.

And anyone who had objects made from gold and silver was a potential supplier. Hoards of beautiful objects have been discovered in places such as modern-day France dating from the middle of the third century AD, preserved because their owners buried them to avoid loss through confiscation or theft.

Buried treasure

The Roman world was urban, more highly urbanised than the medieval world, and that was a source of much of its wealth creation. In its towns and cities craftsmen specialised and produced fine silverware or beautiful glassware, which was traded across their world for money. With the destruction of their currency, it now became more difficult to trade highly specialised skills for needed goods and services, and opportunities for work became more limited. Economic activity declined.

The Roman banking system also appears to have failed in about AD 260. It is from that time that references to bankers in the Roman world disappear from the historical record, and no further references to Roman bankers can be found for well over a hundred years. The collapse of the banking system would have had severe consequences. Much of the money in our world is created by banks when they accept deposits and lend these out. Roman banks also created money in this way. Bank lending was important for commerce, providing loan capital to those who had ideas for trading opportunities but limited funds to start their ventures.

Such trading ventures in turn had generated work for the towns' manufacturers.

Commerce had also depended on the banks for the money transfer system, which allowed goods to be bought and sold across their empire without tonnes of precious metal being transferred to pay for those goods. The purchase and sale of valuable assets, landed estates, and blocks of flats in the towns and cities, had also been facilitated by that transfer system. That method of transfer functioned until the middle of the third century AD.

The collapse of the banking system would have been as crippling as the collapse of our own banking system. In any case, a changed Roman world in which the administration of law was uncertain, the currency had collapsed, and the state regularly confiscated assets to pay for ongoing expenditure, was not one in which a banking system – which depends on the secure enforcement of private property rights and the secure enforcement of contracts, including loan contracts – could thrive.

Catastrophe in the East

A monument, the Ka'ba-ye Zartosht, stands at Naqsh-e Rustam in the Iranian desert; it was erected by a ruler of the area from which the Parthians threatened Roman power in the east during the reign of Marcus Aurelius. But a later ruler, Shapur I, a member of the dynasty that had supplanted the Parthians, added his own inscription to this monument.

He does not celebrate great material wealth or a new peace, as Augustus had done on the monuments he had ordered erected around the empire. Where Augustus talks of the great buildings he had restored, Shapur talks of the sheep that he has arranged to be sacrificed each day into the future. Where Augustus celebrates peace, Shapur celebrates war.

The monument lists town after town that Shapur I and his army had destroyed, towns in what is now Syria, Iraq, Turkey, and Greece. He also celebrates the defeat of the mighty Romans. The army they had been sent out against him numbered 70,000 men, about one fifth of the total military force of the Roman Empire, and he enslaved those he did not slaughter. He goes further than that. He boasts of the protection money that the once-powerful Roman state was forced to pay him, an amount equivalent to between £250 million and £500 million in ours.

The Roman emperor brought to his knees

Carved on the great cliffs at Naqsh-e Rustam in Iran are other images commissioned by Shapur, images that tell an even more crushing story. They show the capture of the Roman emperor Valerian, kneeling before this king from the desert lands. According to one source, Valerian served as a mounting block, kneeling to offer his back for Shapur to step on as he mounted his horse. When Valerian died in AD 260, this once-powerful Roman emperor was said to have been flayed and had his skin stuffed.

If we were to fix the date on which the Roman state had failed, then the year AD 260 is as good a date as any. By that date it had endured a great military defeat and humiliation in its history. Its treasury, well managed for many centuries, was bankrupt. Its currency, carefully developed from the time when Rome's defeat of the only other military superpower had given them access to the Spanish silver mines, had collapsed, with the reforms of Augustus and Vespasian now undone. The trading infrastructure to which Trajan had added so much was no longer maintained. Law on which so much of its commercial life, and therefore the wealth of its citizens, depended, was no longer as predictably enforced as before. The life of its citizens would deteriorate further, and a long economic depression began which would last about one thousand five hundred years.

Chapter 9
Survival

The temple at Baalbek

Some years ago, I went on a business trip to Beirut, my first visit to that beautiful city by the sea. I remember the buildings: some still being rebuilt after civil war and others showing the pock marks left by exploding bombs. The general manager of the company I was visiting to present the results of work we had done for him offered to set up a press conference where I could publicise what I did and generate more business for myself. But I had just started an evening degree in classics in London, and the lecturer teaching me Latin had told me of the ancient temples at Baalbek, in the

A magnificent survival

north of the country. The press conference would have been fun, but I could do only one of the two.

So, the next day, the general manager took me on the three-hour trip to Baalbek, including a stop for lunch at a place that hardly ever saw tourists then. The journey we took would have been difficult a few years previously because of civil war and tensions with Syria, and it is not recommended nowadays. On the day I visited, there were few visitors at the site of this great temple of Jupiter Heliopolis, most of which has survived the centuries. There was much for me to see as I wandered around those ruins with so much of the magnificence enduring. The temple of Jupiter at Baalbek had been one of the most famous temples of the ancient world.

I had learned at school about these architectural styles, the different types of column, names of the temple's various parts, and how Rome had drawn from Greece –and how the Greek architecture had been based on the style of the wooden temples existing when the Greeks first arrived. There was a symmetry to it and a mathematical beauty. The temple was mine to enjoy that day while the general manager, who had perhaps seen it all before or was interested in other things, wandered around elsewhere.

The temple has been perceived differently by the visitors who have come to the site over time. It was in its ruined state partly because at one time it was a source of raw materials. The iron cramps that held the columns in place had been scavenged. It had been cheaper to get scrap metal from a structure that had become alien and was no longer protected rather than sourcing it as the Romans had, using money and trade.

Nineteenth-century visitors had seen a different beauty there. Such a visitor reading his guidebook might "sigh to think that all this magnificence was pride, this worship pagan, and all this skill and grace and beauty defiled by voluptuous and soul-destroying sin". They saw skill and beauty but they distanced themselves from the people who built this. Their values and beliefs were different. Here was something magnificent but alien too.

For me it was closer to my own experiences. This had been a project once, a project like the business that took me to Beirut, a project carrying the same pride in work well done, with a similar organisation of people working together and achieving a similar satisfaction on completion. Sometime around the first century AD people had formed the idea of building it here, persuaded one another to begin and complete the project, and they had done their work well. It had been a creative and energetic time.

There was, however, a sadness there for me, because that magnificence had ended, that time had ended, and that world had fallen apart. Now when I think of those who built that temple I picture a world in which not enough people understood what made all that magnificence possible for them and what they most needed to protect it and keep it going. Perhaps every time has its end.

Even so it never ended totally. That society was not a complete failure. The political institutions of the old world were indeed destroyed and never returned, but the prosperity it had enjoyed at its height did. That prosperity returned in part because enough people survived to encourage new growth, and in part because some things grow back anyway, when the conditions are right.

The loss of self-belief

The world in which the Romans lived when the great temple at Baalbek was built was one of prosperity. The poet Horace celebrated that prosperity: the fields were fertile, the seas were travelled on safely, and law and ancient custom protected them from crime. The poet Virgil wrote of how the world was theirs to rule. That was how the Romans had seen themselves in the time of Augustus and how they saw themselves later in the time of Trajan, for example. They were a confident people, sure of their prosperity and their pre-eminent place in the world.

By the middle of the third century AD, all that had been destroyed. Misery had replaced quiet peace and confidence. There were new writers, men such as the Christian convert Cyprian, and those new writers had different things to say. Cyprian was the leader of the Christian community in the North African city of Carthage, which had been a great trading centre, exporting grain and olive oil around the Mediterranean basin, with a port to equal the ports around Rome, as we saw in Chapter 6.

But Carthage was no longer thriving. Cyprian now wrote that resources were running out, that gold and silver were no longer mined as much as before. There was disorder. The farmer was absent from the field, the sailor from the sea, and the soldier from his camp. There was no justice in the courts and no skill in the work of the craftsman. It was, he said, an old world gone weary. Others saw it differently, blaming Cyprian and his fellow Christians. They had brought all this trouble by refusing to worship the Roman gods. Cyprian was tried for his Christian beliefs under the emperor Valerian and executed, going willingly to his death hopeful of a better life in the next world. He died in AD 258, followed two years later by the emperor who had persecuted him.

In AD 260, stories reached Rome and elsewhere of the cata-strophic defeat in the East and the humiliation of the emperor Valerian, near the border between modern Turkey and Syria. For more than sixty years since the accession of Septimius Severus, the Roman people had been ruled by a military dictatorship, not the delicately balanced constitutional government of Augustus's time and later. The army was now made up largely of mercenaries negotiating their own pay from a state that could no longer rely on secure tax revenues to meet their demands for money. This army had proven itself incapable of its basic purpose of protecting the Roman people and could not even protect the life of the emperor.

The words of Horace, Virgil, and the other Augustan poets continued to be read and studied, appreciated as beautiful poetry. But they were now no longer true. They were no longer believed.

Building new walls

Aelius Aristides, the Greek orator whose words are quoted at the start of Chapter 6 and who had praised the prosperity of Rome, had also praised the Romans for the unwalled cities and towns of their empire. There had been walls built around Rome once, in the fourth century BC, but it had long outgrown them. What protected Rome when Aelius Aristides visited it in the middle of the second century AD was what protects our towns and cities today: not walls, which make entry difficult for those who might want to enter, loot our property, or take our lives, but law and order, which we zealously support because our prosperity and peace depend on them.

The decline in Roman security first became evident in the margins of the empire. In about AD 200, walls were built for the first time around towns in Britain, around London and Exeter, for example. By the middle of the third century AD they were being built everywhere, and in about AD 270, fifteen years after the death of Valerian, the emperor Aurelian started the construction of new and massive walls around the city of Rome, a visible sign to its inhabitants of the new insecurity in their world.

A now fearful city protects itself with walls

These walls still stand and for the very good reason that for centuries they were maintained in good condition because they continued to be needed. It was not until well into the nineteenth century that peace had again been sufficiently established around Rome that the state could protect its citizens without the need for walls. Only then did the Aurelian walls around the city of Rome become, not necessary infrastructure, but markers of what the past had been.

Breaking up into little pieces

Beginning in the middle of the third century AD, the Roman Empire broke into little pieces. The territory once ruled as a single entity from Rome – with a common law and language, rights recognised from one region or town to another, a common currency accepted across an area about equal to half the size of the United States today, with freedom of movement and with rights of settlement, with a single army that policed the whole area and defended its borders – now disintegrated. Not since then have people who live in what is now Germany, Syria, Spain, and Libya, for example, lived as part of a single state.

The impoverishment that Cyprian could see was evident to all, but the causes were not understood. Time and time again new emperors proclaimed themselves *Restitutor Orbis,* restorer of the world. Time and again they tried to restore the old order, the orderly and prosperous world of their predecessors. Time and again they failed. First one currency reform was attempted and then another, but it was too late. For centuries, hundreds of tonnes of gold and silver had publicly circulated around the Roman world in countless small metal coins, but those hundreds of tonnes of gold and silver were now disappearing from circulation. They were scattered across the empire in private hoards or buried or melted down to make items such as tableware. The currency that had been so carefully created and managed, as we saw in Chapter 4, could not be recreated. The authorities tried to curb the high inflation of the third century. An edict was issued which set out in detail the maximum prices that could be charged for goods and which set limits on the wages that could be paid. But the many millions of traders and workers could work out what was in their own best interests and could find workarounds, and so that attempt failed too. The price edict inscriptions still stood, monuments now to the powerlessness of the central authorities and their inability to restore order.

Further and more lasting changes were introduced towards the end of the third century and served to make the problem worse. The success of the Roman economy had depended in part on labour mobility, which allowed the free man or woman to travel to where the work was and to work in whatever occupation best suited them, if they could find the work. Their expanding cities had depended on inward migration, their prosperity on labour specialisation. That now ended. The old Roman collegia, the associations in which those who worked in a particular trade met for social and business reasons, slowly transformed into compulsory guilds rather than voluntary associations. The law placed further restrictions on trade. The young man must follow his father's trade, not seek a trade for which he was better suited. The poor were also now tied to the land. In this world there was less freedom than there had been before; it was a poorer world for that. The land and labour structures of the Middle Ages were being formed and they impoverished the land and its people, as we saw in Chapter 7.

It was a troubled world in which urban living was difficult. The rich moved out to their country estates, and the urban centres depopulated. For some it was safer to live in the country and protect themselves there, build fortified castles, farm their own land for their own benefit and that of their dependants. The urbanisation, on which much of the wealth of the Roman Empire depended, as we saw in Chapter 5, was now being reversed.

Within fifty years of the walls around the Roman town of London being built, the buildings of that town began to be stripped, as their stones and other materials were scavenged for re-use. The amphitheatre in the Roman town of London, which had held audiences greater than the Albert Hall holds today, was stripped by a population that once sourced its building materials through trade and with money, as we saw in Chapter 6, but no longer could.

Economic collapse

We can imagine that world as being so distant from ours, so different from ours, or even so much less sophisticated than ours, that we have little to learn from it. That, however, would be arrogance. The wisest of their great men and women were as wise as the best of ours, and the most foolish of theirs were just as foolish as the worst of ours. The root causes of the economic disasters of our time are much the same as the root causes of what happened in the Roman

Empire, except that what happened then was more severe and lasted longer.

For example, in the late nineteen twenties, the United States stock market increased relentlessly in value. So long as that continued, there was money to be made. Some investors put just their own money into the market, but others borrowed. The money was easy to get; the banks were happy to take the shares bought with the loans as collateral, and only asked their clients to put up small amounts of cash. As more money went into the stock market, prices went yet higher and the ever-increasing riches that the market promised – and was delivering – caused more people to borrow increasing sums of money. Regularly the total amount lent out by brokers to their investing clients was reported to the authorities in the normal way, and it was clear that borrowing was driving the market up. The risk that the market might collapse was also clear. But there was no wisdom in saying that too loudly. It might continue just like this for some weeks more, or months, or perhaps for a year or two. Whoever called the bubble ran the risk of being seen as a fool if the bubble did not burst, or worse still of being the cause when it did.

So, the authorities allowed this madness to continue until the inevitable happened. The bubble burst. Prices fell, and shares ended up worth less than the loans that had financed their purchase. Investors went bankrupt. Their loans were called in, and the shares backing those loans were sold, driving prices down still further until at its lowest the stock market had fallen by 90 percent.

As loans failed, banks became insolvent and closed their doors. The stock market panic spread, and as people saw banks close, they withdrew funds from banks that were still open, exacerbating the problem. As good banks became anxious that they might have a run on their deposits, they held more of their assets in cash and lent less. Then as now, most of the money supply was created by bank lending, and as the banking crisis continued, the money supply dropped, at its worst by about one third. With the loss of confidence and the drop in money supply, business investment dropped, production and demand fell, and unemployment increased to 25 percent. Soup kitchens opened and people queued for food, in one of the most prosperous countries on earth.

Poverty caused by the mismanagement of others

Undoubtedly, some people foresaw the damage that could be caused by a great increase in bank lending backed by assets of questionable value. As we saw in Chapter 8, the damage that would be caused in the Roman world by increasing the pay of soldiers, as happened in the late second century AD, so suddenly and to such an extent was also probably foreseeable at least by some. So too was the likely effect of allowing individuals such as Commodus into the most senior position of the state, individuals who did not have the competence to discharge their responsibilities and whose actions could ruin all.

The economy of the United States recovered from that Great Depression and relatively quickly: it was only about ten years from trough to peak. The political institutions of the country survived that turmoil. For example, the usual four-yearly cycle of United States presidential elections continued. With a new president in 1932 there were new policies and a new confidence to replace the despair of the preceding years and, since much had survived, the rebuilding was possible, and quick. There was now protection for depositors, new bank regulation, and infrastructure building. The political institutions of the Roman Empire, by contrast, had largely been destroyed in the collapse, along with the Roman currency, which did not survive the chaos, unlike the dollar, which survived the chaos of the Great Depression.

The twentieth century saw a yet more severe economic collapse. Germany, following its defeat in the first world war, had been required to pay reparations, in addition to repaying the loans with which it had in part financed the war, printing money to meet its obligations. As it printed more and more money, its currency was increasingly devalued on the foreign exchanges, and inflation in Germany made it increasingly worthless there too. Severe unemployment and economic depression followed. Although a replacement to that currency emerged and the economy recovered, the respite was short.

The economic depression in Germany resumed in 1929 as the contagion from the US stock market spread. Military dictatorship and a new defeat in war devastated much of the country and most of the economy. Nevertheless, Germany, and much of Europe, whose political institutions had very largely been destroyed, recovered. Other countries that had survived provided assistance, and within about twenty years prosperity had been restored.

There was no such assistance for the Roman world. Those who lived along its borders at the time of its economic collapse were not peoples who lived its highly urban and monetised life. They were very largely tribal and iron age peoples who did not have any interest in rebuilding institutions which they themselves did not possess; rather, they looked to take whatever they could from whatever was left over from the chaos. As a consequence, the depths of the depression that followed the collapse of the Roman economic system lasted much longer.

Across much of the now fragmented territory once ruled from Rome an economic depression had started. In some places that economic depression would last for more than a thousand years before the peace and prosperity that had been known in Roman times started to return.

The immediate consequence of the economic depression was a decline in urbanisation, trade, infrastructure, agricultural productivity, labour mobility, personal wealth, and life expectancy. But there was hope in the ruins of all that magnificence for those who could see it, a reminder of what had been and that greater things were possible. And while political institutions and wealth had been destroyed, there was much else that had survived. The thirst for knowledge and improvement remained.

Progress

In time the old prosperity did return but its re-emergence was slow. For several hundred years, all that was noticeable was decline, the re-use of the old building materials, and war. Then, for several hundred years, there was a slow growth, but in most places the change was imperceptible. The progress was such as what forms us as we grow. It was a slow process of building on what was there before, as the constructive forces outdid the destructive ones.

When we were little children, we absorbed words and learned to speak, we absorbed concepts, and the language we learned shaped how we thought. We inherited words from those who surrounded us as we grew, just as the Romans had inherited words when they were children. Language inherited takes many hundreds of years to develop; yet children absorb it in a few years.

Later we learned to read and write and acquired skills which have become part of us. The simple shape of a word triggers images or sensations or associations, and we scarcely see the letters which some years ago we carefully spelt out. Our hand moves across a page and thoughts became marks without any conscious effort by us to direct the pen we hold. All those now innate skills are inheritances from human inventions from thousands of years.

If we were to look back at a country that has grown wealthier over time, we see the same process. Let us imagine a place such as Great Britain, taking this as an example because it has not been invaded and taken over for several hundred years. The surrounding seas have given it protection which its continental European neighbours have not had to the same extent. Let us imagine for the purpose of illustration that its wealth has doubled every fifty years. Thus, children inherited twice as much as those born fifty years before them. There are more and better roads. Buildings have been added to the cities, old building have been improved or replaced. More people can read and write. More of the population has acquired marketable skills, and new skills have been developed, replacing older ones. The body of law has developed, and the institutions of the country have become more respected. All of this and the many other aspects that add to the wealth of a country have, in this illustration, doubled every fifty years. A graph of the country's wealth would look like this:

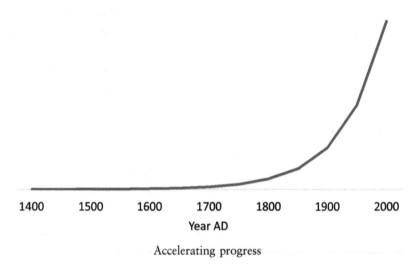

1400   1500   1600   1700   1800   1900   2000
Year AD

Accelerating progress

Looking at this graph, we would scarcely notice the progress that occurred in the first four hundred years. Indeed, the last fifty years of increase counts for as much as was added in all the years between 1400 and fifty years ago. But each generation has added the same proportion as its predecessors, been just as creative and productive. The wealth of the country, in this example, has doubled every fifty years through the period. Each succeeding generation, however, has had more to work from and build on; thus, progress in more recent years looks greater.

When I was a boy, I built a radio with my grandfather, who lived in Dublin. He had run away from home when he was a teenager to join the British Army and later, when he came back to Dublin, he studied to become an aeronautical engineer. We sawed wood to make the casing and varnished it. We bought transistors and capacitors and the other pieces we needed according to a book I had bought, soldered them in the way the book explained, connected the battery, and fitted the dial at the front. After a few hours' work, we were finished and put the new radio in its brown wooden casing on the windowsill of my bedroom, turned it on, and fiddled with the dial. Like magic we heard words in some foreign language, which we guessed was Russian.

A lot of the technology, such as the transistor, had not been invented when my grandfather was born. Long before we built that radio and since then, individuals motivated by pure curiosity and the thrill of discovery had experimented and innovated, each generation adding to what they inherited. It would be difficult to find a radio today that uses the technology of transistors and capacitors. In the years since my boyhood, countless new ideas have emerged, most of them small improvements but a few of them more substantial.

The same process is at work in art. Over time new techniques, new ideas, new styles, new ways of seeing add to what was there before. Our inheritance is richer and will continue to increase if each generation applies curiosity, creativity, energy, and ambition.

Re-emergence

The recovery from the collapse of the Roman economic system was slow. The rediscovery of some of Rome's earlier achievements helped that recovery.

The writings of Virgil, Horace and the other poets, the histories written by Tacitus and Livy and more, the astronomy and medicine developed when the Roman economy was at its height, as well as the work done centuries before in Athens: out of all that philosophy, science, and literature, a portion survived Rome's collapse. It re-emerged in cities such as Constantinople, was copied and spread through cities such as Baghdad. It survived in monasteries across Europe, as far away as in Ireland, where it was copied and studied, preserved for coming generations.

The ruins of the old civilisation were to be seen everywhere and were in some cases re-used. When in the middle of the eighth century

Abd al-Rahman, fleeing Damascus after the overthrow of his family, found his way to what was left of the old Roman capital in southern Spain, he saw the ruins of its infrastructure – its temples, baths, streets, water system, houses – and he rebuilt them. He built what was to be one of the largest cities of the Middle Ages, re-using old Roman columns to support a mosque, mixing the old with the new. Here and elsewhere the scientific and mathematical work of Rome's rich past was rediscovered and added to.

Over the next several centuries, progress continued across the territory once ruled from Rome, although peace had not been re-established. Thus, the castles built in the eleventh and twelfth centuries were better fortified than before, and armour was improved beyond measure. But other developments came into view. A new architectural style emerged: cathedrals were built, spires and towers pointing to the sky and great buttresses supporting walls punctured by stained-glass windows. The surrounding houses were, however, almost all built of wood, not stone.

Some of Rome's former progress remained hidden and unused. Agricultural productivity, the amount of food produced from the same plot of land, was lower, in most cases substantially lower, than it had been. For all the displays of communal wealth, in cathedrals, for example, it was a poorer time than the time when the Romans ruled, and the depression continued.

The collapse in urbanisation was visible too. Rome of the fifteenth and sixteenth centuries was a much-reduced city. Its population had declined from about one million to roughly fifty thousand. The area enclosed by the monumental walls of Aurelian was almost all now empty space, some columns still standing, parts of temples incorporated in churches, but mostly it was overgrown, trees and vegetation creating woodland where before there had been great meeting places, commerce, news, and political scheming. The columns of Trajan and Marcus Aurelius still stood, but were now surmounted by statues of Christian saints. It remained a troubled world. That city contained within the great third-century walls continued to need their protection, and troops. And sometimes the walls were not enough and the city of Rome was sacked and looted.

The re-emergence of the past continued, however. At the end of the fifteenth century, for example, a young Roman broke through into the buried palace of Nero, a personal extravagance. As Raphael, Michelangelo, and others tunnelled down and around, they saw the fresh colours, this different art, this new inspiration. They never uncovered the floors of those rooms but tunnelled on, making caves that were lined with the newly discovered art. They brought into the tunnels food, wine, and candles; they emerged with new images and ideas to refresh what they were creating during the rebirth of culture that would be called the Renaissance. Elsewhere in the city statues were being recovered from the ground and provided a further inspiration, a different way of seeing the human body: more down to earth, less otherworldly, more dynamic. Work of their predecessors, some one thousand five hundred years before, profoundly influenced the work of these artists. Thus, the forgotten art of Rome lived on.

Elsewhere the past was being re-used. Some of the texts produced by the Romans had survived, and from the sixteenth century onwards they became increasingly important to academics. These writings had survived in places such as Alexandria, Baghdad, Cordoba, Toledo, Salerno, Palermo, and Venice. Now with the invention of the printing press, they spread more rapidly. They were read by Elizabeth I of England. She read and translated Tacitus, who had written a history of Rome up to the age of Nero and beyond. Here were stories of intrigues, of the instability of the ruler, of rulers who had fallen and been replaced, of wise rulers who had transformed their country, and of the expansion of an empire, stories of a richer and different life. There was much here to be learned by a queen whose father had executed her mother and whose life had been precarious from childhood, a queen ruling in a country where the succession to the head of state had often been as insecure as it had been in Rome. There was history here that could benefit an England that was emerging from the great upheaval of the Reformation.

Trade was now increasing from the low levels it had reached when Rome's trading empire collapsed. That trading empire had been built on territory gained from conquest across Europe, North Africa, into parts of the Near East, and beyond into places such as India. Now exploration, and sometime conquest, pushed into the newly discovered Americas and further east to India and China.

New trading companies were formed at the beginning of the seventeenth century, the East India Company in Britain and the Dutch East India Company, which needed capital. As we saw in Chapter 6, some Roman commercial enterprises used limited liability companies with managers separate from their owners, with the grant of limited liability being given by the state. That structure allowed those with capital, great landowners, for example, to participate in potentially profitable commercial ventures, but protect themselves from ruin if the venture failed. It provided the sponsors of those ventures with the capital they needed for their ventures and had facilitated trade in the second century AD and earlier. In Europe in the seventeenth century and later, the same structures were again used and again helped trade to flourish. Perhaps those legal structures were copied from the Roman example set out in Justinian's *Digest of Roman Law.*

By the eighteenth century, the world that the Roman people had once ruled was becoming more like what they had experienced at their height. There was a greater freedom, cities were expanding, wealth and trade were increasing. Agricultural productivity was now beginning to return to what it had been in Roman times. Even the size of ships was beginning to come close to the size of the ships that had once docked in the harbours of nearby Portus, now long abandoned. And those ships now docked, in some places, in ports that were equal in size to those of Rome and North Africa.

Monetary reforms were taking place. The currency reforms in Britain at the beginning of the nineteenth century drew on the Roman model. The gold, silver, and copper coins of George III and of Vespasian resemble each other. George III is shown in the style of a Roman emperor, the inscriptions on his coins are in Latin, and the exchange ratios among different metals are broadly similar. In both cases a stable currency was created, which enabled a trading empire to flourish.

Until its collapse, the Roman currency had been a stable currency with scarcely any inflation, universally accepted across a great area for just over two hundred years. No currency in use today has experienced that length of price stability. Few currencies in use today have been in existence that long.

Others drew lessons from that Roman Empire and its heritage. When across the Atlantic English gentlemen set themselves the task of devising a new constitution, they drew freely from the experience of the Roman Empire. They established a new capital and built it in the style that the Romans had used: the round domes that the Romans had invented and the architectural orders they had copied from the Greeks. They called one of their legislative bodies the Senate and created the position of leading citizen, but not for life. They institutionalised the checks and balances which were a feature of the Roman system. Copying from the Romans and with the evidence of what worked and did not work, they were able to build afresh with greater chance of success. The re-emergence of the Roman prosperity was quicker because of this.

There was, however, something that the Romans never experienced, something new in the retelling of the old story. Innovation had not been a great mark of their way of doing things, and the radio that my grandfather and I built together was something they never saw. There are some signs of innovation in the Roman story: the developments of glassware in the first century AD, for example, or in agriculture, but there are only a few such signs. Generating new ideas for their own sake, with individuals competing against one another to generate more and develop further never really happened for them. The hundreds of years of intellectual development that produced all that was needed for us to build my radio is unique to the retelling of the story.

Money has been made from all that intellectual development. Whole industries have emerged from that story of progress. The Romans had the commercial spirit that would have also profited from that. What made their trading empire work and their myriads of workshops in their towns and cities would have helped that grow for them too. But those modern scientific ideas never emerged for them as they later did from the late fifteenth century onwards. Perhaps the peace did not last long enough.

The temple of Mithras

The building that houses the temple of Mithras in the City of London has a display of some of the objects which were found when the site was excavated: a pair of shoes, part of a broken wooden door, a pendant made from amber which came from the Baltic, a millstone made in Germany, nails, roof tiles, and coins.

There was a noise and a clatter around these objects once: the millstone as it was unloaded from one of the ships docking not far from where London Bridge is today, the cry as the pendant was lost and not found, the throwing away of the old door and the hammering of the nails as the hinges of the new one was fixed in place. There was a creativity here once, of the trader who thought it profitable to import that millstone or of the artisan who made those shoes. There was a business acumen in the financiers who lent money to those businesses, and a law that made their financial documents valuable.

Those men and women and children are about eighty generations distant from us. The generations move out quickly, and there is a fair chance that most of the people who stand in front of that display today are related distantly to the people who handled these objects and heard that noise and clatter. I was born in Ireland, but for centuries people have been moving between the islands of Britain and Ireland, so I imagine that I too am related to them. So too very likely are people from across Europe, North Africa, and beyond, places from which immigrants came to this town and who traded with this town.

They lived through different times in their different generations. The fear and panic when London was destroyed in the revolt of Boudicca, the optimism as it was rebuilt and, then after a long period of quiet, a new chaos, and then yet a recovery. And on it goes. There is little of any importance to distinguish us from them, those very distant relatives of ours.

Appendix: Money

We represent modern currencies by symbols such as a £ or $. The Roman unit of account was the sestertius and it is represented by the letters HS.

We have an immediate sense of what £10 means. It is more than enough to buy you a pint of beer, but it is nowhere near enough to buy you a house. We have no immediate sense of what HS100 means. In order to provide that immediacy, I have converted Roman currency amounts into our equivalent.

We can follow an approach which considers money as the power to command the labour of others. Now, as it happens, HS900 was the annual salary payable to a Roman legionary after the pay increases instituted by Julius Caesar. The annual salary paid to a private in the modern British Army is about £25,000. A Roman legionary, like a British private now, was trained, disciplined and fit, fought on the battlefield, provided security against civil unrest and protected the rule of law. The Roman legionary, however, generally was illiterate and uneducated. His labour was only partially equivalent to that of a modern soldier. The modern soldier also has greater labour mobility and consequently more wage bargaining power while the pay of the Roman soldier was enough for his bed, board, clothing and perhaps a third more. Labour was, in any case, relatively cheap until recent times. This approach is likely to over-state the value of the Roman currency.

We could follow an approach which looks at the price then and now of some commodity, silver, for example. Now HS4 was the equivalent of one silver denarius which contained about three grams of silver, although that amount varied. That amount of silver costs about £1 at today's prices. However, silver was more in demand then than now. The state authorities needed that metal to produce coins and modern states do not need it to anything like that extent now. Commonly then the wealthy and the moderately well off had silver tableware for use and display. That demand has also considerably abated. Silver was scarcer then. There have been centuries of extraction of silver from the earth since then and silver is not discarded. The supply of silver is, therefore, much greater now than then. This approach is likely to undervalue the Roman currency.

There is no market in which sestertii and pounds can be exchanged as convertible currencies, both of which can be used to buy goods and services. If there were such a market, then the exchange rate between the two currencies would fluctuate. Over the last several decades £1 has been worth between US$1 and US$4.

In order to give an impression of the value of Roman monetary amounts while retaining the sense of uncertainty, I have converted HS1 as being between £5 and £10.

I use this approach, for example, when I discuss the amount of money that Seneca lent to the native Britons. He lent them in total HS40 million in Roman currency, which is equivalent to between £200 million and £400 million in our terms.

Additional Reading

The analysis of the Roman economy which underlies this book is based on a thesis which I completed in 2016 at King's College London, entitled "The Imperial Roman Economy". It is available from the library of King's College London and will be published in 2021 by Kilnamanagh, the publishers of this book. The thesis, Maher (2021), provides support for the economic conclusions in this book, and sets out current scholarly debates and where I stand in those debates.

The bibliography at the end of this book lists the main books and articles that I have consulted. It is very largely the bibliography of my thesis, with some additions. Almost all of these books and articles are available from the Hellenic and Roman Library in Senate House, Bloomsbury, London. In this Appendix I note for each chapter the ancient sources I have quoted or drawn on and any books and articles that I have particularly relied on for the chapter.

The following reference works provide short detailed articles on specific topics related to the world which is the subject of this book:

Bowman, A., E. Champlin and A. Lintoff (eds.) (2005), *Cambridge Ancient History X: The Augustan Empire, 43 B.C.–A.D. 69*, 2nd edn., Cambridge.

Bowman, A., P. Garnsey and D. Rathbone (eds.) (2005), *The Cambridge Ancient History XI: The High Empire, A.D. 70–192*, 2nd edn., Cambridge.

Bowman, A., A. Cameron and P. Garnsey (eds.) (2005), *The Cambridge Ancient History XII: The Crisis of Empire, A.D. 193–337*, 2nd edn., Cambridge.

Roberts, J. (ed.) (2007), *The Oxford Dictionary of the Classical World*, Oxford.

Hornblower, S. and A. Spawforth (eds.) (1998), *The Oxford Companion to Classical Civilisation*, Oxford.

Chapter 1 Introduction

See Maher (1995) for a description of an actuarial process for understanding a business and analysing the numbers.

Chapter 2 Expansion

The quotation at the start of this chapter is from Virgil, *Aeneid* 1.278–1.283. The translation is my own. The description of the two incursions into Britain by Julius Caesar in 55 BC and 54 BC are taken from his book *de Bello Gallico*, which may have been compiled from the dispatches he sent to the Senate while on campaign. The first incursion is described in book 4.20–4.37 and the second in book 5.2–5.24.

My description of the later invasion of Britain in AD 43 and its settlement are taken firstly from the work of the Roman senator and historian, Tacitus. Tacitus was born in Gaul in around AD 56 and followed a successful political career in Rome. One of his first books, a short monograph, is on the achievements of his father-in-law Agricola in Britain and includes much background information on the settlement of Britain. He later wrote two major works, his *Histories* and his *Annals,* only parts of which survive. He describes the invasion and settlement of Britain in his *Annals* 14.31–14.39.

A later writer, Cassius Dio, also provides relevant material. Cassius Dio was born sometime between AD 155 and AD 164. His family came from Bithynia in modern Turkey. Cassius Dio wrote a history of the Roman world, in Greek, from before the foundation of the city of Rome until AD 229. His work, like that of Tacitus, only partially survives. In book 62.1–62.12 he gives his description of the revolt of Boudicca, complementing that of Tacitus.

I have based my description of the Roman constitution in the time of Julius Caesar partly on the work of Polybius. The Greek historian Polybius lived from about 200 BC to about 118 BC. In his early life he had seen Rome secure domination over his country and had been taken as a captive to Rome. Later he was an eyewitness to the destruction of Carthage and saw first-hand the Romans securing total dominance of the Mediterranean by the elimination of the only remaining superpower. In old age he returned to his native country. He wrote his *Histories* in part because he wanted to explain why the Roman state had been so successful. He attributed this largely to its constitution.

The Roman constitution is described in book 6 of Polybius's *Histories,* written in Greek. For my purposes the major development between his time and the time of Julius Caesar was the automatic entry of the quaestor to the Senate. I have also drawn on *de petitione consulatus*, which is electioneering advice possibly written by Quintus Tullius Cicero, born in 102 BC.

I have taken the translation of the text of the tablet found in the excavations of the Mithraeum from Tomlin (2015).

Chapter 3 Peace

The story of the Catiline conspiracy is taken from Sallust's essay on Catiline. Sallust lived from 86 BC to about 35 BC and attempted to pursue the normal career of the politically ambitious Roman, although the Senate at one stage expelled him. His service as governor in Africa, which should have been followed by election to consulship, was however the last step in that career. On his return to Rome he was accused of maladministration of the province and thereafter confined himself to writing. Cicero's speeches at the trial of Catiline also survive.

Shortly before his death in AD 14 Augustus had a document listing his achievements written up. He left instructions that monuments be erected after his death with that text inscribed. In this text he detailed what he considered the significant events of his life, in particular how he had restored order after he ended the civil war. He also itemises his expenditure on building work, soldiers' pay and donations. This text is known as the *Res Gestae*, or 'things achieved'. I have used this in my description of the transformation that took place after the ending of the civil war and also in my quantification of his wealth.

The life of Augustus is also covered by Tacitus, Cassius Dio and Suetonius. Suetonius was born in about AD 69. He started his career as a lawyer but abandoned that and took up work in the imperial administration, including as correspondence secretary. He wrote biographies of various Roman leaders, including Julius Caesar and Augustus.

Wiseman (2019) describes the modesty of the house in which Augustus lived at Rome.

The translation of the Laudatio Turiae is by E. Wistrand. The quotation from Cicero is from *In Verrem* 1.1.2. The poetry quoted is from Virgil, *Aeneid* 1.198–1.207, Virgil *Eclogues* 1.1–1.15, 9.2–9.6 and Horace, *Odes* 3.30.1–3.30.2. The translations are my own.

My description of the management of the state finances and the system by which the state subcontracted to the private sector is based on book 6 of Polybius's *Histories*. The reference to the Roman legal valuation of pensions is a reference to the writings of the Roman lawyer Ulpian; see the section on financial knowledge in Maher (2021) chapter 6.

Chapter 4 Money

Maher (2021) chapters 7 and 8 provide much of my theoretical work on the Roman currency and provide a summary of the academic debate.

The law to which I refer at the start of this chapter is 31 U.S.C. 5112(k): "The Secretary may mint and issue platinum bullion coins and proof platinum coins in accordance with such specifications, designs, varieties, quantities, denominations, and inscriptions as the Secretary, in the Secretary's discretion, may prescribe from time to time."

For a description of how money is created out of thin air in our modern system see Whelan (2012). See Scott (1910) for a discussion on currencies before the twentieth century, and how money in general works. I have based my account of the threat to the British currency in the eighteenth and early nineteenth centuries, and the successful reforms, on his work. The financial crisis in the early part of the first century AD is described in Tacitus *Annals* 6.16–6.17.

The quantification and description of infrastructure spending under the emperors Augustus to Nero is based on Thornton and Thornton (1989). My description of the events from the death of Nero up to the accession of Vespasian is taken very largely from Tacitus's *Annals*. Mattingley (1921) lists the mints of the empire and shows the consolidation under Vespasian and the later emergence of multiple mints.

Chapter 5 Cities

Maher (2021) chapters 2 and 3 provide a description of urbanisation in the Roman Empire, its relationship to agricultural productivity and its relationship to the transport system. A comparison to urbanisation at later times is also provided. See Holleran (2012) for urban activity in the city of Rome, and Mouritsen (2011) for the contribution of freed slaves to the economy. The list of urban activity as evidenced by inscriptions is taken from Joshel (1992) and Holleran (2012).

The graph at the end of this chapter showing income in a hypothetical country is based on Appendix 3 of Maher (2021). Rural output in the initial case of no urbanisation is calculated assuming a labourer on average has a day rate of one denarius, is idle for half the year and supports three dependants. Low relative urban productivity is assumed to be 150 percent of rural productivity, largely because of less downtime. High relative urban productivity is assumed to be 600 percent of rural productivity, largely because of skilled specialised work.

Chapter 6 Prosperity

This chapter is based on Maher (2021) chapter 4.

The passages quoted at the start of this chapter are taken from the speech 'Regarding Rome' of the Greek orator Aelius Aristides, who was born in AD 117. The translations are by Behr (1981). The story of Pompey clearing the sea of pirates is in Cassius Dio 36.23.

Talbert (2010) describes the itineraries and maps available during the time of the Roman Empire. See Keay (2012) for a description of the port system around Rome and Stone (2014) for the North

African ports. My account of glass manufacturing in the Roman Empire is taken from Sterne (1999).

The description of the Roman system of limited liability is taken from Justinian's *Digest*. This was compiled under the Byzantine emperor Justinian in about AD 530. Roman statute law, case law and juridical opinions had been recorded in various different documents and the emperor Justinian ordered that these be compiled in one document which then had the force of law. Only those laws or opinions which he wanted to continue to be valid were recorded. The limited liability arrangements to which I refer in this chapter are set out in *Digest* 3.4.1.

Chapter 7 Life

The passage quoted at the beginning of this chapter is from Virgil's *Eclogues* 4 60–63. The passage from the agronomist Varro later on in this chapter is Varro, *Res Rusticae* 1.18.7–1.18.8. The translations are my own.

The work on agriculture is from Maher (2021) chapter 2 and on life expectancy from Maher (2021) chapter 5. The grain yields used in the graph comparing productivity in England and France are taken from Slicher van Bath (1963). Spurr (1986) can be referred to for a discussion of primitive grain cultivation and gives comments on Neolithic grain yields. I have drawn on Wickham (2005) for the social and cultural changes in the period between AD 400 and AD 800.

Hinde (2003) discusses the development of mortality in Britain and provides relevant data on the mortality impact of the sixteenth- and seventeenth-century plagues. The data on the progression of life expectancy in the British peerage is taken from Population Investigation Committee (1964).

Chapter 8 Chaos

This chapter draws on Maher (2021) chapter 8, in particular for the cost of the military. I have used Cassius Dio for the history up to the emperor Commodus, and the historian Herodian thereafter.

Herodian was a civil servant, born in AD 170. His *Roman History,* written in Greek, covers the period from the end of the reign of Marcus Aurelius, in AD 180, up to AD 238. There are some differences in the accounts of these two historians where they overlap.

See De Callatäy (2005) for a discussion of lead concentration in the atmosphere as evidenced by deposits in the Greenland icecap and a reconstruction of the history of silver production and Wilson (2002) for Roman mining activity and technology. The graph of the building projects is based on Wilson (2011), which uses data from the *Epigraphische Datenbank Heidelberg.* The graph showing the silver content of the denarius is based on Walker (1976), Walker (1977) and Walker (1978).

For descriptions of the epidemic diseases during the reign of the emperor Marcus Aurelius and the emperor Commodus in AD 165, AD 168 and AD 192 see Galen *Lib. Prop.* 1.16, 3.3, 5.12, Cassius Dio 73.14–15 and Herodian 12.1.2. Galen was born in AD 129 in what is now modern Turkey into a wealthy family. He travelled widely and worked as a physician in Rome. Much of his writing on medicine survives.

Chapter 9 Chaos

The guidebook referenced at the start of this chapter is Cook (1876). The quotations from Cyprian are taken from his speech *Ad Demetrianum.* Cyprian was born in Carthage in about AD 200 and converted to Christianity in his thirties, later becoming bishop of Carthage.

Moller (2019) covers the survival of classical texts. Galbraith provides a description of the events up to and during the stock market crash of 1929, and gives his interpretation of the causes. Bernanke (2004) sets out monetary reasons for the Great Depression.

Acknowledgements

Since my early twenties I had always wanted to write a book, on any subject. Birkbeck, University of London, teaches evening courses and that helped me start this project. I picked Classics from the prospectus because I had never studied Greek at school and thought it would be fun to learn Latin again. I studied for a BA degree at Birkbeck while continuing to work as an actuary. I would like to acknowledge the help I received there from Professor Catherine Edwards, Professor Christy Constantalopoulou, Professor Serafina Cuomo, now of Durham University, and Dr Martin Dinter, now of King's College. I am grateful to Professor Cuomo for her encouragement and recommendation that I study for a PhD in the economy of the Roman Empire under the supervision of Professor Dominic Rathbone at King's College London.

I am indebted to James Martin S.J, for his advice, encouragement and recommendations as I started this project. My colleagues Hugh Rosenbaum and Julian Leigh F.I.A. read each chapter in early and later drafts and helped make what might otherwise have been a lonely project something more enjoyable. I looked forward to their comments and learned a lot from what they said to me. I must also acknowledge my indebtedness to my colleague Dr Daniel Marx for his assistance and advice throughout the project, and to Sue Willett and Christopher Ashill of the Hellenic and Roman Library. My editor Vinita Wright also added to the enjoyment and I appreciate her help very much.

I am indebted to Steven Male, Dr John Cassayd-Smith and Eileen Cooper R.A. who read the final version of the chapters of this book and I enjoyed learning from their own, and different, ways of seeing things, and changing what I had to say as a result. At different stages when I needed a review of some paragraph or parts of a chapter I turned to Dr William Loschert, Mitesh Rajput, Anne-Marie

Harvey, Harjoban Thandi, Matthew Ball F.I.A, Gerry Harvey, Lucie Howitt, Rosemary Fagan and Will Harvey and I am grateful to them for their ever prompt help.

I am grateful to Professor Dominic Rathbone of King's College London for supervising the thesis which underlies this work, for encouragement and helpfulness and especially for making that project so fascinating and enjoyable. I am grateful also to my examiners Professor Michael Crawford of University College, London and Dr Claire Holleran of the University of Exeter for their comments and helpful discussions.

Many other people helped me with my thesis. Professor Andrew Hinde of the University of Southampton helped in my understanding of the history of British demography. The late Professor John Crook of St John's College, Cambridge introduced me to Ulpian's valuation functions and kindly sent me some relevant passages from the *Digest*. Dr Kris Lockyear of University College, London gave me useful background on Roman money and both Professor Henrik Mouritsen and Dr John Pearce of King's College London commented on my early work on Roman agriculture. In addition, I had a number of conversations with Dr Pearce on grain productivity and on mortality. I had discussions with Dr Alexandra Sapoznik of King's College London on medieval and early modern grain productivity and my fellow student Dr Federico Ugolini and I discussed Roman port structures.

I had the benefit of insights into grain productivity from Patrick Mulcahy, a UK agronomist. Phil Skelton and Peter Seymour, both of ACE Insurance, gave me useful context on modern marine transportation. Adrian Gallup of the Government Actuary's Department provided helpful data extracted from the English Life Tables. Michael Townsend of the Institute of Historical Research helped me by identifying sources for population estimates of English towns. James McCormack, Sean McCormack and Martina Maher helped with the input of the over 1,500 data points on Slicher van Bath wheat yields. Helen Maher and Andy Staudt helped in the construction of some of the graphs in my thesis.

The views expressed in this book are my own and not necessarily those of any of the people who have helped me. Any errors that might remain are my responsibility.

228

List of illustrations

Cover   "The Sack of Rome by the Visigoths, 410" (1890) by Joseph-Noël Sylvestre. Photo © Heritage Image Partnership Ltd / Alamy Stock Photo

Cover   Gold, silver and copper coins, first and eighteenth centuries AD, British Museum, London. Photo © The Trustees of the British Museum

Cover   Rock-face relief of Persian emperor Shapur I, third century AD, Naqsh-e Rustam, Iran. Photo © Sahand Ace (CC BY-SA 3.0*)

p3   "The Sack of Rome by the Visigoths, 410" (1890) by Joseph-Noël Sylvestre. Photo © Heritage Image Partnership Ltd / Alamy Stock Photo

p10   "Julius Caesar" (c. 1625/26) by Peter Paul Rubens. Photo courtesy of The Leiden Collection, New York

p14   Map of Roman London: c. AD 120. Image © Peter Froste / Museum of London

p16   Statue head of Mithras, second/third century AD, Museum of London. Photo © Mitesh Rajput

p17   Temple of Mithras, third century AD, Bloomberg Space, London. Photo © Mitesh Rajput

p20   Amber pendant found at site of Temple of Mithras, third century AD, Bloomberg Space, London. Photo © Bloomberg

p21   Statue head of Serapis, second/third century AD, Museum of London. Photo © Museum of London

p31   "Cicero denounces Catiline" (1889) by Cesare Maccari, Palazzo Madama, Rome. Photo © Album / Alamy Stock Photo

p32   Fragment of the Laudatio Turiae, first century BC, Museo Nazionale Romano, Terme di Diocleziano p35   "The victory of Julius Caesar over the Belgians" by Louis van Engelen (1865–1940). Photo © Fine Art Auctions Miami

p43   Imperial and Senatorial provinces in AD 14

p48   Bust of Octavian, first century BC, Musei Capitolini, Rome. Photo © Carole Raddato (CC BY-SA 2.0*)

p50   Aqueduct of Segovia, first century AD. Photo © World Monuments Fund

p60   Gold, silver and copper coins, first and eighteenth centuries AD, British Museum, London. Photo © The Trustees of the British Museum

p64   Bank of Ireland, College Green, Dublin. Photo © James McCormack

p70   Plot of average annual infrastructure expenditure

p71   Tunnels of Claudius, first century AD, Abruzzo. Photo © Claudio Parente (CC-SA 4.0*)

p74   Frescoes at Domus Aurea, first century AD, Rome. Photo © Heritage Image Partnership Ltd / Alamy Stock Photo

p77   Bust of the emperor Vespasian, first century AD, Museo Archeologico Nazionale di Napoli. Photo © Azoor Photo / Alamy Stock Photo

p87   Tomb of Eurysaces the Baker, first century BC, Rome. Photo © Mitesh Rajput

p88   Relief of Eurysaces and Atistia, Centrale Montemartini, Rome. Photo © Adam Eastland / Alamy Stock Photo

p90   The Meroë Head of Augustus, first century BC, British Museum, London. Photo © The Trustees of the British Museum

p96   Map of journeys of St Paul

p99   "An Irish Peasant Family Discovering the Blight of Their Store" (1847) by Daniel MacDonald. Photo © National Folklore Collection, University College Dublin

p103   Pula Arena, first century AD. Photo © Ella Rock

p105   Mosaïque du cortège rustique d'Orbe-Boscéaz, detail, second century AD. © Archéologie cantonale de l'État de Vaud, photo Archéotech SA

p107   Modern model of aeolipile by John R. Bentley. Photo © John R. Bentley

p108   Plot of changes in city sizes

p109 Plot of real income per capita against population living in urban areas. Created by Daniel Marx with data from UN World Urbanization Prospects (2018), Maddison Project Database (2018), collated by Our World in Data

p111 Plot of productivity as a function of urbanisation

p115 The treasure of Jerusalem, Relief under the Arch of Titus, first century AD, Rome. Photo © Mitesh Rajput

p117 Bust of Emperor Trajan, sixteenth century, Musei Capitolini. Photo © Mitesh Rajput

p118 Detail from Trajan's Column, second century AD, Rome. Photo © Mitesh Rajput

p122 Via Ostia. Photo © Mitesh Rajput

p125 "Cato Warning his Senate Colleagues about Carthage" by Severino Baraldi. © Look and Learn / Bridgeman Images

p128 Plot of wharf length changes

p131 Amphora, Dr William Loschert's private collection. Photo by the author

p132 "Hay Barge off Greenwich" (1835) by Edward William Cooke, National Maritime Museum, Greenwich, London. Photo © Royal Museums Greenwich

p134 Glass jug, Dr William Loschert's private collection. Photo by the author

p143 Plot of agricultural productivity of France and England since the Middle Ages

p145 Plot of gain in productivity

p147 Luttrell Psalter facsimile, Dr William Loschert's private collection. Photo by the author

p150 Military discharge diploma, AD 103, British Museum, London. Photo © The Trustees of the British Museum

p157 Cartoon from *Fun*, 1866. Image © Chronicle / Alamy Stock Photo

p158 Roman latrines, Rome. Photo © Mitesh Rajput

p159 Papal throne in red marble, Musei Vaticani. Photo © Governatorato SCV – Direzione dei Musei

p160 Plot of life expectancy of the British peerage

p168 Extent of Roman Empire. Image © Varana (CC BY-SA 3.0*)

p170 Milecastle 39, Hadrian's Wall, second century AD

p171 Detail from Column of Marcus Aurelius, second century AD, Rome. Photo © Mitesh Rajput

p174 Map of Arshakuni Armenia, around the year 150 AD. Image © Sémhur / Wikimedia Commons (CC-BY-SA-3.0*)

p176 Commodus as Hercules, 192 AD, Musei Capitolini, Rome. Photo © Mitesh Rajput

p179 Plot of soldiers' pay and deductions

p182 Bust of Septimius Severus, ca. 200 AD, Glyptothek Munich

p183 Bust of Caracalla, ca. 212 AD, Museo Archeologico Nazionale di Napoli

p180 Plot of changes in army pay

p189 Plot of building projects

p192 Plot of silver content in a denarius

p195 Chaourse Treasure, second/third centuries AD, British Museum, London. Photo © The Trustees of the British Museum

p197 Rock-face relief of Persian emperor Shapur I, third century AD, Naqsh-e Rustam, Iran. Photo © Sahand Ace (CC BY-SA 3.0*)

p199 Temple of Bacchus, second century AD, Baalbek, Lebanon. Photo © Jerzy Strzelecki (CC BY-SA 3.0*)

p203 Aurelian Walls, third century AD, Rome. Photo © robertharding / Alamy Stock Photo

p207 Great Depression, 1931, Chicago. Photo © IanDagnall Computing / Alamy Stock Photo

p210 Plot illustrating hypothetical growth in GDP

* Licence details may be found on https://creativecommons.org/licenses

While every effort has been made to contact copyright holders of illustrations, the author and publisher would be grateful for information about any illustrations that have not been properly credited and would be glad to make amendments in further editions.

Bibliography

Allen, R (2009), "How prosperous were the Romans? Evidence from Diocletian's Price Edicts (A.D. 301", in A. Bowman and A. Wilson (eds.), *Quantifying the Roman Economy – Methods and Problems,* Oxford: 327–45.

Alston, R. (1994), "Roman military pay from Caesar to Diocletian", *Journal of Roman Studies* 84: 113–23.

Alston, R. (2007), "Warfare and the state – the military and politics", in P. Sabin, H. Van Wees and M. Whitby (eds.), *The Cambridge History of Greek and Roman Warfare,* Cambridge: 158–177.

Andreau, J. (2010), *L'économie du Monde Romain,* Paris.

Arnaud, P. (2007), "Diocletian's Prices Edict: the prices of seaborne transport and the average duration of maritime travel", *Journal of Roman Archaeology* 20: 321–36.

Austin, R., M. Ford and C. Morgan (1989), "Genetic improvements in the yield of winter wheat: a further evaluation", *The Journal of Agricultural Science* 112 3: 295–301.

Bagnall, R. and B. Frier (1994), *The Demography of Roman Egypt,* Cambridge.

Bailey, D. (1996), "Honorific columns, cranes and the Tuna epitaph", in Bailey, D. (ed.), *Archaeological Research in Roman Egypt,* Ann Arbor: 155–68.

Bang, P. (2007), "Trade and empire: in search of organizing concepts for the Roman economy", *Past and Present* 195: 354.

Barclay, W., A. Coale, M. Stato and T. Trussell (1976), "A reassessment of the demography of traditional rural China", *Population Index* 42 4: 606–635.

Barsby, A. and C. Barsby (1996), *Manorial Law,* Epsom.

Bastianelli, S. (2008), *Centumcellae (Civitavecchia), Castrum Novum (Torre Chiaruccia): Regio VII, Etruria,* Rome.

Behr, A. (1981), *Aelius Aristides: the Complete Works. Orations XVII–LII,* Leiden: 73–97.

Bernanke, B. (2004), *Money, Gold and the Great Depression,* Virginia.

Blayo, Y. (1975), "La mortalité en France de 1740 à 1829", *Population* 30: 123–42.

Bloom, D., D. Canning and G. Fink (2008), "Urbanisation and the wealth of nations", *Science* 319: 772–5.

Blum A. and I. Troitskaya (1997), "Mortality in Russia during the 18th and 19th centuries: local assessments based on the Revizii", *Population: An English Selection* 9: 123–46.

Bowman, A., A. Cameron and P. Garnsey (eds.) (2005), *The Cambridge Ancient History XII: The Crisis of Empire, A.D. 193–337,* 2nd edn., Cambridge.

Broadberry, S., B. Campbell, M. Overton, B. van Leeuwen and A. Apostolides (2009), "Historical National Accounts for Britain, 1300–1850: some preliminary estimates", *Reconstructing the National Income of Britain and Holland, c. 1270.1500 to 1850.*

Brunt, P. (1950), 'Pay and superannuation in the Roman army', *Papers of the British School at Rome* 18: 50–75.

Brunt, P. (1981), "The revenues of Rome", *Journal of Roman Studies* 71: 161–72.

Burn, A. (1953), "Hic breve vivitur: A study of the expectation of life in the Roman Empire", *Past & Present* 4: 2–31.

Burnett, A., M. Amandry and P. Ripollès (1992), *Roman Provincial Coinage. Volume I: From the Death of Caesar to the Death of Vitellius (44 BC–AD 69),* London.

Butcher, K. and M. Ponting (2014), *The Metallurgy of Roman Coinage: From the Reform of Nero to the Reform of Trajan,* Cambridge.

Cairncross, A. (1949), "Internal migration in Victorian England", *Manchester School* 17: 67–87.

Cairncross, A. (1953), *Home and Foreign Investment,* Cambridge.

Carroll, M. (2014), "Mother and infant in Roman funerary commemoration", in M. Carroll and E-J. Graham (eds.), *Infant Health and Death in Roman Italy and Beyond,* Journal of Roman Archaeology Supplementary Series: 159–78.

Bibliography

Casson, L. (1965), "Harbour and river boats of ancient Rome", *Journal of Roman Studies* 55: 31–9.

Casson, L. (1995), *Ships and Seamanship in the Ancient World*, 2nd edn., Baltimore.

Champlin, E. (1991), *Final Judgements: Duty and Emotion in Roman Wills 200 B.C. to A.D. 250,* California.

Coale, A. and P. Demeny (1983), *Regional Model Life Tables and Stable Populations,* New York.

Collins, H. (2001), "Tacit knowledge, trust and the Q of sapphire". *Social Studies of Science* 31: 71–84.

Cook, T. and Son (1876), *Cook's Tourists' Handbook for Palestine and Syria,* London.

Cotterall, B. and J. Kamminga (1990), *Mechanics of Pre-Industrial Technology,* Cambridge.

Crawford, M. (1970), "Money and exchange in the Roman world", *Journal of Roman Studies* 60: 40–8.

Crawford, M. (1975), "Finance, coinage and money from the Severans to Constantine", in J. Vogt, H. Temporini and W. Haase (eds.), *Aufstieg und Niedergang der römischen Welt: Geschichte und Kultur Roms im Spiegel der neueren Forschung* Berlin: 560–93.

Crawford, M. (1974), *Roman Republican Coinage,* Cambridge.

Cuomo, S. (2011), "A Roman Engineer's Tales", *Journal of Roman Studies* 101: 143–65.

Davies, R. (1971), "The Roman military diet'" *Britannia* 2: 122–42.

de Callatäy, F. (2005), "The Graeco-Roman economy in the super long-run: Lead, copper and shipwrecks", *Journal of Roman Archaeology* 18: 361–72.

Dessau, H. (1908), "Afrikanische Munizipal – und afrikanische Militärinschrift", *Klio*: 8: 57–63.

de Vries, T. and W. Zwalve, (2003), "Roman actuarial science and Ulpian's life expectancy table", in L. de Ligt, E. Hembrijk and H. Singor (eds.), *Roman Rule and Civic Life*, Amsterdam: 277–98.

Develin, R. (1971), "The army pay rises under Severus and Caracella and the *annona militaris*", *Latomus* 30: 687–95.

Dixon, J., L. Nalley, P. Kosina, R. La Rovere, J. Hellin and P. Aquino

(2006), "Adoption and economic impact of improved wheat varieties in the developing world", *The Journal of Agricultural Science* 144 6: 489–502.

Duncan-Jones, R. (1978), "Pay and numbers in Diocletian's army", *Chiron* 8: 541–60.

Duncan-Jones, R. (1982), *The Economy of the Roman Empire,* 2nd edn., Cambridge.

Duncan-Jones, R. (1990), *Structure and Scale in the Roman Economy,* Cambridge.

Duncan-Jones, R. (1994), *Money and Government in the Roman Empire,* Cambridge.

Edgerton, D (2008), *Shock of the Old: Technology and Global History since 1900,* 2nd edn., London.

Edmondson, J. (1989), "Mining in the later Roman empire and beyond: continuity or disruption?", *Journal of Roman Studies* 70: 84–102.

Edmondson, J. (2005), "Family relations in Roman Lusitania: Social change in a Roman province?", in M. George (ed.), *The Roman Family in the Empire: Rome, Italy and Beyond,* Oxford: 183–229.

Erdkamp, P. (2001), "Beyond the limits of the 'Consumer City'. A model of the urban and rural economy in the Roman world", *Historia*: 332–56.

Erdkamp, P. (2005), *The Grain Market in the Roman Empire – a Social, Political and Economic Study,* Cambridge.

Evans, J. (1981), "Wheat production and its social consequences in the Roman world", *Classical Quarterly* New Series 31: 428–42.

Fifoot, C. (1932), *English Law and its Background,* London.

Finley, M. (1965), "Technical innovation and economic progress in the ancient world", *The Economic History Review* 18: 29–45.

Finley, M. (1977), "The ancient city: from Fustel de Coulanges to Max Weber and beyond", *Comparative Studies in Society and History* 19: 305–27.

Finley, M. (1999), *The Ancient Economy*, 2nd edn., Cambridge.

Foxhall, I. and H. Forbes (1982), "Sitometreia: the role of grain as a staple food in antiquity", *Chiron* 12: 41–90.

Frank, T. (1940), *An Economic Survey of Ancient Rome* 5 Volumes, New York.

Friedman, M. (1990), "Bimetallism revisited", *Journal of Economic Perspectives* 4 85–104.

Frier, B. (1982), "Roman life expectancy: Ulpian's evidence", *Harvard Studies in Classical Philology* 86: 213–51.

Frier, B. (1994), "Natural fertility and family limitation in Roman marriage", *Classical Philology* 89 4: 318–33.

Frier, B. (2000), "Demography", in A. Bowman, P. Garnsey and D. Rathbone (eds.), *The Cambridge Ancient History XI: The High Empire, A.D. 70–192*, 2nd edn., Cambridge: 787–816.

Frier, B. and D. Kehoe (2007), "Law and economic institutions", in W. Scheidel, I. Morris and R. Saller (eds.), *The Cambridge Economic History of the Greco-Roman World*, Cambridge: 113–43.

Fulford, M. (2009), "Approaches to quantifying Roman trade: Response" in A. Bowman and A. Wilson (eds.), *Quantifying the Roman Economy: Methods and Problems*, Oxford: 250–8.

Galbraith, K. (1954), *The Great Crash, 1929*, Boston.

Garnsey, P. (1983), "Grain for Rome", in P. Garnsey, K. Hopkins and C. Whittaker (eds.), *Trade in the Ancient Economy*, London: 118–31.

Gilliam, J. (1952), "The minimum subject to the *Vicesima Hereditatium*", *American Journal of Philology*, 73 4: 397–405.

Goldsmith, R. (1984). "An estimate of the size and structure of the national product of the early Roman Empire", *Review of Income and Wealth* 30: 263–88.

Gowland, R., A. Chamberlain and R. Redfern (2014), "On the brink of re-evaluating infanticide and infant burial in Roman Britain", in M. Carroll and E-J. Graham (eds.), *Infant Health and Death in Roman Italy and Beyond*, Journal of Roman Archaeology Supplementary Series: 69–88.

Graham, E-J. and M. Carroll, "Introduction", in M. Carroll and E-J. Graham (eds.), *Infant Health and Death in Roman Italy and Beyond*, Journal of Roman Archaeology Supplementary Series: 9–22.

Greene, K. (1986), *The Archaeology of the Roman Economy*, London.

Greenwood, M. (1940), "A statistical mare's nest?", *Journal of the Royal Statistical Society* 103: 246.

Gregg, S. (1988), *Foragers and Farmers: Population Interaction and Agricultural Expansion in Prehistoric Europe*, Chicago.

Halstead, P. (1987), "Traditional and ancient rural economy in Mediterranean Europe: Plus ça change?", *Journal of Hellenic Studies* 107: 77–87.

Harari, Y. (2014), *Sapiens: A Brief History of Humankind*, London.

Harl, K. (1996), *Coinage in the Roman Economy, 300 BC to AD 700*, Baltimore.

Harris, W. (2006), "A revisionist view of Roman money", *Journal of Roman Studies* 96: 1–24.

Harris, W. (2009), "Comment on Andrew Wilson: 'Approaches to quantifying Roman trade'" in A. Bowman and A. Wilson (eds.), *Quantifying the Roman Economy: Methods and Problems*, Oxford: 259–68.

Harris, W. (2011), *Rome's Imperial Economy*, Oxford.

Heinzelmann, M. (2008), "Supplier of Rome or Mediterranean marketplace? The changing economic role of Ostia after the construction of Portus in the light of new archaeological evidence", *Bollettino di Archeologia*: 5–10.

Hicks, J. (1969), *A Theory of Economic History*, Oxford.

Hinde, A. (2003), *England's Population: A History since the Domesday Survey*, London.

Hinde, A. (2004), "The use of nineteenth-century census data to investigate local migration", *Local population studies* 73: 8–28.

Holden, P. (1980), *Studies in the Auxilia of the Roman Army from Augustus to Trajan*, Oxford.

Holleran, C. (2012), *Shopping in Ancient Rome*, Oxford.

Hong, S., J.-P. Candelone, C. Patterson and C. Boutron (1994), "Greenland ice evidence of hemispheric lead pollution two millennia ago by Greek and Roman civilisations", *Science* New Series 265 5180: 1841–3.

Hopkins, K. (1966), "On the probable age structure of the Roman population", *Population Studies: A Journal of Demography* 20 2: 245–64.

Hopkins, K. (1978), *Conquerors and Slaves*, Cambridge.

Hopkins, K. (1980), "Taxes and trade in the Roman Empire (200 B.C. -A.D. 400)", *Journal of Roman Studies* 70: 101–25.

Hopkins, K. (1983), "Models, ships and staples", in P. Garnsey and C. Whittaker (eds.), *Trade and Famine in Classical Antiquity*, Cambridge: 84–109.

Hopkins, K. (1987), "Graveyards for historians", in F. Hinard (ed.), *La Mort, les Morts et au-delà dans le Monde Romain. Actes de Colloque de Caen 20–22 Novembre 1985*, Caen: 113–26.

Horden, P. and N. Purcell (2000), *The Corrupting Sea*, Oxford.

Hornblower, S. and A. Spawforth (eds.) (1988), *The Oxford Companion to Classical Civilisation*, Oxford.

Houston, G. (1988), "Ports in perspective: Some comparative materials on Roman merchant ships and ports", *American Journal of Archaeology* 92: 553–64.

Howgego, C. (1990), "Why did the ancient states strike coins?", *Royal Numismatic Society* 150: 1–25.

Howgego, C. (1992), "The Supply and Use of Money in the Roman World 200 B.C. to A.D. 300", *Journal of Roman Studies* 82: 1–31.

Howgego, C. (1994), "Coin circulation and the integration of the Roman economy", *Journal of Roman Archaeology* 7: 5–21.

Humphries, A. and R. Biffen (1907), "The improvement of English wheat yields", *The Journal of Agricultural Science* 2 1: 1–16.

Johnson, A. (1959), *Roman Egypt: to the Reign of Diocletian*, Baltimore.

Jones, A. H. M. (1953), "Inflation under the Roman Empire", *The Economic History Review* 5 3: 293–318.

Jones, A. H. M. (1964), *The Later Roman Empire*, Oxford.

Jones, A. H. M. (1974), "Taxation in antiquity", in P. Brunt (ed.), *The Roman Economy: Studies in Ancient Economic and Administrative History*, Oxford: 151–86.

Jones, A. H. M. (1974), *The Roman Economy*, Oxford.

Jones, D. (2006), *The Bankers of Puteoli: Financing Trade and Industry in the Roman World*, Stroud.

Jones, G. (1980), "The Roman mines at Riotinto", *Journal of Roman Studies* 70: 146–65.

Jongman, W. (1988), *The Economy and Society of Pompeii*, Amsterdam.

Jongman, W. (2006), "The rise and fall of the Roman economy: population, rents and entitlements", in P.F. Bang, M. Ikeguchi and H.G. Ziche (eds.), *Ancient Economies, Modern Methodologies* Bari: 237–54.

Jongman, W. (2007a), "Gibbon was right: the decline and fall of the Roman economy", in O. Hekster, G. De Kleij and D. Slootjes (eds.), *Crisis and the Roman Empire,* Leiden: 183–99.

Jongman, W. (2007b), "The early Roman empire: Consumption", in W. Scheidel, I. Morris and R. Saller (eds.), *The Cambridge Economic History of the Greco-Roman World,* Cambridge: 592–618.

Joshel, S. (1992), *Work, Identity, and Legal Status at Rome: A Study of the Occupational Inscriptions,* London.

Kay, P. (2014), *Rome's Economic Revolution,* Oxford.

Keay, J. (1993), *The Honourable Company: A History of the East India Company* 2 edn., London.

Keay, S. (2009), "Scientific approaches to the study of Roman ports", *British Academy Review* 14: 25–7.

Keay, S. (2012), "The Port System of Imperial Rome", in S. Keay (ed), *Rome, Portus and the Mediterranean,* London: 33–67.

Kehoe, D. (1988a), "Allocation of risk and investment on the estates of Pliny the Younger", *Chiron* 18: 15–42

Kehoe, D. (1988b), *Economics of Agriculture on Roman Imperial Estates in North Africa,* Göttingen.

Kehoe, D. (1997), *Investment, Profit and Tenancy. The Jurist and the Roman Economy,* Michigan.

Kehoe, D. (2007), "The early Roman empire: Production", in W. Scheidel, I. Morris and R. Saller (eds.), *The Cambridge Economic History of the Greco-Roman World,* Cambridge: 543–69.

Keppie, L. (2005), "The army and the navy", in A. Bowman, E. Champlin and A. Lintott (eds.), *The Cambridge Ancient History X: The Augustan Empire, 43 B.C. –A.D. 69* 2nd edn., Cambridge: 371–96.

Kessler. D. and Temin, P. (2007), "The organization of the grain trade in the early Roman empire", *The Economic History Review* 60 2: 313–32.

Kron, G. (2008), "The much maligned peasant. Comparative

perspectives on the productivity of the small farmer in classical antiquity", in L. de Ligt and S. Northwood (eds.), *People, Land and Politics: Demographic Developments and the Transformation of Roman Italy, 300 BC–AD 1*, Leiden: 71–120.

Kron, G. (2011), "Food production", in W. Scheidel (ed.), *The Cambridge Companion to the Roman Economy*, Cambridge: 156–74.

Krugman, P. and R. Wells (2013), *Economy*, 3rd edn., New York.

Kucharik, C. and N. Ramankutty (2005), "Trends and variability in U.S. corn yields over the twentieth century", *Earth Interactions* 9: 1–29.

Laurence, R. (1999), *The Roads of Roman Italy.* London.

Laurence, R., S. Cleary and G. Sears (2011), *The City in the Roman West c. 250 BC–c. AD 250.* Cambridge.

Lawton, R. (1968), "Population changes in England and Wales in the later nineteenth century: an analysis of trends by registration district", *Transactions of the Institute of British Geographers* 44: 55–74.

Lendon, J. E. (1990), "The face on the coins and inflation in Roman Egypt", *Klio* 72: 106–34.

Lo Cascio, E. (1981), "State and coinage in the late Republic and early Empire", *Journal of Roman Studies* 71: 76–86.

Lo Cascio, E. (2007), "The early Roman Empire: the state and the economy", in W. Scheidel, I. Morris and R. Saller (eds.), *The Cambridge Economic History of the Greco-Roman World*, Cambridge: 619–47.

Lo Cascio E. and P. Malanima (2005), "Cycles and stability: Italian population before the demographic transition (225 B.C. –A.D. 1900)", *Rivista di Storia Economica* 21: 197–232.

Lockyear, K. (1999), "Hoard structure and coin production in antiquity – an empirical investigation", *The Numismatic Chronicle* 159: 215–43.

MacKenzie, D. and G. Spinardi (1995), "Tacit knowledge, weapons design, and the uninvention of nuclear weapons". *The American Journal of Sociology* 101 1: 44–99.

MacMullen, R. (1984), "The Roman Emperor's army costs", *Latomus* 43: 571–80.

Maddison, A. (2007), *Contours of the World Economy, 1-2030 A.D.: Essays in Macro-Economic History*, Oxford.

Maher. G. (1995), "Loss reserves in the London Market", *British Actuarial Journal* 1 4: 689–760.

Maher, G. (2021), *The Imperial Roman Economy*, Kilnamanagh.

Mattingley, H. (1921), "The mints of the empire: Vespasian to Diocletian", *Journal of Roman Studies* 11: 254–264.

Mattingley, H. and Sydenham, E. (1923), *The Roman Imperial Coinage.* London.

Mattingly, D. (1997), "Beyond belief: drawing a line beneath the consumer city", in H. Parkins (ed.), *Roman Urbanism: Beyond the Consumer City.* London: 210–8.

Mayer, E. (2012), *The Ancient Middle Classes: Urban Life and Aesthetics in the Roman Empire, 100BCE–250 CE.* Cambridge.

Mayerson, P. (1984), "Wheat in the Roman world: an addendum", *The Classical Quarterly*: 243–5.

Meiggs, R. (1973), *Roman Ostia*, 2 edn., Oxford.

Mitchell, B. (2007), *International Historical Statistics 1750–2005: Europe*, 6th edn., New York.

Moller, V. (2019), *The Map of Knowledge*, London.

Mommsen, T., P. Krueger and A. Watson (1998) (eds.), *The Digest of Justinian*, Pennsylvania.

Morley, N. (1996), *Metropolis and Hinterland*, Cambridge.

Morley, N. (2000), "Trajan's engines", *Greece and Rome* 47: 197–210.

Morley, N. (2007), "The early Roman empire: Distribution", in W. Scheidel, I. Morris and R. Saller (eds.), *The Cambridge Economic History of the Greco-Roman World*, Cambridge: 570–91.

Morley, N. (2011), "Cities and Economic Development in the Roman Empire" in A. Bowman and A. Wilson (eds.), *Settlement, Urbanisation and Population*, Oxford: 143–60.

Mouritsen, H. (2011), *The Freedman in the Roman World*, Cambridge.

Neesen, L. (1980), *Untersuchungen zu den direkten Staatsabgaben der römischen Kaiserzeit (27 v. Chr.–284 n.Chr.)*, Bonn: 135–140.

Nissen, J., P. Damerow and R. Englund (1993), *Archaic Bookkeeping:*

Early Writing and Techniques of Economic Administration in the Ancient Near East, Chicago.

North, D. (1990), *Institutions, Institutional Change and Economic Preformance,* Cambridge.

Parker. A. (1980), "Ancient shipwrecks in the Mediterranean and the Roman provinces", British Archaeological Reports, Supplementary Series.

Parker, A. (1990), "Classical antiquity: the maritime dimension", *Antiquity* 64: 335–46.

Parker, A. (2008), "Artifact distribution and wreck locations: the archaeology of Roman commerce", in R. Hohlfelder (ed.), *The Maritime World of Ancient Rome,* Michigan: 177–98.

Parkin, T. (1992), *Demography and Roman Society,* London.

Parkins, H. (1997), "The 'consumer city' domesticated? The Roman city in elite economic strategies", in H. Parkins (ed.), *Roman Urbanism: Beyond the Consumer City,* London: 83–7.

Patten, J. (1978), *English Towns 1500–1700,* Kent.

Pitts, M. and R. Griffin (2012), "Exploring health and social well-being in late Roman Britain: An intercemetery approach", *American Journal of Archaeology* 116 2: 253–76.

Polanyi, K. (1944), *The Great Transformation,* Boston.

Pope, C. (1992), "Adult Mortality in America before 1900: A View from Family Histories", in C. Goldin and H. Rockoff, (eds.), *Strategic Factors in Nineteenth Century American Economic History: A Volume to Honor Robert W. Fogel,* Chicago: 267–96.

Population Investigation Committee (1964), "The demography of the British peerage", *Population Studies Supplement.*

Purcell, N. (1985), "Wine and wealth in Roman Italy", *Journal of Roman Studies*:1–19.

Rathbone, D. (1991), *Economic Rationalism and Rural Society in Third-Century A.D. Egypt: the Heroninos Archive and the Appianus Estate,* Cambridge.

Rathbone, D. (1996a), "Monetisation, not price-inflation, in third-century A.D. Egypt?", in C. King and D. Wigg (eds.), *Coin Finds and Coin Use in the Roman World,* Berlin: 321–39.

Rathbone, D. (1981), "The development of agriculture in the 'Ager

Cosanus' during the Roman Republic: Problems of evidence and interpretation", *Journal of Roman Studies*: 10–23.

Rathbone, D. (1996b), "The imperial finances", in A. Bowman, E. Champlin and A. Lintott (eds.), *The Cambridge Ancient History X: The Augustan Empire, 43 B.C.–A.D. 69*, 2nd edn., Cambridge: 309–23.

Rathbone, D. (1997), "Price and price formation in Roman Egypt", in A. Andreau, P.Briant and R. Descat (eds.), *Economie Antique: Prix et Formations des Prix dans les Economies Antiques*, St-Bertrand-de-Commings: 183–244.

Rathbone, D. (2000), "The 'Muziris' papyrus (SB XVIII 13167): financing Roman trade with India", *Bulletin de la Société d'Archéologie d'Alexandrie* 46: 39–50.

Rathbone, D. (2003), "The financing of maritime commerce in the Roman Empire, I–II AD", in E. Lo Cascio (ed.), *Credito e moneta nel mondo romano* Bari: 197–229.

Rathbone, D. (2007a), "Military finance and supply", in P. Sabin, H. Van Wees and M. Whitby (eds.), *The Cambridge History of Greek and Roman Warfare* Cambridge: 158–77.

Rathbone, D. (2007b), "Roman Egypt", in W. Scheidel, I. Morris and R. Saller (eds.), *The Cambridge Economic History of the Greco-Roman World*, Cambridge: 698–719.

Rathbone. D. (2008), "Poor peasants and silent sherds", in L. Ligt and S. Northwood (eds.), *People, Land and Politics: Demographic Developments and the Transformation of Roman Italy, 300 BC–A.D.*, Leiden: 305–32.

Rathbone, D. (2009a), "Earnings and costs: living standards and the Roman economy (first to third centuries A.D.)" in A. Bowman and A. Wilson (eds.), *Quantifying the Roman Economy: Methods and Problems*, Oxford: 299–326.

Rathbone, D. (2009b), "Nero's reforms of *vectigalia* and the inscription of the Lex Portorii Asiae", in M. Cottier, M. Crawford, C. Crowther, J. Ferrary, B. Levick, O. Salomies and M. Wörrle (eds.), *The Customs Law of Asia*, Oxford: 251–78.

Rathbone, D. and P. Temin (2008), "Financial intermediation in first-century AD Rome and eighteenth-century England", in K. Verbowen, K. Vandorpe and V. Chankowski (eds.), *Pistoi dia tèn technèn. Bankers, Loans and Archives in the Ancient World. Studies in Honour of Raymond Bogaert,* Leuven: 371–419.

Rathbone, D. and S. van Reden (2015), "Mediterranean grain prices in classical antiquity", in R. van der Speck, B van Leeuwen and J. van Zanden (eds.), *A History of Market Preformance: From Ancient Babylonia to the Modern World,* London: 149–235.

Rickman, G. (1971), *Roman Granaries and Store Buildings,* Cambridge.

Rickman, G. (1980), *The Corn Supply of Ancient Rome,* Oxford.

Rihill, T. (2013), *Technology and Society in the Ancient Greek and Roman Worlds,* American Historical Association.

Roberts, J. (ed.) (2007), *The Oxford Dictionary of the Classical World,* Oxford.

Robinson D. and A. Wilson (2011), "Introduction: maritime archaeology and the ancient economy", in D. Robinson and A. Wilson (eds.), *Maritime Archaeology and Ancient Trade in the Mediterranean,* Oxford: 1–11.

Roby, H. (1886), *De usufructu: Iustiniani Digestorum Lib. VII Tit. I,* Cambridge: 188–91.

Romer, P. (1990), "Endogenous technological change", *Journal of Political Economy* 98 5: 71–102.

Rosenstein, N. (2004), *Rome at War: Farms, Families and Death in the Middle Republic,* North Carolina.

Rosenstein, N. (2008), "Aristocrats and agriculture in the Middle and Late Republic", Journal of Roman Studies 98: 1–26.

Rostovtzeff, M. (1957), *The Social and Economic History of the Roman Empire,* 2nd edn., Oxford.

Roth, U. (2007), *Thinking Tools, Food for Thought: Agricultural Slavery between Evidence and Models,* London.

Ruffing, K. (2008), *Die Berufliche Spezialisierung in Handel und Handwerk. Untersuchungen zu ihrer Bedingungen in der Römischen Kaiserzeit im Östlichen Mittelmeerraum auf der Grundlage Griechischer Inschriften und Papyri,* Rahden.

Russel, B. (2009), "The dynamics of stone transport between the Roman Mediterranean and its hinterland", *Facta: A Journal of Roman Material Cultural Studies* 2: 107–26.

Russell, C. (1948), *British Medieval Population,* Albuquerque.

Sallares, R. (1991), *The Ecology of the Ancient Greek World,* Cornell.

Saller, R. (1994), *Patriarchy, property and death in the Roman family*, Cambridge.

Saller, R. (2012), "Human capital and economic growth", in W. Scheidel (ed.), *The Cambridge Companion to the Roman Economy,* Cambridge: 71–88.

Scheidel, W. (2001a), *Death on the Nile – Disease and the Demography of Roman Egypt*, Leiden.

Scheidel, W. (2001b), *Debating Roman Demography*, Leiden.

Scheidel, W. (2007), "Disease and death", in P. Erdkamp (ed.), *The Cambridge Companion to Ancient Rome,* Cambridge: 45–59.

Scheidel, W. (2011), "A comparative perspective on the determinants of the scale and productivity of Roman maritime trade in the Mediterranean", in W. Harris and K. Iara (eds.), *Maritime Technology in the Ancient Economy: Ship-Design and Navigation,* Journal of Roman Archaeology Supplement 84: 21–37.

Scheidel, W. and S. Friesen (2009), "The size of the economy and the distribution of income in the Roman empire" *Journal of Roman Studies* 99: 66–91.

Scott, S. (1932), *The Civil Law,* Cincinnati.

Scott, W. (1910), *Money and Banking,* New York.

Sealey, P. (2009), "New light on the wine trade with Julio-Claudian Britain", *Britannia* 40: 1–40.

Shaw, B. (2008), "After Rome: transformation of the early Mediterranean world", *New Left Review* 51 89–114.

Silver, M. (2008), "The rise, demise, and (partial) rehabilitation of the peasant in Hopkins' model of Roman trade and taxes", *Classics Ireland* 15: 1–33.

Slicher van Bath, B. (1963), *Yield ratios, 810–1820,* Wageningen.

Speidel, M. A. (1992), "Roman army pay scales", *Journal of Roman Studies* 82: 87–106.

Speidel, M. P. (1970), "The captor of Decebalus, a new inscription from Philippi", *Journal of Roman Studies* 60: 142–53.

Speidel, M. P. (1973), "The pay of the *auxilia*", *Journal of Roman Studies* 63: 141–7.

Sperber, D. (1991), *Roman Palestine, 200–400: Money and Prices,* 2nd edn., Ramat-Gan.

Spurr, M. (1986), *Arable Cultivation in Roman Italy*, London.

Stein, P. (1962), "Generations, life-spans and usufructs", *Revue Internationale des Droits de l'Antiquité* 9: 335–56

Sterne E. (1999), "Roman glass blowing in a cultural context", *American Journal of Archaeology* 103: 441–84.

Stewart, W., D. Dibb, A. Johnston and T. Smyth (2005), "The contribution of commercial fertilizer nutrients to food production", *Agronomy Journal* 97 1: 1–6.

Stone, D. (2014), "Africa in the Roman Empire: Connectivity, the economy and artificial port structures", *American Journal of Archaeology* 118 4: 565–600.

Szaivert, W. and R. Wolters (2005), *Löhne, Preise, Werte. Quellen zur Römischen Geldwirtschaft*, Darmstadt.

Szilágy, J. (1961), "Beiträge zur Statistik der Sterblichkeit in den Westeuropäischen Provinzen des Römischen Imperiums", *Acta Archaeologica Academiae Scientarum Hungaricae* 13: 125–55.

Szilágy, J. (1962), "Beiträge zur Statistik der Sterblichkeit in der Illyrischen Provinzgruppe und in Norditalien (Gallia Padana) ", *Acta Archaeologica Academiae Scientarum Hungaricae* 14: 297–396.

Szilágy, J. (1963), "Die Sterblichkeit in den Städten Mittel- und Süd-Italiens sowie in Hispanien (in den Römischen Kaiserzeit) ", *Acta Archaeologica Academiae Scientarum Hungaricae* 15: 129–224.

Szilágy, J. (1965), "Die Sterblichkeit in den Nord Afrikanischen Provinzen III", *Acta Archaeologica Academiae Scientarum Hungaricae* 17: 309–34.

Szilágy, J. (1966), "Die Sterblichkeit in den Nord Afrikanischen Provinzen III", *Acta Archaeologica Academiae Scientarum Hungaricae* 18: 235–77.

Szilágy, J. (1967), "Die Sterblichkeit in den Nord Afrikanischen Provinzen III", *Acta Archaeologica Academiae Scientarum Hungaricae* 19: 25–59.

Talbert, R. (2010), *Rome's World: The Peutinger Maps Reconsidered*, Cambridge.

Tchernia, A. (1983), "Italian wines in Gaul at the end of the Republic", in P. Garnsey, K. Hopkins and C. Whittaker (eds.), *Trade in the Ancient Economy*, London: 87–105.

Tchernia, A. (1988), *Le Vin de l'Italie Romaine*, Rome.

Tchernia, A. (2011), *Les Romains et le Commerce*, Naples.

Temin, P. (2004), "Financial intermediation in the early Roman empire", *Journal of Economic History* 64 3: 705–33.

Temin, P. (2006a), "Estimating GDP in the early Roman empire", in E. Lo Cascio (ed.), *Innovazione tecnica e progresso economico nel mondo romano*, Bari: 31–54

Temin, P. (2006b), "The economy of the early Roman empire", *Journal of Economic Perspectives* 20 1:133–51.

Temin, P. (2012), *Roman Market Economy*, Princeton.

Thornton, M. and R. Thornton (1989), *Julio-Claudian Building Programs* Wauconda.

Tillott, P. (ed.) (1961), *A History of the County of York: City of York (The Victoria History of the Counties of England)*, Oxford.

Tomlin, R. (2017), *Roman London's First Voices: Writing Tablets from the Bloomberg Excavations, 2010–2014*, Museum of London Archaeology.

Trenerry, C. (1926), *The Origin and Early History of Insurance*, London.

Turner, P. (1989), *Roman Coins from India*, London.

van Nijf, O. (1997), *The Civic World of Professional Associations in the Roman East*, Amsterdam.

Walker, D. (1976), *The Metrology of the Roman Silver Coinage Part I From Augustus to Domitian*, Oxford.

Walker, D. (1977), *The Metrology of the Roman Silver Coinage Part II From Nero to Commodus*, Oxford.

Walker, D. (1978), *The Metrology of the Roman Silver Coinage Part III From Pertinax to Uranius Antoninus*, Oxford.

Walsh, P. (1997), *Petronius. The Satyricon*, Oxford.

Wassink, A. (1991), "Inflation and financial policy under the Roman empire to the Price Edict of 301 A.D.", *Historia* 40: 465–92.

Watson, G. (1956), "The pay of the Roman army: Suetonius, Dio and the *quartum stipendium*", *Historia* 5: 332–40.

Weber, M. (1930), *The Protestant Ethic and the Spirit of Capitalism*, London.

Weber, M. (1978), *Economy and Society*, California.

West L. (1929), *Imperial Roman Spain: The Objects of Trade*, Oxford.

Whelan, K. (2012), "ELA, promissory notes and all that: The fiscal cost of the Anglo-Irish Bank", *University College Dublin Centre for Economic Research Working Papers Series*: 12/06.

White, K. (1963), "Wheat-farming in Roman times", *Antiquity* 37: 207–12.

White, K. (1965), "The productivity of labour in Roman agriculture", *Antiquity* 39: 102–7.

Whittaker, C. (1990), "The consumer city revisited – the vicus and the city", *Journal of Roman Archaeology* 3: 110–8.

Wickham, C. (2004), *Framing the Early Middle Ages: Europe and the Mediterranean, 400–800*, Oxford.

Wilson, A. (2002), "Machines, power and the ancient economy", *Journal of Roman Studies* 92: 1–32.

Wilson, A. (2009), "Approaches to quantifying Roman trade", in A. Bowman and A. Wilson (eds.), *Quantifying the Roman Economy: Methods and Problems*, Oxford: 213–49.

Wilson, A. (2011), "City sizes and urbanisation in the Roman Empire", in A. Bowman and A. Wilson (eds.), *Settlement, Urbanisation and Population*, Oxford: 161–95.

Wilson, S. (1996), "Voluntary associations: an overview", in J. Kloppenborg and S. Wilson (eds.), *Voluntary Associations in the Graeco-Roman World* New York: 1–15.

Wiseman, T. (2019), *The House of Augustus: a Historical Detective Story*, Princeton.

Woods, R. (1993), "On the historical relationship between infant and adult mortality", *Population Studies* 47 2: 195–219.

Woolf, G. (2009), "Literacy or literacies in Rome?", in W. Johnson and H. Parker (eds.), *Ancient Literacies: The Culture of Reading in Greece and Rome*, Oxford: 46–68.

Zhao, Z. (1997), "Long-term morality patterns in Chinese history: evidence from a recorded clan population", *Population Studies: A Journal of Demography* 51 2: 117–27.

Zimmer, G. (1982), *Römische Berufsdarstellungen*, Berlin.

Index

Abd al-Rahman
  rebuilding of Roman ruins in Spain
    212
AD 33 economic crisis 68–70
Aelius Aristides (Greek orator)
    113–114, 202
aerarium militare *see* treasury
Agricola 12–13
agriculture *see* agronomists, diet, food,
    grain, land consolidation
agronomists, Roman 153–155
Alexandria
  population of 107–108
  maritime trade 131
  slaughter of city's youth by
    Caracalla 184–185
amphitheatres
  London 15, 205
  Pula 102–103
  Rome 76, 101, 176
amphora 131
Anglesey, Roman army base at 12
Antioch 97, 107–108
Antoninus, emperor 167, 170–171
aqueducts 34 , 49–51, 68, 70–72,
    156–157, 163, 170, 177, 185,
    190
Armenia 165, 166, 171–172
army, Roman
  during Caracalla's reign 184
  during Commodus' reign 177–178
  during Hadrian's reign 170
  during Nero's reign 76
  during Septimius Severus' reign
    183
  in Britain 12–13, 18, 149
  military dictatorship 202

military superiority over Carthage
    125
  pay 40, 41, 44, 48, 60–61, 86,
    115–116, 178–191
  pensions 48, 54–56, 151
  professionalising of 53–56
  see also booty
art, Roman 213
Augustus, emperor
  and agriculture 100
  and the army 53–56
  and Cicero 34
  and Praetorian Guard 181
  and Senate 39–40, 44, 52, 177
  Augustan poets 202
  coming to power of 38–39
  comparisons with Trajan 117
  death of 46–47
  Forum of 52, 120
  monetary policies of 62, 79, 82
  monuments to 47–48
  private wealth of 48–49
  public works of 49–53, 68–69, 72,
    185
  relationship to Julius Caesar 26
  Res Gestae 52, 221
aureus 60, 62, 63, 79, 86, 134, 150,
    155

Baalbek, temple at 199–201
Baghdad 172, 211, 213
banking
  crises ancient and modern 68–70
  crisis in USA in 1920s 206–208
  failure of Roman banking system
    195–196
  lending to ancient Britain 11

modern central banks 57–58
partnership structures of Roman
    banks 66
practices ancient and modern 63–67
Bank of England 68
barbarians 3–4, 113
baths, public 51, 72, 76, 135–136,
    156, 170, 188, 212
Beirut *see* Baalbek
Bithynia 122–123, 129
Boadicea 11–13
booty 9, 27, 30, 40, 43, 52, 55,
    60–61, 191
Britain
  Great Britain
    currency problems and solutions
        80–82, 112, 214
    land consolidation, effects of
        97–100
    importance of Battle of
        Trafalgar to trade 119
    rights of the individual 144
  Roman Britain
    invasion and revolt 9–13
    building of defensive walls 167,
        170
    building of walls around towns
        203
    death of Septimius Severus 183
    military revolt 177
  see also England
British peerage, life expectancy of
    159–162

Caligula
  infrastructure expenditure of 70–71
Caracalla, emperor 183–188
Carthage
  and grain trade 134
  as a port 130
  decline of 202
  population of 107
  rivalry with Rome 125, 191
Catiline 30–31, 34
Cato
  as agronomist 153

as grain trader 137–138, 155
  opponent of Carthage 124–125
China, modern 130
cholera (in London in 19th century)
    156
Christianity 2, 123, 164, 201–202,
    212
Cicero 26, 30, 34, 41, 51, 151
cities *see* migration, population,
    urbanisation
civil war
  AD 193 civil war 182, 194
  Caesar's civil war 27, 29, 33–34,
      38, 41, 49, 142, 162
Claudius, emperor
  infrastructure spending 71–72, 75,
      126–128
  military expedition of 10–11
coinage, debasement of 58–59, 81–83,
    192
Colchester 12
Colosseum 1, 76, 103, 115
Commodus, emperor
  army pay during his reign
      177–178, 186, 191
  assassination of 181
  civil war after his death 194
  mocking of Senate 176
  revolts, fire, disease, and food
      shortages 177
  unsuitability of as emperor 173,
      177, 207
constitution, Roman 28, 31–32, 36,
    38–40, 44, 74, 202
contracts *see* law and finance
copper coins, 58–60, 63, 73, 82, 214
corporations *see* societas
councils, local 101–102, 150
currency
  attempts to revive Roman currency
      204
  basis of Roman currency 59–63
  collapse of Roman currency
      192–198
  properties of metal currencies
      79–82

properties of modern currencies
58
strength and universality of Roman
currency 5, 82–84, 110, 140,
172, 214–215
trust in currency 58, 86–87, 95
weakness of Roman money system
79–80
Cyprian 201–202, 204

Dacia 36, 118–119, 166, 167, 171,
191
Danube, river 8, 118, 166, 171
denarius 60, 62, 63, 79, 86, 134,
191–193
Didius Julianus, emperor 182
diet 135, 143, 161
see also food
Domitian, emperor 115–116, 178,
181, 186
drains 156–159

economic depression 197, 208–209,
212
Egypt
currency in 82–83
grain trade from 133–134
Roman papyrus documents found
in 178
treasures of appropriated by Rome
49, 53, 60
England
agricultural productivity 142–145
construction of canals 106
Elizabethan period 213
English civil war 29
migration of labour 110
size of towns 107–108
Eurysaces (wealthy baker) 88–89, 90,
91, 94, 97, 100, 110, 120
eviction 53–54, 97–101, 148

food
and land consolidation 100
and life expectancy in 16th and
17th century England 159–162

and life expectancy of Roman elites
162–163
and urbanisation 97–98, 109–111
baking trade in ancient Rome
87–88
in London in 19th century 106
productivity 142–145, 148, 212
shortages during reign of
Commodus 177
see also diet, grain
Forum
of Augustus 52, 68, 120
of Julius Caesar 52
of Trajan 117–124
France
agricultural yields from medieval to
early modern period 143–146
Fucine lake tunnel 71

Galba, emperor 76–77
Gaul
and Britain 9–11
conquest of and enslavement of its
people 35–36, 42, 49
GDP
and urbanisation 108–109
Germany
ancient 177, 204, 216
modern 57, 81, 208
glassware, production of 133–137,
194–195, 215
see also windows
gold
and the currency 59–63, 68–69,
79–84, 134, 187, 191–196, 204
mining of 190, 191, 192, 202
Golden House *see* Nero
grain
production, science of 152–155
trade 133–34, 155–156, 188, 190
yields 6, 142–145
Great Depression (1930s) 207–208
Greece, ancient 44, 96, 196, 200
Guildhall, London's 37–38, 95

Hadrian, emperor 167, 170–171

Herculaneum 103
Hero of Alexandria 106–107
Homer 45, 135
Horace 44, 46, 201, 202, 211

Iberia 188–191
India
    trade with Rome 23, 113, 131,
        133, 140
    trade with Europe in early modern
        era 138, 213–214
inflation 184, 193–194, 204, 214
information, flow of 18–19, 24,
    120–124, 129, 156
infrastructure
    army's construction of 118–119
    building of under Augustus 49–53,
        68–69
    disrepair of 34, 198, 208
    lack of spending on by Nero 75,
        and by Domitian 115
    maintenance of 163, 170
    see also roads, ports
inheritance 25, 49, 89
inheritance tax *see* tax
Iraq 8–9, 171, 196
Ireland
    since 19th century 13, 29, 59,
        63–64, 85, 97, 101, 121
    monasteries of preserving classical
        learning 211
Iron Age 9, 10, 208
Italy
    borders breached 172
    governance of 42
    land in awarded to military
        veterans 53–54
    land use 135
    Rome's control over 4

Jerusalem 78, 114–115, 191
Judaea 63, 114, 163, 167
Julius Caesar
    and army pay 41, 54, 61–62, 116
    and Augustus 26, 49
    and Britain 9–11

and enslaving of the Gauls 35, 42,
    98
and rivalry with Pompey 28
see also civil war
Justinian's *Digest of Roman Law*
    214

labour mobility 95, 204–205,
    208–209
land consolidation 98, 100, 110
Lateran Palace 158
latrines 158
Laudatio Turiae 33
law
    common legal system, importance
        to trade of 66
    law and finance 22–24, 66,
        138–140
    magistrates 26–27
Lebanon 104
Libya 104, 204
life expectancy 159–163, 209
limited liability 139, 214
    see also societas
literature, flourishing of 44
Livy 44–45, 159, 211
London
    Battle of Trafalgar, importance of
        to London's financial sector in
        19th century 119
    City of London 37–38, 95
    in medieval times 93–95, 107
    in Roman times 11, 14–24, 56,
        203, 205, 216
    population over time compared to
        Rome 108
    ports 130–133
    railways in 19th century 106
    sacking of by Boadicea 12
    sanitation in 19th century 156–158
Luttrell Psalter 146–149, 152–153

Macrinus, emperor 187
Marcus Aurelius, emperor 171–173,
    181, 191, 196, 212
Mark Antony 34, 38, 182

medieval era
  fragmentation of Europe during
    145–146
  guilds 93
  grain yields during 142–145, 153
  life in 146–149
  mobility, lack of in 95–96, 150–151
  see also England
Mediterranean
  and extent of Rome's empire 8–9
  Rome's dominance of 125, 137
  Rome's trade across 125–130,
    133–137, 170, 172
Michelangelo 213
migration 94–98, 109–111, 204–205
mining *see* gold, silver
minting (of coins) 53, 57, 61, 68,
    79–83, 116, 190–194
Mithras, temples dedicated to
  in London 16–18, 20, 22–24, 216
  in Rome 93
monasteries 96, 142, 148, 211
money *see* coinage, copper, currency,
    denarius, gold, inflation,
    minting, price stability, silver,
    treasury

Naples 72, 176
Naqsh-e Rustam, reliefs depicting
    defeat of Valerian at 196–197
Nelson, Admiral Lord Horatio 119,
    125–126
Nero
  death of 76, 81
  fire during reign of 177
  Golden House of 74–76, 137, 213
  power of Senate over 44, 76, 78,
    177
  spending on public works 115,
    127–128
Nerva, emperor 116–117
Nicomedia 129–130
North Africa
  expansion in port capacity 130
  trade from 133–135, 156, 170,
    172–173, 213

Ostia, port of 71, 92, 123, 126–127,
    158
Otho, senator 77
Ovid 44, 46

Parthia 171–172, 191, 196
Pertinax, emperor 181
Pescennius Niger, emperor 182, 194
Petronius *see* Trimalchio
Philip the Arab, emperor 193
piracy 124, 126
plague (in England) 160–161
plebeians 31–32, 39, 126
Pliny 122–123, 129
Pompeii 103–104, 107
population
  growth in ancient Rome 91, 94
  growth in cities ancient and
    modern 95, 107
  Rome's small population in 15th
    and 16th centuries 212
ports
  and flow of information 123–124,
    156
  and maritime trade over time
    124–134, 137–138, 156,
    162–163, 170, 172–173
  container ports, importance of to
    modern China 130
  disrepair during Rome's decline
    188
  Rome's ports not equalled in size
    until 18th century 214
Portus 127–131, 214
postal system, Rome's 121–122
Praetorian Guard 55, 77, 181–182
price stability 193–194, 214–215
Pula 102–103
Puteoli, port of 126

Raphael 213
Reburrus (Roman soldier) 149, 151,
    154, 184
Reformation 146, 213
Renaissance 212–213
Rhine 8–9, 166, 172

roads 13, 18, 49, 86, 95, 121–122, 185
Roman world, survival of and influence on modern world 211–215
Russia 165–166

sanitation *see* aqueducts, baths, drains, latrines, water
Scipio Africanus 136
Senate
    and bankers 69
    and Cato the Elder 124–125, 137
    and silver mines 190
    power and finances of 40–44
    role appointing officials 27
    US politics, influence on 215
    wealth needed to be a member of 25, 151
Seneca 11, 51, 136, 218
Septimius Severus, emperor
    accession and reign 182–183, 202
    and army pay 186
    and price rises 193–194
    and public expenditure 189
Shapur I 196–197
ship size ancient and modern, 127, 131–134, 214
Sicily 41, 113, 133–134
Sidon 135–136
silver
    and the currency 58–63, 69, 79–83, 86, 116, 134, 187, 197, 202, 204, 214
    content of coins 192–194
    mining of 36, 188–192
slaves
    and expansion of empire 9, 27, 166, 196–197
    and land consolidation 98
    enslavement of Gaul 35–36, 49
    freed slaves 23, 72–73, 46, 87–89, 93
    medieval serfdom 95
    silver mines 190
    slave farms 100–101, 155

societas 137–140
Soviet Union 165–166
Spain
    and extent of Roman empire
    and Julius Caesar 25
    and Galba 76
    glass production 136
    olive growers 166
    silver mines and mints 82
    swords 136
    see also Abd al-Rahman
St Albans 12
St Paul 96–97
Syria 8–9, 42, 196, 200, 202, 204

Tacitus 211, 213
tax
    decline of tax system 187–188
    in occupied Britain 11–13
    in occupied Gaul 36
    increased tax revenue from urbanisation 112
    inheritance tax 55
    local taxes 102
    revenues of the Senate 40–41, 43–44, 52
    taxes for infrastructure 70
    increases under Commodus 177–178
Terentia (wife of Cicero) 151, 154–155
Tiber, river 126, 159
Tiberius, emperor 69–70, 75, 116, 190
Titus, emperor 103, 114–115
trade
    and prosperity 5, 36–37, 112, 117, 134, 140
    banks, importance of to 62, 65
    Battle of Trafalgar, importance of to Britain's trade in 19th century 119
    common legal system, importance of to 66
    decrease in due to decaying infrastructure 188

decrease of as empire fragmented
145, 208
expansion of under Augustus 53
from Roman empire to ancient
Britain 9, 11, 13, 14, 20–24
laws governing 27
limited liability, importance of to
214
maritime peace, importance of to
124–126, 137
port infrastructure, importance of
to 126–133
sanctions in modern era 83
strategy of 138
universal currency, importance of
to 86
see also societas, Trimalchio
trades
multiplicity of in Rome 89–94
restrictions on entering after
decline of empire 205
Trajan
baths of 137
Christianity, discouragement of 164
death of 166
military campaigns of 166
Pliny, correspondence with
122–123
ports, building of 127–133,
155–156
successful reign of 117–120, 162,
166–167
treasury
aerarium militare (military
treasury) 55
and Augustus 49
and Caracalla 187–188
and coinage 192
and Julius Caesar 28
and Tiberius 69–70
bankruptcy of 197
operation of 43–44
Trimalchio (fictional trader) 72–74
Troy 45–46
Turkey 47, 121, 122, 194, 196, 202

United States
constitution, Roman influence on
214
dollar as world's dominant
currency 83
Treasury and Federal Reserve of
57–58
urbanisation
ancient and modern 107–112, 195
decline of in medieval era 212
decline of in Roman empire 205,
208–209
in England 94–98, 144

Valerian, emperor 197, 202, 203
Van Bath, Slicher see grain yields
Varro 153–154
Verres, governor of Sicily 41
Vespasian
and currency 59–60, 82–84, 115,
194, 214
death of and succession 114–116
reign of 77–79, 86, 103, 106, 189,
198
Vesuvius 103
Virgil 8, 44–45, 54, 141–142, 201,
202, 211
Vitellius, emperor 77–78

walls
around settlements 15, 202–203,
212
of Hadrian and Antoninus
167–170
water
clean water, supply of 26, 49–51,
70–71, 91, 156–159, 162–163,
170, 177, 185, 212
water power 190
Whittington, Richard 94–95, 97, 146
wills 152
windows 136–137
women
and business 9, 25–26, 114
and property rights 151